Being Spiritual

in an

Anti-Spiritual

Society

Being Spiritual in an Anti-Spiritual Society

KIM MICHAELS

MORE TO LIFE PUBLISHING

www.morepublish.com

For foreign and translation rights,

contact info@ morepublish.com

ISBN: 978-87-93297-74-6

The information and insights in this book should not be considered as a form of therapy, advice, direction, diagnosis, and/or treatment of any kind. This information is not a substitute for medical, psychological, or other professional advice, counseling and care. All matters pertaining to your individual health should be supervised by a physician or appropriate health-care practitioner. No guarantee is made by the author or the publisher that the practices described in this book will yield successful results for anyone at any time. They are presented for informational purposes only, as the practice and proof rests with the individual.

For more information: *www.ascendedmasterlight.com and www.transcendencetoolbox.com*

CONTENTS

Introduction: Growing up in the most
sophisticated civilization 9

1 | What kind of beings are we? 17

2 | Modern societies and mental illness 35

3 | Are we changeable or unchangeable beings? 53

4 | Why can't we all get along? 63

5 | Changing the world or changing ourselves? 81

6 | How do we know what is real? 93

7 | Is there only one truth? 109

8 | The dilemma of human understanding 125

9 | Plausible deniability and plausible plausibility 143

10 | What's the purpose of life 173

11 | The big contrast 181

12 | Death, the ultimate explanation problem? 189

13 | Life: One-shot deal or ongoing process? 201

14 | Everything is energy-and so what? 231

15 | The real currency on earth 257

16 | Approaching an explanation of evil 273

17 | How we create our circumstances 285

18 | Is the earth a feed-back machine? 293

19 | How we program the subconscious computer 305

20 | What can we do about evil? 327

21 | Are we all trapped in an illusion? 345

22 | The reality simulator called earth 357

23 | Why can't we talk about religion? 369

24 | Why can't we talk about Jesus? 381

25 | Why can't we talk about God? 393

26 | What kind of beings are we (Part 2) 417

27 | Re-parenting ourselves 439

28 | Why spiritual people are on earth 445

29 | The Neutralist Manifesto 477

INTRODUCTION: GROWING UP IN THE MOST SOPHISTICATED CIVILIZATION

This is my personal, subjective story of how I experienced being a spiritual person who grew up in an anti-spiritual society. As I was growing up, I was told many times that I lived in the most advanced and sophisticated civilization ever seen on this little, blue planet. It was implied that because of our advanced science and technology (we sent a man to the moon), my society could answer all questions about life and would soon have solved most of our problems. I was not very old when I started realizing this simply wasn't true. I had questions society couldn't answer and I saw so many things that I knew could have no place in a truly sophisticated society. My childhood was like a series of shock-treatments, taking me from one shocking realization to another and sometimes I seriously wondered what kind of planet I was on.

A pivotal point in my childhood came during my school years when I learned that 500 years ago, people believed the earth was flat. It wasn't just uneducated people who believed this, but even the leaders of society. The way this was presented by the teacher was that people back then were really primitive, but see how much more sophisticated we were because we had realized the earth is round. My spontaneous reaction to this was: "But how will people look at us 500 years from now?" It was completely obvious to me that progress will continue and that 500 years into the future, people will know a lot more than we know today. I had no doubt that they would look back at us and think we were primitive for believing in many things that we think are absolute truths but that they would see as illusions.

Society could not meet my most important need

Despite the bold claims I heard over and over gain, my experience was that my society could not meet what was my most important need. I had a very strong need to find answers to my questions about life, yet none of the people around me (from my parents and family to my teachers in school and to the supposedly most intelligent people of society) could answer these questions in a way that satisfied my need for knowing. Even worse, there was no one with whom I could have an open and free conversation about life's deeper questions. At a very young age, it became clear to me that none of the adults I knew could talk about the fundamental questions of life, mainly because they had never found any answers for themselves and they had simply given up looking. I was a little older when I realized that my society at large also could not help me find answers, mainly because it was divided into two camps that both claimed to have the final answers. Yet none of those camps had answers that rang true to me.

To me, it was obvious that if my society could not answer the most basic questions about life, how could it claim to be sophisticated and advanced? I knew, even as a young child, that there were answers to my questions and I knew I would never give up looking. I was never going to accept incomplete or contradictory answers. I was never going to accept that some authority figure told me to believe something that did not meet my personal, inner criteria for what feels real.

The inconsistencies and contradictions I saw in society

Another reason I did not feel I lived in a sophisticated society was that, from a very young age, I observed many issues that contradicted my inner sense of what is right or natural. I also saw some contradictions between what society claimed and what was the actual reality. Here are just a few examples, as I will give more later:

- I grew up in a society where I always had all the food I could eat, but I saw on television that in Africa children like me were starving or severely malnourished.

- I grew up in a society that claimed to be peaceful, yet I very early learned that there is something called war. There was the possibility that someone from outside my peaceful society could come and kill me and my parents. I later learned that if someone in Soviet Russia pushed a button, my entire country would be obliterated by nuclear bombs eight minutes later (and this is still the case today).

• If I really lived in a sophisticated society, how come none of the adults I knew seemed truly happy? It seemed to me that they all had something missing in their lives, yet they had no idea what it was and neither did society. And nobody was talking about it.

• I was given an education in all kinds of practical, material topics. Yet, I experienced that both I and the children and adults around me had various problems of a psychological nature. Despite this, I was never given any education in dealing with the one thing that affects everything I do in life: my own psyche.

• I was told I lived in a society that knew more about the universe than any previous civilization, yet it had not resolved the obvious contradiction between a religious and a materialist view of life. What am I: a sinner, an evolved ape or something else entirely?

• The biggest contradiction was the existence of evil. On the personal scale, I could not understand how children could be cruel to each other and how adults could treat each other unkindly. On the larger scale, I could not understand war, crime, torture and all the other forms of human evil that I learned about as I grew older. How come the most sophisticated civilization on earth could not even explain the origin and nature of evil? This only became worse when I learned about the fate of 6 million people in Nazi concentration camps and saw the pictures of human beings like myself that looked like walking skeletons. It was one thing that such things could happen, it was another that a society, which claimed to know more than any previous civilization, had no plausible explanation.

The explanation problems of my civilization

My society's inadequate understanding of life made my childhood and youth much more difficult than it needed to be. In this book I will outline my personal journey of seeking answers outside the mental boxes defined by society. I will show how this (after 44 years) has given me answers to my questions and allowed me to become a human being who is at peace with himself and with living on a planet like earth. I have even come to the point where I consider myself a happy human.

My personal experience has shown me that all of the questions I had about life have plausible and satisfactory answers. I will therefore look at some of the explanation problems that I saw growing up and present an alternative explanation. Our modern democracies are still acting as if the answers to life's questions must be found either within the religious mental box or the "scientific" materialist mental box. It has been my clear experience that answers to life's deeper questions can be found, but not in any of these mental boxes. And it has always been blatantly obvious to me that if answers cannot be found in the official boxes, then I simply have to look elsewhere. The idea that if the official boxes do not have the answers, I should not be asking the question simply did not compute to me.

An unrecognized minority

I was born in prehistoric times when there was no Internet (1957), and I grew up in Denmark, which is one of the countries I would like to call the "modern democracies." From a material viewpoint, my childhood was good, and my material needs were adequately taken care of. From a psychological and spiritual (psycho-spiritual) viewpoint, my childhood was like a long walk in the desert where I was constantly thirsty but never found a watering hole.

At the age of 18, I realized that I am not the only spiritual person on the planet, and this brings up another inconsistency. My society claims to be an open and tolerant democracy with respect for minorities. In my lifetime, I have seen several minority groups gain acceptance and legal recognition. One example is gays and lesbians, and they probably make up a smaller percentage of the population than spiritual people. Despite this, spiritual people are still unrecognized and unaccepted. In the media we are on a regular basis portrayed as crazed cult members who are mindlessly following a guru, eating strange food and talking about astrology and chakras. Our view of life is often put down as being stupid and defying common sense. This is at best stereotyping and at worst a malicious campaign against us.

I have reached a point where it is time for me to speak out about this. I find it reasonable that spiritual people demand to be treated in a way that is in line with the democratic ideals that our societies claim to be based on. In a way, this book is me saying to modern democracies: "Put your foot where your mouth is! Let me be a spiritual person in an open and tolerant society that is not antagonistic to the fact that I have a non-standard view of life. Let us have an open conversation about the deeper questions of life and let us dare to think beyond the two mental boxes that have so far failed to answer those questions."

I hope this book will inspire other spiritual people to also tell their stories so that society will eventually recognize that a sizable percentage of the population has legitimate needs that society has failed to understand and acknowledge. I even hope that society might one day recognize that spiritual people have something to offer because we have been willing to look outside the mental boxes that keep society stuck between two groups of equally closed-minded people (fundamentalist Christians and fundamentalist materialists). We have been willing to work on our personal psychology and this gives us experiences that the modern democracies will need as they face the next big challenge, namely how to move from focusing on material welfare to psychological wellbeing.

In summary, I will look at some of the explanation problems that I have seen in society and show how a more open-minded approach can give us a different perspective. I will start by taking a fairly universal approach that does not require the reader to believe in ideas that are too far beyond the mainstream. Later in the book, I will look at more specific spiritual ideas and how they can make the explanation problems of modern society evaporate into this air.

1 | WHAT KIND OF BEINGS ARE WE?

Here is the first explanation problem I will discuss: If our civilization is so sophisticated, how come people aren't happy? I don't see that people in general have become happier since my childhood. In fact, I think one could argue that the opposite is the case. There are more psychological problems today than ever, such as people going down with stress or experiencing depression or even more severe psychological illnesses.

Could it be that people are not happy because our civilization has failed to move from focusing on material welfare to psychological wellbeing? Could it be that society has not been able to make this transition because it has failed to resolve the question of what kind of beings we are? If we don't understand what kind of beings we are, how can we know how we truly function? And if we don't know that, how can we understand what it takes for a human being to be happy?

So what kind of beings are we? I was brought up to think I am a human being, but my society could never give me a clear, consistent definition of what exactly that means. On the contrary, my society had a schizophrenic approach to the question. My society was deeply divided between two competing thought systems that claimed to have the final answers as to what kind of beings we are. I was not very old when I realized that these systems were incompatible, even mutually exclusive.

The message I got from my society was that because of its democratic principles, it allowed both viewpoints to co-exist, and I simply had to choose one over the other. Yet from a very early age, I had a strong inner knowing that neither of the two gave a complete understanding of who we are. I could not choose one of them because I knew there had to be something else for me to find, something that was beyond both of them. Had I lived in today's Internet age, I might have found it at an earlier age. As it was, I did not find an alternative explanation until I was 18. And that did indeed make my childhood much more difficult than it would have been, if I had found something that satisfied my quest for understanding. Or if I had been able to talk openly about my questions with adults who could steer me in the direction of finding my personal answers.

The irony of democracy

To me, the biggest irony of the modern democracies is that we claim to be open and tolerant societies, yet there is very little tolerance for viewpoints that go beyond Christianity or Materialism. I think the reason we can't have an open and neutral conversation about the deeper issues is that we have this irreconcilable split between a Christian and a materialistic view of life. I think most people reason that since the so-called authority figures in the religious and scientific fields can't agree on what kind of beings we are, then the rest of us surely can't have anything to say about the issue so we better stay out of the debate. The result is that we are not able to talk about the topic. The materialists are waiting for Christianity to finally lose all influence on society and die out, and the Christians are waiting for Jesus to come back and take the scientists to hell. In the meantime, our societies are caught in a no-man's land and unable to move on.

The irony I see is that democracy is fundamentally a form of government based on non-violent conflict resolution. Non-violent conflict resolution can only happen through open debate and dialogue. If there is no open debate, how can there be resolution? And if there is no resolution, how can there be progress?

Open dialogue is the key to progress

Since I was a very young child, I have been focused on progress. It has been a very important topic for me, and one might say that beyond all of my other studies, I have been a student of progress. I have studied what leads to progress, and it has become obvious to me that progress in society is proceeded by progress in the minds of its citizens. To me, it is plainly obvious that our failure to talk about the fundamental questions of life prevents our modern democracies from making progress in certain areas.

I grew up during the cold war, and at an early age, I became aware of the split between the communist East and the capitalist West. For the first thirty-some years of my life, my society thought there was no resolution to this conflict. Yet, we then witnessed the seemingly miraculous fall of the Berlin wall and the end of the conflict between capitalism and communism.

Some people say this was the victory of capitalism over communism, but I don't see it that way. In Denmark and many other modern democracies, we don't have a strictly capitalistic system in which the fittest exploit the unfit. We have a form of society that is beyond the traditional divisions between a communist and a capitalist economy. Instead of allowing the capitalists to monopolize the economy, we have developed an alternative, even a compassionate, approach to the economy.

One might say there was no open dialogue between East and West about communism and capitalism. Yet there was an open dialogue in the modern democracies about whether the economy should allow a small elite to take advantage of the rest of us. I believe this eventually led to a raising of the collective awareness, an awareness that our only choice isn't to have a strictly communist or a strictly capitalist economy.

Another interesting example of how progress happens is the issue of slavery. For thousands of years, various societies allowed slavery and it was an institution that was rarely questioned. The official abandonment of slavery did not happen as the result of a violent revolution. It happened as the result of a debate about many issues related to democratic principles, including what kind of beings we are.

It gradually became clear to people in the democratic world that it is not consistent to have a society that claims to be democratic, yet it allows people to be bought and sold as property. What happened was that we raised our collective awareness of what kind of beings we are, namely that we are not merchandise to be bought or sold. One class of human beings cannot own another class of human beings. Thus, there came a point where the modern democracies started abandoning slavery. It simply became obvious that this was the next logical step for society.

The missing growth in happiness

Well, I believe that as a natural part of progress, our modern democracies are on the brink of another breakthrough, but we haven't yet been able to leave our heritage behind. And precisely because we haven't resolved the question of what kind of beings we are, we have failed to acknowledge that the tremendous progress in material living conditions has not led to a corresponding growth in happiness and well-being.

It is as if no one will openly say that while we are becoming more and more wealthy in a material way, we are becoming more and more psychologically impoverished. The welfare society has not produced well-being. To me, this means we have (for some time now) been treading water on the topic of how people become happy. We are not making progress on the issue of what makes us tick. Yet the clock is still ticking.

The main reason is of course that we have not resolved the split between Christianity and Materialism. So let me talk about how these two thought systems affected me.

Why Christianity didn't satisfy my curiosity

Obviously, I could never accept that the authority figures of religion and materialistic science were the only people who could know anything about the deeper questions. I always knew that I have the ability to know and decide this on my own. Here is how this looked for me as a child.

Although many people in the modern democracies seem to have lost faith in Christianity, it still has a very subtle influence on our thinking. Denmark has a Lutheran state church, and people automatically become members at birth. My family was a typical Danish family in that they were not religious, but they had not renounced their membership of the state church. I was baptized in the church in infancy, but I have forgotten that event so it didn't play a big role in my childhood. I think I went to church once or twice during my early childhood (a wedding and a funeral), but my next close contact with the church was at my confirmation. This event was a big disappointment to me.

Some time before our confirmation, a priest from the state church started coming to our classroom twice a week to give us lessons. They were meant to prepare us to confirm our Christian faith. I think most of my classmates only agreed to go through the confirmation in order to have the big party and all of the gifts that is part of Danish tradition. Yet I was looking forward to the lessons because it was the first time in my life I had been close to a priest, and I thought he would be able to give me some answers to my questions.

During the first two lessons, I was very alert and asked several questions. Yet, I quickly realized that the priest didn't have any more answers than the other adults I had met during my childhood. This was stunning to me! I simply couldn't wrap my mind around a person who had chosen to become a priest, yet who apparently hadn't thought about the deeper questions of life. I had the sense that the purpose of religion was to help people deal with the deeper questions (I have later realized what is the true purpose of religion). I assumed that if a person had chosen to educate himself as a priest, it was because he or she had a personal interest in these questions. And surely, an institution that had survived for centuries and claimed to represent God and Jesus, must have found a way to help its own priests resolve these questions.

It soon became obvious to me that this priest had no personal resolution. All he could give me was a set of predefined answers based on what was to me a very strange concept, namely "church doctrine." He told me that this is what the Christian religion defines as the truth so this is what I had to believe as a Christian. This was monumentally disappointing to me because these standard doctrines simply did not resonate with what I knew inside myself. How did I know church doctrines were not the complete truth? Well, this is a profound topic so I will talk more about it later. My point for now is that the Christian religion could not satisfy my need for answers to the fundamental questions. Let me focus on the question of what kind of beings we are.

Here is another inconsistency. Denmark is a democracy and it guarantees its citizens certain basic human rights, one of which is freedom of religion. Because of freedom of religion, Danish society didn't quite know how to teach religion in the school system. When I was a child, there was no obvious religious education until I was old enough for the confirmation. Yet in the third grade, I did receive lessons in something called "Bible History," which taught us the main events of the Old Testament.

These lessons told me that I am a descendant of two people, called Adam and Eve, who lived a long time ago in the Middle East. God had created only these two people, and all the rest of us descended from them. At the age of 8, this made no sense to me at all. I didn't know anything about genetics and inbreeding at the time, but I knew this simply wasn't true.

The lessons told me that Adam and Eve had lived in a wonderful place that was far better than what I experienced in my world. Now, this had a certain resonance with me. At that age, I was acutely aware of war and many other man-made atrocities. I also had an inner knowing that it was possible to have a world where war simply could not exist. So I did have an inner sense that we human beings had originally come from some state that was better than what we have now. I also knew we have the potential to return to that state, even here on earth. Yet to say that paradise was a small garden in the Middle East with only two people in it made no sense to me whatsoever.

Worst of all, the lessons told me that Adam and Eve had done something to disobey the God who lived in this garden. This had made him angry, and as a result God had thrown them out of the garden. This punishment by the angry God was the real cause of all the misery I saw in the world around me. In other words, I (and all other people to this day) were being punished by God for the choices of two other people that I didn't even know and probably wouldn't have liked.

Even though I was 8 years old, there was no way you could make me believe this. I just knew inside myself that this could not be the real God and there had to be another explanation (which I will describe later). The consequence of Adam and Eve being thrown out of paradise was that according to the Christian religion, we are all sinners. We were born into sin because of what Adam and Eve did thousands of years ago. In other words, the Christian religion wanted me to believe that I am a sinner as a result of me being punished by an all-good God for choices made by other people.

I knew this simply wasn't true. I knew that I am an individual with free will. I would be held responsible for my own choices by a higher power, but this power would never hold me responsible for the choices of other people. I simply knew this, and I never accepted myself as a sinner. I never accepted that a God, whom Christianity claims is all-knowing, all-powerful and all-good, had created me as a flawed being who needed to be saved by my very nature. I knew that the real God had given me the same choice as Adam and Eve. I was not being held responsible for the choices of Adam and Eve. I was in this world because of choices I had personally made. I just had no way to explain when I had made those choices (I do now, but the answer will have to wait until I have given more background information).

On top of all this, Christianity told me that because I am a sinner, the only way for me to be saved is to live a life according to the rules defined by the Christian religion (believe in doctrines that made no sense to me and follow rituals that seemed mechanical to me). If I did this, then after I died, Jesus would come and take me to heaven where I would live for all eternity, supposedly sitting on a pink cloud and playing the harp. I knew this was not true, precisely because I always knew that I am responsible for my own choices. My salvation is not a matter of following outer rules and rituals. It is all about going through an inner process that depends on the choices I make regarding how I change my state of mind. I knew that salvation is a state of mind. There is no way that Jesus or any other celestial being can change my mind for me. I knew this even as a child, but I was not able to describe this process at the time (I am now, and will do so later).

The result of this was that I knew certain basic ideas promoted by the Christian religion had some reality to it. Yet I also knew they were mixed with a lot of incomplete understanding and even some direct untruths. I knew this inside myself even as a child, but I obviously didn't have a very clear understanding of these topics. And because I had no one to talk to and no books to read, it was very difficult for me to deal with all of the questions this brought up. I simply could not fathom how the self-declared sophisticated society I lived in could have a state religion that could not answer my questions about life, but instead gave me a set of doctrines that were clearly self-contradictory.

Why Materialism didn't satisfy my curiosity

Because my society was deeply divided between two opposing views on what kind of beings we are, it wasn't able to deal with the deeper questions, and this created some inconsistencies. One example of this was that at the same age as I was going through the preparations for my confirmation in the state church, I was given biology lessons that told me about evolution and Darwin's claim that we descended from the apes. It's still amazing to me that a self-proclaimed sophisticated society can subject its children to this kind of inconsistency and all of the conflicting questions this created in our ill-prepared minds. Worst of all is that we had no one to talk to about this, as the adults around us also received no help to resolve this conflict and were therefore unable to have a conversation about it.

So here I am, at the age of 13. I have been told that I descended from Adam and Eve, which I didn't believe for a second. One would think I would then happily accept the theory of evolution (note the word "theory," which some people tend to forget) and deny the spiritual side of my nature. And truly, I always accepted that there is a gradual, evolutionary process on this planet. At an early age, I had been given a book about dinosaurs, and it was obvious to me that there is a very old process that has led from primitive life-forms to more sophisticated life-forms. However, it seemed equally obvious to me that this cannot explain where I came from.

I am not sure I could have articulated this at the age of 13, but inside of me I knew that I am not an evolved ape. I had no problem with the idea that my physical body is the result of a gradual, evolutionary process. Yet what has that got to do with what kind of being I am and where I came from? During my entire childhood, it was completely obvious to me that I am not my physical body. I am more than my physical body. This isn't something I believed and it certainly wasn't something anybody told me. It was something I experienced as a daily reality. This experience was so real to me that no argument presented by any authority figure in society could override it.

I was always fascinated by animals, especially birds. Yet it seemed obvious to me that animals have a lower form of consciousness than us humans. I remember once watching a television program about monkeys, and it showed a chimpanzee doing its typical grin. It was obvious to me that there is no missing link between the consciousness of an ape and the consciousness of a human. The jump from the animal level of consciousness to ours is not a matter of gradual evolution. It is a fundamental difference that to me could not be explained by gradual changes. It was what physicists call a "quantum leap," which I didn't know about at that age.

It was clear to me that I am an individual, and my individuality is a product of my consciousness. It was also obvious to me that my consciousness is a matter of how I think about and look at myself. So here comes what they called science and tells me that all of who I am is a product of some material processes in this lump of gray matter that resides between my ears. You could no more make me believe in this than you could make me believe in Adam and Eve.

Again, I had a daily experience that showed me the limitations of this so-called scientific claim, and the primary element of this experience was self-awareness. I experienced that I am able to mentally step outside of myself, look at myself and then consciously decide to change my behavior. I had several times during my childhood had an experience of suddenly seeing a certain aspect of my behavior and then consciously deciding to change it. For example, at the age of 10, I suddenly saw that I had gradually started using swear words, and it hit me how primitive this was. From one moment to the next, I decided to stop using swear words—and I did. Now, you show me an animal who is able to do that.

We had two dogs during my childhood, and I loved them both. The first one was a wild dog that I simply couldn't connect to. The second one was a very gentle dog, and I could get a sense of connection with her, but obviously not the same kind of connection as I could have with another human being. It was obvious to me that no animal has the ability to step back, look at itself and decide: "Hey, I'm fed up with chewing the cud, I wanna know what it's like to be a horse." As a child I had watched the animated Disney movie *The Jungle Book,* in which the king of the apes sings: "I wanna be a man, man-cub, and stroll right into town … I'm tired of monkeying around." Yet I had no problem realizing that in the real world, animals don't think and feel like humans. Nor can they learn to behave like humans.

To me, the "missing link" in the materialist explanation is self-awareness, the ability to mentally step outside of myself, look at myself, decide that there is a certain type of behavior that I no longer want, and then consciously choose to change that behavior. I have done that so many times in my life that this is a self-evident reality for me. I know no animal can do this. I also know that the lump of inert matter between my ears cannot do this. I can step outside myself, but my brain cannot step outside my skull. So when "scientific" Materialism tells me that my entire consciousness is a product of my physical brain, it is completely and utterly unbelievable to me. Why so? Because it contradicts my daily experience. I know I am more than a material being and I have known and experienced this since I was born (actually much longer, but let's not get ahead of ourselves).

I knew, with an inner certainty, that when my teacher told me that science had proven the theory of evolution, there had to be more to it. When the priest told me that everything I needed to know could be explained by Christian doctrines, I also knew there had to be more to it. And that is why neither the religion of Christianity, nor the religion of Materialism could satisfy my curiosity about life. I had questions that they could not answer, and that is why I knew I had to look for answers elsewhere. I knew my questions were valid and that somewhere there were answers to be found.

What kind of beings are we then?

So what kind of beings do I think we are? Well, I could not have answered that during my childhood, so let me jump to the view I have developed during my 44-year journey into the unknown.

To get started, I will again reach back to my childhood. My father was born in the early 1920s when Danish society, and especially the school system, was very different from when I was a child. My father was born in a working class family (that was back when Danish society still had a working class), and he went to public school. He was very intelligent and for the first years he did very well in school. Back then, the children were seated in the classroom according to how well they did. The best student would sit right in front of the teacher's desk and the worst student would sit in the back of the classroom. My father was at the very front, and he was sometimes taken into other classrooms to demonstrate how good he was at basic math. He could calculate large numbers in his head very quickly (impressive at a time when the pocket calculator had not been invented).

One might say that my father was a savant, but he was no idiot. He had a very strong inner sense of fairness and honor.

This soon put him in conflict with the Danish school system because he saw that some teachers were clearly unfair. For example, he had one teacher who enjoyed punishing the students by having them come up to his desk, hold out their hand and then hit the palm of their hand with a steel ruler. The teacher would clearly get a sadistic enjoyment out of this, as his eyes would shine, and he would stick the tip of his tongue out of one side of his mouth. If a student cried after being hit a couple of times, he would be sent back to his desk. Since my father thought this was unfair, he refused to cry so the teacher kept hitting his hand until he came to his senses and realized he had gone too far. My father was sent back to his desk and his hand hurt for hours afterwards.

Another situation was when a teacher noticed that my father was writing with a very short pencil. The reason was that my father knew his parents had very little money. He didn't want to ask them for money for a new pencil so he kept using the old one as long as he could. The teacher got angry and ordered my father to bring a new pencil to school the next day, and he specified that it had to be a certain brand. My father got 10 ore (the smallest unit of the Danish currency) from his mother and went to buy a pencil. The brand specified by the teacher cost 10 ore, but they had another brand that only cost 5 ore. My father bought the cheaper pencil and now had the incredible luxury of being able to buy 5 ores worth of day-old Danish pastry at the bakery. He thought it was a great deal until he got to school and the teacher inspected his pencil. When the teacher saw that it was not the specified brand, he got angry and threw the pencil against the wall. Needless to say, the graphite stick broke and my father constantly had to sharpen the pencil. Because of many other incidents like this, my father decided (at the age of 10) that he no longer wanted to have anything to do with the Danish school system, and he simply refused to study and learn. He was soon moved from the front to the back of the classroom.

Now, this might be an interesting story about the bad old days, but here is the twist. My father was a story teller, and he told me how he had read books about foreign lands, and it was his great dream to become an engineer who traveled around the world, building bridges. I have no doubt that he had the intelligence to become a good engineer, but of course in order to do so, he would have had to work his way through the Danish school system. Back then, it would have been very difficult for a child from a working class family to get any higher education, but I still think that a child with extra-ordinary abilities might have been given a way through. Obviously, this could only have happened if that child knew how to work with the system, and you can't do that from the back of the classroom.

When I heard my father talk about how he wanted to become an engineer, I could contrast this with him spending decades working at the same factory, cleaning printing machines with turpentine that rotted his brain. I felt a deep compassion for the fact that he had been unable to realize his life's dream. I also felt his inner pain, not only about having to spend most of his time at a boring job, but also about the lost opportunity. His life obviously had not turned out the way he had hoped as a child. Yet at the same time, it was clear to me that my father had aborted his life's dream at the age of 10 when he decided to stop working with the school system. It was obvious to me that the other 25 students had the same teachers, but not all of them made the same decision as my father.

At the age of 10, I knew that my father had aborted his life's dream not because of the outer circumstances, as difficult as they were. No, my father had aborted his life's dream because of his inner circumstances, meaning his personal psychology. I had also observed other adults inside and outside of my family who had done exactly the same thing. By simply observing people, it had become obvious to me that the main limitation we face in life is our own psychological conditions.

This brings me back to the question of what kind of beings we humans are. Obviously, this will not be the full definition (more will follow), but as a starting point, we human beings are _psychological_ beings. Everything we do as individuals is determined by what goes on in our psyches. Everything we do as a society is determined by how our individual psyches combine to form what we call a culture, a society, a civilization, but which we might as well call the collective psyche.

We can change our psyches

At the age of 10, I decided that I was not going to go through what my father had endured. This didn't mean that I decided to conform to school (which I already did) and become an engineer. I decided that I would not let my life be dominated by conditions in my own psychology. I clearly saw that it was my father's temper and stubbornness that had set his life on a track. I saw that it was his way of reacting to the world that had dominated his life and was still doing so. I was absolutely determined to find a way to become free of my own psychological mechanisms so I could reach a higher degree of psychological or mental freedom.

This wasn't easy for me, as my society didn't offer me much help. When I was a child, the common assumption was that there wasn't much you could do about your psychology, and if you were relatively normal, you didn't _have_ to do anything. The common attitude was that you had to be really crazy before you went to see a psychologist. If you were relatively normal, you just muddled through with the psychological make-up you had. What we today call books on popular psychology or even self-help were non-existent in the society of my childhood. I am sure such books would have made a tremendous difference for me.

Today, the attitude to psychology has clearly changed, and there is not the same stigma associated with seeking help for psychological problems. At the same time, there seems to be a growing awareness in the modern democracies that psychological issues is not something society can ignore. Denmark has a highly developed public healthcare system that also covers mental illness. During the last few years, several experts have publicly stated that the greatest challenge for the healthcare system over the next couple of decades will be mental illness. The same shift seems to he happening in other modern democracies.

Although Denmark is consistently ranked among the happiest nations in the world, not all Danes are constantly happy. Substance abuse is increasing and more and more people get institutionalized with debilitating mental illnesses. It is now expected that two-thirds of the population will have a depression during their lifetime. Surveys have also shown that an increasing number of people suffer from stress-related mental issues or even burnout. Out of a population of 5 million, 700,000 take some form of psychiatric drugs, every third person receives a psychiatric diagnosis, and mental illness costs society 10 billion Dollars a year (a lot for a small country). In my mind, this underscores my observation that we are psychological beings, and it points to another inconsistency in society.

2 | MODERN SOCIETIES AND MENTAL ILLNESS

Danish society is based on a sophisticated set of views about equality and fairness. It is claimed that in Denmark "few have too much and none have too little." This is often referred to by ourselves as the "Danish model," and there is a certain pride in Danish society about what we have achieved. I am not generally critical about my society. I acknowledge that all of the modern democracies have made tremendous progress over the past century.

Even in my lifetime, I have experienced how my working class grandparents lived in the poorest apartments in town. Both of my parents grew up on the same street in what could be called a kind of barracks. These were built specifically for poor people, and each apartment had two rooms, a kitchen, and a back corridor. Four apartments were together in a block, and they shared two outside toilets and one room for doing laundry and taking baths. The only way to heat water was a large kettle drum under which one could light a fire. My father and mother grew up on opposite sides of this street. They each had two siblings so there were only five people living in these two rooms that were probably 20 square meters each. Yet some other families on the same street had seven children. Needles to say, these apartments no longer exist but have been replaced by more modern buildings. The kind of poverty I saw in my grandparent's generation is simply unthinkable today, and I fully acknowledge this progress.

Based on the poverty and inequality that existed in the early 1900s, I consider it both logical and necessary that society has gone through a period of focusing on improving people's material living conditions. There is no criticism in me of the need to do this. However, I also see that this is only a phase, and I think it is based on an underlying assumption that I have never heard anyone articulate. It seems to me that the Danish welfare society is based on the assumption that we are materialistic beings. Meaning that if society improves the material living conditions of its citizens, then they will automatically become happy and satisfied with their lives. Happiness is something that takes care of itself.

This clearly has not happened. I sometimes joke that in Denmark, we lost the right to complain decades ago, but this hasn't stopped anyone. Complaining is our national sport. How do we explain that we have a group of nations that have seen tremendous improvements of people's material living conditions, yet they have not seen an increase in people's non-material living conditions? Despite the fact that people have less and less reason to complain, people are becoming more and more dissatisfied with their lives. Go back to what I said about the increase in mental illness, substance abuse, depression, suicide and stress. We now have a large part of the world where people have both adequate and even abundant material conditions. According to the underlying materialist assumption, this should have resulted in people becoming deliriously happy.

To me, there is only one conclusion, and it is a very obvious one. *If* we were material beings, happiness should have been the automatic result of giving people the right material conditions. After all, our approach to physical health has been that the body is a machine, and illness means something has gone wrong with the machinery. You find what has gone wrong, and you fix it with surgery or a chemical, and health should be restored. Again, I recognize that modern medicine has made tremendous progress even in my lifetime, yet I also see that disease has not been eradicated.

Likewise, our approach to mental health has been that happiness is a product of the brain, which is a mechanical device depending on chemistry and electromagnetism. Given all of the experimentation with drugs, one would think that by now science should have come up with a pill that produced happiness. Instead, I see that more and more doctors and psychologists are recognizing that it is not possible to cure mental illness or induce happiness the chemical way.

To me, this reinforces my conviction that we human beings are not material beings. We are more than *material* beings, we are *psychological* beings. When I come to a conclusion like that, it immediately releases an impulse to change my worldview and my actions accordingly. In my view, the modern democracies are right now being forced to reconsider the materialistic approach to making people happy.

To pay up or face up

The situation we face is simple. Most of the modern democracies have public healthcare systems. In the coming decades, experts agree that these systems are in danger of being overwhelmed by mental illness. The same holds true for the social welfare systems because mental illness often robs people of their capacity to work. There is no question that businesses are losing huge amounts of money on the lost productivity caused by mental issues. This is not even talking about the lost creativity coming from people not developing their creative potential as a result of psychological issues (like my father). In Denmark, there is already now a lack of qualified workers and this is expected to increase.

My conclusion is simple. If we continue with our current approach, we are likely to see that social safety nets (that we have so carefully developed during the past century) will be brought to their knees by mental illness. Therefore, it is plainly obvious to me that we need a better approach. Our approach so far has been that happiness and mental well-being is a personal matter. Society's role is to provide the right material conditions, and then people will automatically become happy—except for a few more extreme cases.

From a certain viewpoint, one could argue that mental illness was less common decades ago. I think this was in large part because of the stigma associated with mental illness. Many cases simply did not get diagnosed because people didn't seek help. They went to the bottle instead of the psychologist. So from another viewpoint, one could say that what used to be an exception has become more mainstream. When experts predict that two-thirds of the population will experience a depression during their lifetimes, I think mental health has become an issue that society cannot afford to ignore.

So what do we do? Well, here is how I see our options. We have a nation that provides public health-care. If someone develops a mental illness, they go to the system and the system is obligated to seek to help them, with the associated cost to society. It seems clear to me that if we continue with our current approach, society will simply have to pay up. The only way out is to change our approach. We have to pay up or smarten up.

The alternative I see is that we create a kind of buffer-zone between the population and the mental health-care system. We naturally still need a public system that is able to deal with more severe cases of mental illness. Yet, based on my personal experience, I know many mental health issues could be dealt with by people themselves—if only they were given the right tools.

During my childhood, I remember there was talk about the health-care system being overwhelmed by physical illness and an aging population. Then, Danish society made an effort to focus on prevention rather than cure, by, for example, promoting a better diet, encouraging people to stop smoking and to exercise. To me, we need to do something similar about mental health. We need to shift from *curing* mental illness to *preventing* it from becoming so severe that people cannot deal with it themselves.

Obviously, my primary motivation for suggesting this is not economical. As I described, I felt a deep compassion for my father having his life's dream aborted by his psychological issues. I had a deep desire for being able to help him, and of course the many other people I saw who also had psychological issues. In fact, I have met very few people who did not have some psychological issues that severely impacted their lives. One could say that my main focus in life has been to find a way for us human beings to rise above our psychological limitations.

Help to self-help

Obviously, the changes I am envisioning will require a major shift, a systemic shift. It will require us to adopt an entirely new paradigm because we have already proven that we cannot prevent mental illness by having people pop pills. We will have to develop a paradigm that equips people with the knowledge, attitude and tools to deal with mental health on their own (unless it becomes too severe, but this is what we can often prevent). I even think we need to start in kindergarten and schools by teaching children basic knowledge about psychology and how to deal with their own emotions and attitude to life.

I have personally had many psychological issues during my life. I have not had to burden the public system with them because my spiritual approach to life has empowered me to deal with them on my own. The same holds true for thousands of spiritual people I have personally met, and millions more I have not met. These many people could be a resource for society because we have learned how to take care of our own psychological needs, and most of us would love to help others.

During my 44-year journey I have found insights and tools that have helped me heal my psychological issues and find a deep sense of happiness and peace. I am not expecting that my approach will work for everyone, and I am certainly not expecting that modern democracies will start promoting my spiritual worldview. Yet I do see that society is being forced to consider alternatives to the current materialistic approach, and I think it needs to begin with us becoming willing to have an open debate about what kind of beings we are. What does it mean to be a human being? What does it take for us to actually function as human beings? What are our basic needs?

To me, we have a set of material needs, but we also have a set of non-material needs. The material needs take care of the survival and function of our physical bodies, but they do not ensure our psychological survival or well-being. Therefore, I think the modern democracies are right now facing a mental health crises that will force us to make the shift from a *welfare* society to a *wellbeing* society.

As I said, what millions of spiritual people have gone through over the past decades is a pioneering effort that has the potential to help society make this transition. After all, we spiritual people have direct, personal experience in how to take command over our mental health and psychological well-being. We are further along than the average person, and I see this as a resource that society could benefit from using. However, here comes the "but."

A universal approach

In my view, spiritual people have something to offer society, *but* it is not what most spiritual people think. When I was young and had recently found spiritual teachings, I was overwhelmed by youthful exuberance and thought the solution to all of society's problems was to convert everyone to follow my particular spiritual teaching and movement. Today, I see this as hopelessly naive on my part.

When I look at the thousands of spiritual people I have personally met, and when I look at spiritual or New Age people in general, one thing stands out to me. We are spiritual people because we have accepted a certain view, a certain approach to life. When I step far enough back, I see this view as being neutral and universal. Behind it all is a set of universal ideas about how the human psyche functions. These ideas are as neutral as knowledge about the force of gravity or the functions of the body. They are not specific to a particular religious tradition, but they are sometimes incorporated in a specific religious tradition. They are not specific to a particular spiritual teaching or teacher, but they are sometimes found in a specific teaching and expressed by a specific teacher.

When I look at spiritual people in general, I see that most of them belong to a specific spiritual teaching, organization or teacher. Most of them think that the solution to all of society's problems is that society officially recognizes their tradition, teaching or guru—as society recognized Christianity as the official state religion. To me, this simply is not realistic. I don't think it will ever happen. We have simply moved out of the age where one religion can dominate society (at least in the modern democracies). Yet maintaining this dream prevents spiritual people from having the positive impact on society that we could have—if we could shift from promoting a specific teaching to promoting universal ideas. Let me put this in a larger context.

I lived in Denmark until 1987 when I moved to the United States. I lived there for 22 years and then moved to Estonia where I lived for a five-year period (with ten months in Sweden). I then moved back to Denmark in 2014. My point is that I grew up in the middle between the capitalist West and the communist East. I have lived in the most capitalistic country in the world, and I have lived in a former Soviet republic. During my time in Estonia, I studied how people had reacted to being forced to live in a communist society.

A couple of things stood out. One was that I asked a good friend how they looked at the potential for war, especially nuclear war, which I had been so afraid of as a child. His response was that they never worried much about it because they knew most of the Russian technology simply wouldn't work. I wish I had known that at the age of 12.

I also realized that in Estonia hardly anyone had ever believed in communism. During my childhood, a sizable percentage of Danish intellectuals were firm believers in communism, or at least socialism. I have no doubt that during the 1960's and 70s there were far more believers in socialism in Denmark than there were in any country in eastern Europe. So why didn't people believe in Marxism when they experienced it firsthand? For the same reason that I didn't believe in Christianity and Materialism: Theory cannot override your daily experience. It doesn't matter how much propaganda you are given about the wonderful principles of Marxism when you experience that the stores have empty shelves and you have to stand in line for two hours to buy a loaf of bread.

The Age of Ideology is over

One day, as I was contemplating the incredible historical changes that Estonian society had gone through, it hit me: The fall of the Soviet Union signaled the end of the "Age of Ideology!"

Just look at what our societies have been doing for the past thousands of years. Starting with the Greek philosopher Aristotle (perhaps even before), we have been on a quest to find the ultimate truth. We have sought the one true religion, the ultimate political theory and the scientific theory of everything. What have we been doing? We have been approaching life based on thinking that if we find the ultimate theory, we can solve all of our problems. Yet where have we been looking for that theory? Well, outside ourselves. One of the most monumental events in western history came in the year 325 when the Emperor Constantine created the Roman Catholic church as his instrument for exercising political power and controlling the people. For over a thousand years, this institution dominated life and thinking in Western Europe. The basic approach behind Catholic Christianity was this: It is possible to create a theory, an ideology, a thought system, a set of doctrines and then force people to live their lives according to the system. And doing so is beneficial, meaning that it will solve society's problems and make people content, even happy.

What was communism? Another example of the same approach. This time, it was the theories of Karl Marx that were used to form an ideology and then it was forced upon society. Those who actually believed in Marxism had the same basic approach as believing Christians. They were convinced that the ideology of Marxism could solve all of society's problems and make people happy.

Now, why did the Catholic church, as willing as it was to torture or kill its own members, lose its grip on society? Why did communism, as willing as it was to torture or kill its own citizens, lose its grip on society? To me, the answer is obvious, and it can be described by referring to a scientific law, called the second law of thermodynamics. This law states that in a closed system, disorder and chaos (entropy) will increase until the system breaks down. Another way of saying this is that a closed system will eventually self-destruct.

Medieval Catholicism was a closed system. All alternative views of life had been banned as heresy, even to the point of burning most books. The system had created a highly structured society in which the majority of people were the virtual slaves of a small minority of noblemen, kings and church officials. This led to various forms of tension and the system became increasingly repressive in order to sustain itself, with the Inquisition and witch hunts as obvious examples. The same with communism. The Soviet Union was shut off from the rest of the world, and Stalin was willing to kill 21 million Soviet citizens in order to maintain his grip on power. This created an obvious tension, and eventually Soviet society faced a situation where it had to change or die. Yet as Gorbachev came to realize, the system could not change so it ended up collapsing under its own weight.

Why did the Soviet Union collapse? Because the closed system could no longer sustain itself economically. And why not? Because it was based on a theory of how the economy *should* work, but the Soviet Union demonstrated that the economy simply doesn't work that way. We might say that Marxism was based on a view of the economy that was akin to denying the force of gravity, and gravity eventually caught up with it.

The difference between science and Materialism

When I was a fairly young child, I grasped what is the essential principle behind science. I saw that science developed because of the Catholic church and its so-called infallible doctrines, including some claims that I knew were untrue. I saw that the real intent behind science is to bring society into an era that is not dominated by human beliefs, superstitions and theories. The real purpose of science is to look beyond all theories and instead make observations and experiments to determine how the world *actually* works. The goal is to create a society that is not based on an ideology, a religion or a theory of how somebody thinks the universe *should* work. Instead, our society is based on observations and experiments to determine how the world actually *does* work. To me, this is the promise of science.

So why didn't I accept the materialist philosophy? Well, I couldn't have put words on it at the time, I simply experienced that the claims made by "materialistic" science contradicted my inner knowledge, first of all that I am not a material being. It was obvious to me that science has never proven that we are material beings. Science has never proven that there is nothing beyond the material universe. Science has never proven that there is no spiritual world beyond the material.

The way I explain this today is that Materialism is just another ideology, another theory, another attempt at defining how some people think the world *should* work. Yet, from early childhood I have known that it contradicts the way I experience that the world *does* work.

I think this has been proven by the failure of a materialistic society to make people happy. Our modern democracies have become prisoners to an ideology of Materialism. This has turned our, supposedly open, democracies into a closed system, and the inherent tension in all closed systems is breaking the system down. How can we observe the breakdown of the system? Well, nowhere more clearly than in the rise in mental illness and psychological problems, including the observable fact that material wealth does not automatically lead to psychological well-being.

As I see it, the rise of psychological problems is a message to our modern democracies that we are in a blind alley, and we need to get out before the system collapses under its own weight. How can we get out? By realizing that the "Era of Ideology" is over. It is time to let go of the dream that we will one day find the ultimate theory that will enable us to solve all of society's problems and make people happy. It is time to give up the drive to develop a theory and then use our resources to try to force the universe into conforming to our theory. And when we can't force the universe, we instead seek to force other people, thinking this will prove the theory right.

Instead, we need to adopt an open-ended approach of continually monitoring ourselves to see what actually makes us happy. Instead of thinking that the world and our psyches *should* work a certain way, we need to look at how things *actually* work. We need to look at what kind of beings we are and how our psyches function. We need to stop looking for answers *outside* ourselves and instead look *inside* ourselves. And to me, this is the essence of spirituality. Spiritual people are (ideally) scientists who are experimenting with the psyche and observing how it *actually* works, not how some pope, scientist or guru says it *should* work.

We need to stop looking for the answers in the far reaches of the cosmos. We need to look inside and realize that on the personal level, our happiness and wellbeing is primarily determined by the conditions in our psyches. Even at the level of society, the key to solving most problems is to understand the psychological component of those problems. Will we allow a small elite of financiers to keep us as economic slaves of a system based on greed (as was demonstrated beyond doubt by the 2008 financial crises), or will we find a more compassionate approach to the economy? Well, that depends on what kind of beings we see ourselves as being. Are we beings who can be divided into two categories, with some the masters and others the slaves? Or is there only one type of human beings where all of us have equal rights and deserve equal opportunity to determine our own destiny?

What do I mean with an open-ended approach? During the Age of Ideology we have been driven by the belief that it is possible for us human beings to define some absolute or highest truth. What we need is to give up this closed-ended approach. Instead, we need to look at history and realize that progress is an ongoing process with no end in sight.

History shows us that we human beings have gradually raised our understanding and awareness. History also shows us that this has not been a steady upward climb because there has been a number of periods where progress stagnated. What made progress come to a halt? It was when a society had accepted a closed-ended ideology that claimed to have some truth that we could not go beyond. Yet history has proven that all such "infallible" truths have eventually been replaced by a higher understanding.

Do we really need to go into the same trap that so many past civilizations have been caught in, of thinking our current understanding is the highest one possible? Can't we just make the quantum leap and accept that progress will continue and that humanity will attain a progressively higher understanding of all aspects of life? Can't we just accept that if we want to keep pace with progress instead of being trapped in some blind alley, we need to always be open to an insight that goes beyond what we currently have? Instead of seeking to defend our "infallible" truth, we are always open to that next revelation that will help us take the next step on the never-ending staircase of progress.

The problem with religion and science

When talking about "scientific" Materialism, I have put "scientific" in quotation marks. This is because I do not consider Materialism to have anything to do with science. As I said, the deepest intent behind science is to free people and society from theories so we can base our lives not on a dream of how the world *should* work but on experience of how it actually *does* work. Materialism has nothing to do with this goal. Materialism is a political ideology that has hijacked science. It uses science only as a way to demonstrate its authority and get people to accept its view of life (as religion uses God and Jesus to claim authority). It is another attempt at formulating a theory and trying to make the universe conform to it.

On an immediate level, science is the primary tool for moving people and society away from the religious superstition that dominated the middle ages, the so-called dark ages. Yet on a deeper level, science has the potential for being the tool to move us completely out of the Era of Ideology, the era in which we attempted to create a man-made theory and force the universe to work according to the theory.

The larger irony here is that science only came to stand in opposition to religion because religion had been perverted from its original purpose. In my view, scientific Materialism has no more to do with pure science than Catholicism has to do with pure spirituality. The original purpose behind spirituality is to enable us to live happy and fulfilled lives. Spiritual teachings were meant to give us a frame of reference for living our lives in a way that was in line with how the world and our psyches actually work, thereby giving us the knowledge and tools to attain mastery over our psychological conditions.

Obviously, some of these old spiritual teachings were expressed in an age when people had less knowledge of how the world works than we have today. Thus, it is mind-boggling to me when fundamentalist Christians can believe that no spiritual being has anything more to tell us about the spiritual side of life today than what was said 2,000 years ago. I have come to understand that the original teachings of Jesus described a path to help us gain mental freedom. These teachings have been hijacked by the Catholic church (and later Lutheran churches) and used as a justification for political control. Science brought us out of this control, but now Materialism has used science to create a new form of thought control. It is *comical* to me that those who promote Materialism cannot see how similar its approach is to that of medieval Christianity. Materialists are simply seeking to set themselves up as the unquestionable authority of society, just as the Catholic priests were in the Dark Ages. When will we ever learn?

It is self-evident to me that spirituality needs to be an open-ended activity that is constantly refining itself as society changes and people's needs change. The rise in mental health problems proves that Christianity has completely failed to adapt to the changing times and give people what they need in today's complex world. If Christianity had fulfilled its responsibility to help people deal with the fundamental questions, I don't think we would see the amount of psychological issues we have today. Of course, the question is whether official Christianity would be able to adapt, given its starting point, but I will talk about that later.

To me, there is no inherent contradiction or conflict between pure spirituality and pure science. Science is naturally focused on the material side of life. It is a matter of using our physical senses, and instruments that extend the senses, to observe and then using our rational minds to see patterns. Spirituality is naturally focused on the world that is outside the range of the physical senses, including the deeper aspects of the psyche. We can also make observations about how the psyche works, and we can then use another faculty of our minds, often called intuition, to see patterns. Ideally, I see scientific exploration and spiritual exploration as going hand in hand.

Elitism is an unrecognized problem

So how did we ever come to have a split between science and religion and why are our modern democracies dragging this conflict with us, being unable to talk about what kind of beings we are and how to make us happy? Well, this is a topic I will comment on later when I have given more background and can therefore explain how I reached my conclusion. Let me hint at one way to answer this question by pointing out a basic observation.

When I look at history, I see a pattern that I was never told about in school. In every society, there is a tendency for a small elite to set themselves up in a position of power and privilege where they basically dominate the population. In my view, this elitism is precisely what democracies are meant to stop. Yet we now see the emergence of societies where power and privilege are acquired not through physical force but through economic force. As the financial crisis of 2008 demonstrated, our modern democracies have allowed the evolution of a situation in which the majority of the wealth is becoming increasingly concentrated in the hands of a small elite. And their grip on the economy has created another closed system that in 2008 threatened the collapse of the world economy.

I would therefore propose that the end of the Era of Ideology is also the end of the "Era or Elitism." After all, wasn't it a small elite that attempted to use ideology to dominate the population? Wasn't ideology (from the Catholic church over communism to scientific Materialism) simply a tool to force people to accept a worldview that established the power and privilege of a small elite? Those who define how the world *should* work, can define it in such a way that society works in their favor.

I want to reach back to what I said about spiritual people having an impact on society. In my view, we can only hope to be constructive by realizing that the Era of Ideology is over. We have gone through the Era of Catholicism, the Era of Marxism and the Era of Materialism, but the solution is not to usher in the era of a specific spiritual ideology. I don't think society will ever accept a particular spiritual teaching or guru. But society might be influenced by certain universal ideas about how the psyche works and what makes people happy.

In my mind, the Era of Ideology is over, and it is time to give up the dream of the ultimate theory or system. It is time to stop trying to force the universe and ourselves to function according to a theory. It is even time to stop dreaming about creating a Utopian society in which all problems are solved and all people are happy. Such a society would be another closed system and it would self-destruct due to the same historical necessity that caused Marxist societies to self-destruct. Instead, I think we need to realize that the task of finding a way to be happy is an ongoing process that will go on indefinitely. Instead of constantly hoping to find some ultimate result, we need to embrace the *process*. And this leads me to the next topic I want to talk about.

3 | ARE WE CHANGEABLE OR UNCHANGEABLE BEINGS?

When I was two or three years old, there was a song that was popular on Danish radio. It was a father singing to his son, and every verse was about some bad thing that happened to him. The refrain contained the words: "My son, my wish for you is that you shall become better than I." My father once sang the song to me, and when he sang those words, I got very upset, jumped up and down and yelled: "*No* Dad, *you* shall become better too, *you* shall become better too!" This is the essence of my psychological make-up. Even as a child, I was dedicated to improving myself and helping other people do the same. My entire life has revolved around improving myself, and by this I primarily mean improving my mind, my consciousness, my psyche. However, this hasn't been an ego-trip because it has always had the underlying purpose to improve conditions for other people as well.

How can society explain that I was born with this passion? According to Christianity, everything is created by God. The underlying assumption must be that

God created each and every one of us with the psychological make-up that we have. So God supposedly created my entire family without any interest in self-improvement, and then he created me with a dominant interest in self-improvement and placed me among people with no interest. This begs the question of how a supposedly all-mighty God would need to create me with a passion for improving myself? If he wanted me to reach a higher state, why not create me in that state? Furthermore, if all I need to do is to wait for Jesus to come and save me, why would I need a drive to change myself? According to official Christian doctrines, I am not a changeable being, I am a sinner who can only behave according to Christian rules and then hope Jesus will save me. So how come I had this drive to change myself?

Materialism likewise has no explanation that makes sense to me. I was told in biology class that my body and brain are the products of my genetic heritage (no one in my family has the self-improvement gene). I was later told my psychological make-up is a product of the material processes of my brain. In other words, because of my genes, I was born with a certain psychological make-up and there is nothing I can do about it. Psychology then tells me that my psychological make-up is also affected by my environment and my upbringing, by nurture, but again, nothing in my upbringing stimulated any drive to improve myself. Materialism makes it clear that I have no power to change my genes, my basic brain functions or my past. Materialism says I am not a changeable being, so how come I had the drive to change myself?

Both of these supposedly authoritative thought systems portray me as a being whose psychological make-up is a product of factors over which I have virtually no control. Thus, according to all of the experts in my society, I am not a changeable being. I am a static being, and there is not much I can do about it. I cannot consciously decide to remake my psychological make-up and become a different person.

Yet if I really were a being with no powers or limited powers for changing myself, how can it be explained that I have been passionate about changing myself from early childhood? How can it be explained that I have indeed changed my psychological make-up in fundamental ways and that millions of spiritual people have done the same? Did God make a mistake when he created those millions of people? Or did some genetic mutation give us a desire to improve ourselves, a desire which other genes make sure can never be fulfilled? Or do we need to look beyond the two dominant thought systems of our time to find an explanation?

Of course, I am not saying that official thought systems are completely incorrect. There are indeed many people who have no desire to improve themselves but who instead seem to want to live their lives a certain way without changing it. Most members of my family are examples of this. They lived or live as if our basic psychology is something we cannot change. When we reach adulthood, our lives are set on a track and there is not much we can do about it.

Is there real hope or only imagined hope?

As I have said, from a very early age, I was acutely aware that I live in a world that needs a lot of improvement. On an overall scale, war and human conflict is something that I never saw as natural or inevitable. According to Christianity and Materialism, there is little hope for overcoming conflict. Yet, then how do we explain that we have actually made some progress towards overcoming conflict? Are not our modern democracies a clear demonstration of the fact that we have a longing for a more free and peaceful society? And do they not also demonstrate that it is possible for us to change ourselves in such a way that we can manifest a society that has a peaceful approach to resolving human conflict? After fighting for centuries, we now have a group of nations that are dedicated to non-violent conflict resolution. So doesn't the very fact that we now have democracies prove that we are capable of changing ourselves?

As a child, I remember reading a book about stone-age people and how they were afraid to walk outside their huts after dark (a clear example of how our psychological make-up limits us). When I compared their material standard of living to my own, I was struck by the amazing progress we have made. Doesn't this technological progress prove that we are changeable beings, that we are capable of improving our outer situation?

As I see it, humanity is on a path that gradually leads towards progress. All we need to do is to take the next logical step and realize that as we are capable of changing our outer circumstances, we are also capable of changing our inner circumstances. There are societies in the East where they have a very old tradition for systematically raising people's consciousness beyond what we today call normal. As I discovered at the age of 18, they have a millennium-old tradition for defining a gradual, systematic path that can lead anyone willing to apply themselves above the conflict-ridden state of consciousness to a state of inner well-being. As I discovered later, we also have a tradition for this in the West, but unfortunately it has been actively suppressed, first by the Catholic Inquisition and then by the Materialist Inquisition. I have always known that we humans are capable of deliberately and consciously changing ourselves, meaning our psychological make-up. If that was not the case, there would be no hope of improving society or the "human condition." If we have no hope of improvement, then why are we bothering? Our modern democracies are based on there being hope of improvement, so imagine that we made a shift and more consciously sought to help people improve their psychological make-up in order to give them psychological well-being and peace of mind.

Another way to look at this is in terms of freedom. Democracies are more free than dictatorships in the sense that they give their citizens more political and economic freedoms. Yet as the rise in mental illness and depression demonstrates, giving us outer freedoms doesn't necessarily mean that we are free. What truly limits us is the inner conditions of our psyches. My father was politically a free man, but he was not psychologically free. I was not psychologically free for the first decades of my life, but I have now attained a much higher degree of psychological freedom. I see it as the next step for modern democracies that we shift from focusing on outer freedom to helping people attain inner freedom, mental freedom, psychological freedom. The freedom to consciously choose our state of mind instead of having it be determined by our reactions to external conditions.

Everybody believes we are changeable

Our society has an explanation problem because we have not resolved the conflict between Christianity and Materialism. We have not done this partly because we have not been willing to have an open debate that can show us the inherent contradictions in both systems of thought. Here is how this relates to us being changeable beings.

Official Christian doctrines state that we are born as sinners, and if you look at the consequence, it would seem that we have no power to change this by ourselves. You are who God created you to be, you have the psychology you were created to have. Yet Christianity does not leave people without hope. It says that we can escape our condition of sin, but not in this world, only in the next world. We need the external savior to take us to heaven, but this can only happen if we obey the external church that supposedly represents this savior on earth. So on one hand, Christianity gives us hope but it also says salvation is not in this world but in a coming world.

At the same time, Christianity is actively seeking to reform people's outer behavior by making them follow a set of rules. Yet if we are not changeable beings, why is it necessary to attempt to scare us into following these rules? And what mechanism allows us to decide to follow these rules, unless we have the ability to consciously and willfully change ourselves? And if we do indeed improve ourselves, are we still sinners? In other words, Christianity acts as if it does actually believe we are changeable beings. We can be forced to change our behavior from without, but we cannot decide to change from within.

The problem is that Christianity has not changed with the times. It has not realized that in today's world people know and understand a lot more about life than when Christian doctrines were defined. Christianity has failed to adapt to the fact that in a democratic society, fear of going to hell is no longer a primary motivating factor. As I said, Christianity was set on a track when the emperor Constantine made it the official religion of the Roman Empire. At that moment, Christianity became a political apparatus for controlling the population, and it remained so for over a thousand years (to some degree it still is). The effect was that society remained a highly elitist society that kept the population as slaves of a small elite of Kings, clergy and noblemen. What made it possible to sustain this society was fear. People could not overthrow the feudal societies because they feared their leaders. And this fear was very much based on the fear of burning forever in a fiery hell by going against God's order. Going against the king and the noblemen was going against the church—and that was going against God.

Yet with the advent of modern democracies, we have created a fundamentally different society. Democratic citizens do not fear our leaders, we do not fear authority. Therefore, the Christian thought system that was defined in a time when people feared authority no longer has validity in today's age. Christianity has failed to adapt and change its doctrines from being based on fear to giving people real understanding. This is why Christianity can offer people no help with their psychological issues in today's complex world. This is why, as a child and youth, I found nothing of real value in the Christian religion, and the same holds true for millions of spiritual people. I think it even holds true for many more millions of people who are not aware that they are spiritual.

Now, let's look at Materialism. One of the prominent proponents of Materialism is the English professor Richard Dawkins. On the one hand, he claims that we are the products of our genes and that we have no power to deliberately override our genetic make-up. He also claims that everything that goes on in our consciousness is the product of the purely materialistic processes in our brains. At the same time, he has been engaged in a decades-long crusade to eradicate religion and turn all people into materialists. Yet why should I believe what he says, when he clearly does not believe it himself?

Here is what Dawkins actually says: I am a product of my genes and the electro-chemical processes of my brain, and I have no conscious control over any of these factors because mind cannot change matter. Therefore, the fact that I see myself as a spiritual being is a matter of my genetic make-up (it cannot in any way be the product of my upbringing, as it was distinctly anti-spiritual). At the same time, he is telling me that my spiritual outlook on life is wrong and that I should make a conscious decision to abandon it and accept his materialistic outlook on life. But if I really am the unwitting product of my genes, which faculty do I have that gives me the ability to change my mind and become a materialist? Wouldn't I have to consciously override my genes in order to accept Dawkins' materialist view? And according to that view, my brain came first and my mind came later, therefore my mind has no power over my brain. So if he really believes this, why doesn't he just shut up instead of telling people to do what his religion says they can't do? Why doesn't he simply wait for evolution to eradicate the genes that make people believe in religion instead of thinking he has to give evolution a helping hand?

There is another proponent of Materialism, named Sam Harris. He has written a book in which he denies that we human beings have free will. So, on one hand he presents arguments for why we don't have free will, but he obviously doesn't believe in his own argumentation. Why do I say that? Because the purpose of his book is to convince me that I am wrong when I think I have free will, and therefore I should consciously decide to abandon my position and accept his position. But if I really don't have free will, which faculty would allow me to make such a change?

My point is simple. Even the most outspoken proponents of Materialism do not believe we are unchangeable beings. The very fact that they are trying to convince other people to change their minds proves that they must believe people have the ability to change their minds. This means we are fundamentally changeable beings. We have the ability to deliberately and consciously change ourselves. This means we are not exclusively the products of our genetic make-up. It proves that not everything that goes on in our minds is the product of the materialistic processes of the brain. To me, all of this proves that we are not material beings.

I am not saying that we are not affected by material conditions, such as our genes, our brain chemistry and our upbringing. I am saying that we are not the *exclusive* products of these material conditions because if we were, we could not change ourselves. And if we could not change ourselves, then the progress we have seen in society has no meaning and should not have happened. Furthermore, our personal lives would have no meaning. Most people are not happy with their current state, and if there was no hope of improving it, life would be unbearable.

I agree with science that we are indeed affected by nature and nurture. I agree that most people are so affected by the conditions in which they grow up that their lives are set on a track that they cannot deviate from (my father is again a typical example). Yet I also see that we human beings have a potential to rise above our upbringing, to refuse to conform and stay on that predefined track. I see that we have the capacity to deliberately pull ourselves above the station in life into which we are born and rise above our upbringing. I see that we can claim our freedom to remake our psychology so we can choose the life experience we want.

It has always been clear to me that I have the ability to change my psychological make-up. For 44 years this has been the main focus of my life, and given how much I have actually changed during that time, I feel my experience validates that we human beings can indeed change ourselves. We now need to consider how we might do so, but first I want to talk about an issue that dominated my childhood and youth, namely why we human beings can't agree on anything.

4 | WHY CAN'T WE ALL GET ALONG?

Another explanation problem of our sophisticated society can be expressed in the old question: "Why can't we all just get along?" As a small child I was deeply shocked by human disagreement and conflict, especially war, which was something I simply could not fathom. It gave me a deep psychological pain to realize that I am on a planet where people regularly decide to commit wholesale slaughter of other people, even women and children. This gave me a very strong need to understand why there is so much conflict among human beings. After studying both psychology and spiritual teachings for over 40 years, I have found explanations that make sense to me. These explanations are complex and have several layers, but I will begin with what I consider the most basic or universal.

I want to reach back to what I said about the Age of Ideology being over. Why did we get into this age in the first place? Why do we human beings have this obsessive-compulsive need to create theories that can supposedly explain everything? And why do we have the even stronger need that, when we think we have such a theory, we simply have to force the universe and other people to conform to the theory? And if other people won't conform, then we feel that the epic importance of spreading our theory justifies killing, or at least forcing, those people.

The pyramid of human needs

In order to explain this, let me refer to a famous American psychologist, named Abraham Maslow. He studied human needs and said that everything that happens in our psyches relates to some kind of need. Maslow created a hierarchy of human needs, often depicted as the pyramid below.

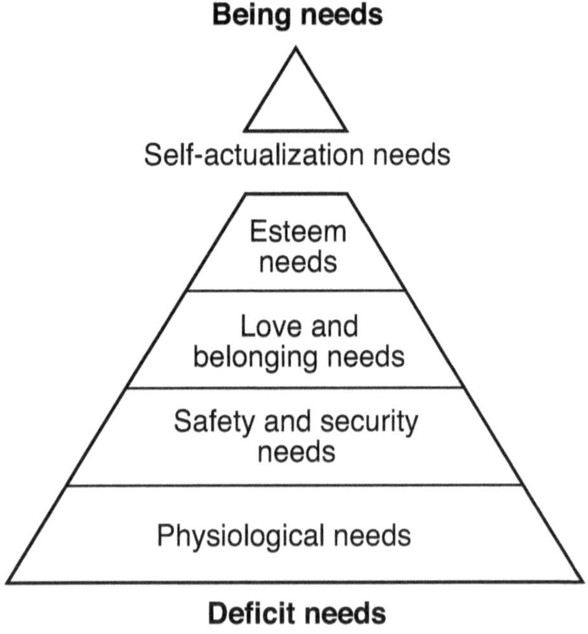

According to Maslow, there is a certain progression in these needs. For example, one of the physiological needs is obviously that we need to eat. If you are really hungry, any of the needs that are higher up in the pyramid fade away in your mind and the need to eat becomes dominant. Likewise, if you feel your life is threatened, getting esteem from others suddenly doesn't seem so important. However, when these basic needs are met, they fade from our awareness and the higher needs become more important. When your belly is full, you focus on other aspects of life. Let us just take a brief look at the needs as described by Maslow, from the bottom of the pyramid and upwards:

- Physiological needs. These needs relate to the short-term survival of the physical body. We need to breathe, drink, eat and sleep. We need to be protected from immediate threats to our lives.

- Safety and security needs. These needs relate to the long-term survival of the body. We need long-term physical safety and a sense that our basic needs are taken care of.

- Love and belonging needs. When we feel that the survival of the body is somewhat taken care of, our attention becomes focused on meeting needs that go beyond physical survival. This includes the needs for a spouse, for friends and for a sense of belonging to a family, a community, a religion, a political movement or any other group.

- Esteem needs. These needs relate to self-esteem. Maslow talked about two levels of esteem needs. The lower level relates to the respect we receive from outside ourselves, such as from a spouse, children, friends, superiors at work or society at large (fame). The higher level is the respect we receive from inside ourselves, namely self-respect. It comes from knowing what kind of beings we are and that we have intrinsic worth. Once we attain self-respect, it is much harder to lose than respect from others.

The needs described so far are what Maslow calls deficit needs. This means that we notice them only when they are not met. In other words, if the lower needs are met, they fade away and we then have attention left over to focus on the higher needs.

For example, in all of the modern democracies, we have had a situation for decades where most people do not need to worry about physiological and safety needs. Most people know that they will have a place to live, enough food to eat and clothes to put on. They also know they live in a relatively safe country where there are few internal threats and also relatively few external threats. This means that in the democratic world most people are focused on love and belonging needs and esteem needs, and some are moving out of the deficit needs and into the higher needs, what Maslow called the self-actualization needs.

The dominant but unrecognized human need

In order to explain human conflict, I will go beyond Maslow because I have come to see that Maslow and most other psychologists have overlooked some of the most dominant of human needs. Let me make a distinction. We human beings have physical bodies that are programmed to ensure the survival of our species. So the two lower needs defined by Maslow are very much based on the needs of the body, namely eating, propagation and physical safety. These needs are what we often call instinctual, meaning they are programmed into our bodies and our subconscious minds. In a sense, we could say that physical survival is the most basic need, but I do not consider it the most basic *human* need. Survival is the most basic needs of our bodies, but it is not a human need because it is not our bodies that make us human.

What makes us human is our minds or our psyches. According to Maslow's pyramid, we are more than our bodies, and that is why we have the higher needs. To me, this is also proven by the development of art, literature and any form of culture. That is why I am saying that the physiological needs and the needs for physical safety are almost animalistic, they are instinctual to our bodies. If we feel another human being is threatening our lives, we might very well kill that person in order to ensure our own survival.

As I said earlier, I cannot see any animal species that has the ability to consciously and deliberately change its behavior. We can do this because we human beings have self-awareness. This ability has many ramifications that I will talk about later. In this context I will focus on one aspect, namely that self-awareness gives us the ability to project what might happen in the future. According to scientific consensus, a deer grazing in the meadow is not consciously worrying about being attacked by a wolf. It has an instinctual programming that causes it to react very quickly when a threat is perceived, but the deer isn't consciously thinking ahead. We human beings obviously do think ahead, and this points to a basic human need.

We human beings have certain instincts, but we also have the ability to consciously think about how we follow, or do not follow, those instincts. We are consciously aware of what we do, and therefore a basic human need is to have some understanding of how our environment works and how we can relate to it. Let me compare this to the progression implied in Maslow's pyramid.

The progression of human needs

If we go back to our ancestors who lived in a hunter-gatherer culture, they were primarily focused on their physiological needs. They had a need to understand their environment, such as what food was available where and when, what predators were present and what weather conditions might threaten them. Yet according to anthropologists, they also developed some ideas about what was behind natural phenomena, such as nature spirits or gods. To me, this is an expression of our need to understand and explain our environment.

As a result of having the ability to project into the future, we also have the ability to deduce cause-effect sequences. Our ancestors observed that as the days grew shorter, birds would start appearing in the sky, flying in a certain direction. They learned that the onset of winter was causing the birds to migrate. This led them to the understanding that there is an unseen cause behind physical events, and this gave them the need to understand these hidden causes in order to be able to predict what would happen in the future. Yet their understanding of the world was very much related to their needs for physical survival.

The hunter-gatherers lived in small, nomadic tribes that rarely had contact with other tribes because the population was so small. As the population grew, there was more competition between tribes for hunting grounds, and this led to a phase where people became more focused on security from human enemies. In many parts of the world, this phase has continued until the advent of modern democracies and a dedication to resolving conflict with non-violent means. Before then, the threat of being attacked was stronger than it is today.

What we see during this phase is that people still had a need to explain their environment, and because of the safety concerns, they needed to explain the presence of enemies. This caused many groups of people to develop some abstract concepts of good and evil. They came to see themselves as good and their enemies as evil.

Despite the frequent conflicts, we then saw the development of societies where people could feel that their physiological needs and safety needs were taken care of to a degree where they could focus more on love and belonging needs. It now became important for people to belong to a clearly defined group, and this led to the development of many different tribes, cultures and civilizations. Because people in ancient times were more isolated (due to the lack of modern communication), each group developed its own understanding of how their environment worked and how they as a group fit into it. The Bible gives us an important example of how a small tribe in the Middle East gradually developed the idea that they were set apart from all other people and belonged to a special race.

The Bible also shows us that after developing this strong group identity, the Jewish people moved to the next level and began focusing on esteem needs. In an environment where each tribe had their own deity, whom they thought was partial to their group, the Jews developed the idea that they had the superior God, the only true God. Next came the idea that they were the chosen people of this superior God, giving them the ultimate level of self-esteem. This developed into the sense that a particular area was a land promised to them by their superior God. Unfortunately, this land was already occupied by other people, but the Jews felt that their God had given them the authority to commit what was essentially genocide against these people (If you have forgotten this, pick up a Bible and read Deuteronomy).

Of course, I am using the Jews only as an example with which we are all familiar. Throughout history, we see many other groups of people who have gone through the same process. They gradually developed an explanation of the world that put themselves in a position of superiority to certain other groups of people, perhaps even as being superior to *all* other groups of people. In many cases, this led to incredible atrocities because these people felt that a deity, a political philosophy, historical necessity or evolutionary demands justified that they killed those who refused to submit to their explanation of the world.

My conclusion is that a very important human need is the need to explain how our environment works. We now need to look at why this leads to conflict.

Why our worldview becomes the source of conflict

Once we have developed an explanation that can tell us how our environment works, we feel it gives us the ability to predict what will happen in the future. This gives us the sense that we are in control of our future, our destiny. Our idea gives us a sense of security. This means that our worldview serves as the primary way for us to satisfy the needs for physical safety and security described by Maslow.

We could look at this from another perspective and say that this human need springs from the fact that we live in an environment that contains a high degree or uncertainty or unpredictability. We experience that we are never quite safe in this world because a variety of factors (starvation, bad weather, earth changes, predators, human enemies, illness—to name a few) make it difficult for us to feel that we can predict how long and how well we might live. This uncertainty is the underlying threat we experience in this world and thus another basic human need is to find a way to deal with this threat.

Again, this relates to us having self-awareness. If we did not have self-awareness, we could not project that in the future we might starve, die from flooding or be attacked by enemies. There is no animal species that can predict its own death, but we human beings can. Our self-awareness gives us the awareness that we will one day die, and that we might die prematurely due to the actions of other people. Because we can predict what *might* happen, we have this basic need to be able to control what *will* happen. From this perspective, a basic human need is the drive to feel we are in control of our future. Our need to explain how the world works could be seen as a means to achieve the sense of being in control.

This explains why we become so attached to our explanations, our worldview. Once we have adopted an explanation that gives us a sense of having control over our environment, this explanation becomes the source of our sense of being secure. If our worldview is proven incorrect, then it is not just an opinion that is threatened, it is our sense of being in control and thereby our sense that we can live with the uncertainty of the world. We have linked our sense of survival to the idea, and that is why defending the idea seems like a life-and-death issue. We literally feel that if our idea is threatened, our survival is threatened. As I said, if we feel our survival is threatened, we might indeed be capable of killing other human beings. To me, this explains why we are capable of killing physical people in order to defend an abstract idea.

We could also say that because of the uncertainty of our environment, combined with our ability to project into the future, a basic fear is that something bad can happen to us or that our needs will not be met. This can lead us into a fear so strong that it becomes psychologically crippling. The world's mental institutions contain many people for whom such an existential fear has become so dominant that they simply cannot function and lead a normal life. Incidentally, I think this proves that we are more than animals, more than our bodies.

Based on this, we could say that the basic driving factor in human existence is the need to overcome our fear of what might happen in the future. In order to beat back this primal fear and be able to function, even enjoy the moment, we need to develop a sense of being in control of our situation. And the primary tool for getting to feel we are in control is to develop a worldview (a religion, a political philosophy or scientific Materialism), which makes us certain that we know how the world works. Once we have such a theory and have accepted it as absolute, it can help us beat down our existential fear and live what we call a normal life in our culture.

This explains why it is seen as such a threat when our worldview is brought into question. If our religion, for example, is proven wrong, it is not something superficial that is threatened. It is the very psychological foundation of our lives. It is the very tool we have used to be able to function. It is our sense of psychological survival. Thus, if our worldview is threatened, so is our very sense of having life under our control. Coupled with our survival instinct, this can lead us to feel that if our worldview is threatened, it is our very survival that is threatened.

How can we kill other human beings?

No animal species kills members of its own species to any noteworthy extent. My conclusion is that the survival instinct of a particular species prevents individuals from killing other individuals of the same species. For human beings, this survival instinct has obviously been overridden by some factor—this is simply an observation we can all make by looking at history or the headlines of today. So another explanation problem our society has is how human beings have become able to kill members of its own species by the millions?

I have now presented at least a partial explanation. As a result of our love and belonging needs, we human beings have developed many different groups. Each group has had to face the existential human problem of how to overcome our fear of the future. We could say that the uncertainty we face on this planet makes life psychologically unbearable, but since we have to live here, we have to find a way to deal with our own psychological reaction to the uncertainty.

In order to establish a sense of being in control of their destiny, each group has developed a specific worldview. Yet because each group has developed a different worldview, there is an inevitable tension between various groups. We can all see how the existence of many different religions has led to major conflicts. I grew up in an environment where two different political systems (each claiming to have the superior truth) created a constant threat of a third world war even more devastating than the previous two.

Another factor is that because of our esteem needs, we tend to use our worldview to develop a sense of superiority to other groups of people. This is what Maslow described as the lower esteem needs where we need to get esteem from a source outside ourselves. We tend to feel that because we belong to this superior group, we have esteem, but this also means anyone who does not share our worldview becomes a threat to that esteem.

We now see the underlying mechanism. Groups of people have attempted to fill the basic need for control by coming up with different explanations of how they think the world works. This is not in itself a problem because the basic goal is that a group of people attain a sense of control that allows them to function psychologically. If Hindus do it one way, Muslims another way and Christians a third way, what's the problem as long as it works for them? Each group is trying to solve the same human problem, and they do it according to their background and culture. If it helps that group beat back their existential fear, why should that be a threat to another group?

Why we cannot get along

Well, the problem is actually explained by Maslow because he says that the lower needs, the deficit needs, can never be filled in an ultimate way. A deficit need can only exist in a polarity to its opposite. The most obvious example is that no matter how big of a meal you might eat, it cannot prevent you from becoming hungry in the future. We can see many celebrities today who have attained fame, but no matter how much attention they get, it never seems to be enough. We can see people who cannot get enough money and who in 2008 allowed their short-term greed to go so far that it threatened a collapse of the entire financial system. The people who precipitated this situation were already billionaires so in actuality they had more money than they could spend during the rest of their lifetimes.

Yet they didn't feel they had enough and this blinded them to the consequences of their actions. This is precisely the effect of the deficit needs when they are combined with the need for control. Even though this goes beyond Maslow, what I have called the need for control is also a deficit need. This means it can never actually be fulfilled. But just as with billionaires, there is the illusion that one day we might have enough. There is the dream of the pot of gold at the end of the rainbow. If a group really had the ultimate thought system, based on an absolute truth that could explain every single factor in the universe, then that group would have ultimate control—or so the lower needs project at us. Of course, this group would then also have the ultimate esteem because it would indeed be superior to all these other groups who have a lesser "truth."

The real reason we can't all get along is that we have developed all of these different attempts to gain control over our future by explaining how the world works. This sense of being in control could be threatened if our worldview (or even parts of it) were proven wrong. The existence of other worldviews is a threat against our worldview so the only way to establish the ultimate sense of being in control would be to eradicate all competing worldviews. This is why Hitler killed 6 million people in concentration camps. This is why Stalin killed 21 million of his own citizens in order to maintain his personal power. This is why the great Chairman Mao killed 70 million Chinese in order to maintain the illusion that his cultural revolution would lead to the ideal society. And this is why radical Muslim groups today dream of eradicating all other religions and establishing Islam as the only religion on earth. It is, for that matter, why many less radical Christians have the same dream about Christianity, or why some so-called militant atheists dream of eradicating all religion.

The human dilemma

The basic human dilemma is that the world presents us with threats and insecurities that we cannot live with in a psychological sense. As I said, we cannot function psychologically in the world we live in. Yet because we have to live in this world, we have had to find ways to deal with it psychologically. And it is our different ways of dealing with this human dilemma that leads to conflict. People feel threatened by other people being different, and the more threatened they feel, the more they are driven to change those other people. If the other people will not be changed, then the first group may feel it is necessary and justified to kill those people in order to (supposedly) remove the threat to their worldview, their sense of security. It is one group's drive to change other people by making them conform to their own worldview that is the source of most large-scale conflicts.

The real issue here is that as long as we are approaching the human dilemma from the position of the deficit needs, we will *never* overcome human conflict. A group trapped in the deficit needs will always feel that its worldview is threatened by different views. Does that mean I think there is no way out? Of course not, because Maslow makes it clear that the solution is to rise above the deficit needs and consciously embrace the self-actualization needs.

According to Maslow, it is a natural progression that as we become better at satisfying the deficit needs to a critical degree, we become less driven by our existential fear. Instead, we begin to focus on the higher needs, the self-actualization needs. As we focus on these needs, they become more and more important. It now becomes more important to discover who we really are than to feel better than other people or to feel that we have the ultimate truth. We can also say that as we begin to focus on the self-actualization needs, our attention is drawn away from the outside world and towards the inner world of the psyche. We become more focused on changing ourselves than on changing other people. We actually begin to do what Jesus told us to do 2,000 years ago, namely to stop looking at the splinters in the eyes of our brothers and instead look at the beams in our own eyes.

It is when we go through this transformation that we can stop feeling threatened by other people being different from ourselves. We can stop seeing differences only as the source of conflict and instead develop respect for other people's right to be different from us—and our right to be different from them. This is what can potentially lead to a more peaceful world because we can begin to approach problems without having this obsessive-compulsive drive to make other people conform to our worldview. Can we actually achieve this state of mutual respect? Well, if we couldn't, how could we possibly have developed democracies? A democracy is based on the recognition that all people have the same basic rights, and the most basic right of all is the right to be different. This is what can lead us to mutual respect for our differences rather than seeing our differences as threats.

The very fact that we now live in democratic societies proves that humankind has already begun this process. We just haven't been consciously aware of what we have been doing, and that is why we haven't made as much progress as we might have.

I was born different

You might recall that I said I grew up in a society that claimed to be the most sophisticated civilization seen on earth. This is an example of how even modern democracies can have developed a worldview that people think is the ultimate explanation of how life works. You might also recall that I said my society could not meet my most basic need, namely an understanding of the deeper questions of life.

The simple fact is that I was born with a focus on self-actualization, and that is why my society's worldview did not satisfy my need to understand the deepest questions. My society's worldview was (and is) based on the need for security. When people are focused on the security needs, they seek an explanation that claims to have some ultimate authority, and then they do not think further. If someone else thinks further, they will feel threatened by this, and that is why we see that Christians and materialists feel threatened by spiritual people.

My need for understanding the deeper questions was not driven by my need for security. It was driven by my need to know what kind of being I am, so I could improve myself, actualize myself. The same holds true for millions of spiritual people found in every nation and culture. We are born at the level of Maslow's pyramid where our main focus in life is self-actualization. Therefore, we cannot be satisfied with an authoritative thought system that says: "Believe this and you will be safe." We don't need to be safe; we need explanations that allow us to raise our level of consciousness. Our primary need is not security but growth.

This is why I see spiritual people as a potential resource for modern democracies. The survival of any society can only be secured by growth. As I said, all closed societies eventually die out. The stark reality of life is that we must either change or die. As I said, the advent of democracies proves we are in the process of changing, but this is driven by people who are willing to change themselves. And we spiritual people have the potential to be forerunners for this process of change. However, in order to do this, we have to fully move out of the safety needs.

When I say that I was born with a focus on self-actualization, it doesn't mean I had no need for security. I felt threatened by war and other human atrocities and I felt very disturbed by human suffering. I wanted to end these threats and end suffering, and I thought the way to do this was to find an ultimate worldview. When I did find my first spiritual teaching, I had a brief period where I was so enthusiastic that I thought the way to end suffering was to get everyone to accept my new spiritual teaching. I have since grown out of this and now see it differently, as I will explain later.

What I want to mention here is that if we spiritual people are to have a positive impact on society, we have to stop clinging to a particular spiritual philosophy or guru because it gives us a sense of security or superiority. We have to realize that it is not a matter of getting society to accept another ultimate truth or another closed system. It is a matter of helping society move towards a higher understanding based on a set of universal ideas. If we spiritual people do not move completely out of our security needs, we will not have the impact on progress that we might have. We will be like all other security addicts who can only fight to make *their* ultimate truth replace all the other ultimate truths.

5 | CHANGING THE WORLD OR CHANGING OURSELVES?

The central human dilemma is that we live in a world that has a lot of uncertainty. Coupled with our ability to project what might happen in the future, this gives us an existential fear of the future, and it can be psychologically crippling. Yet, given that we have to live in this world, we have to find a way to deal with this condition.

The world may present us with many uncertain conditions, but the fear I am talking about is not an *external* condition, it is an *internal* condition, a *psychological* condition. This underscores my conclusion that we are psychological beings. From time immemorial, we human beings have been focused on controlling our external conditions, but our very reason for doing this is to change our internal conditions. We are seeking to change the world in order to overcome a feeling in our own psyches.

We are seeking to change other people in order to change how we feel inside ourselves. Given that all human beings are seeking to change others in order to change how they feel inside, how likely is it that we can all be successful? How likely is it that *any* of us can be successful? If everybody is trying to change everybody else, where will that get us? This deficit psychology puts us in conflict with people who have developed a different way to deal with the same fear. So the cause of all human conflict is a psychological mechanism, and I think people in the modern democracies are ready to become aware of it and rise above it.

The very source of human conflict is that we are seeking to change our inner condition based on our deficit needs. These needs could also be called fear-based needs. There is a fear that we might go hungry or be killed, and our actions are motivated by seeking to overcome the paralyzing psychological effects of this fear.

Maslow said that we are changeable beings. It is possible for us to gradually grow to a state where we are no longer dominated by this paralyzing fear. We can then begin to focus on our self-actualization needs. These needs are not fear-based, they are love-based.

Changing internally by changing external conditions

Self-actualization is a matter of changing our inner condition. Essentially, we could say that while we are dominated by fear-based needs, we are trying to change the universe in order to change how we feel inside ourselves. Once we transcend fear and go into the love-based needs, we begin to change how we feel inside by changing ourselves, by working with the psyche directly.

While we are trapped in the deficit needs, we are still trying to change our internal condition. We are psychological beings and everything we do relates to changing something in our psyches. The problem with the deficit needs is that they focus our attention on conditions outside ourselves. What is the main characteristic of such external conditions? It is that we have either little or no control over them. Thus, how effective can it be to try to change our internal feeling by trying to change the external conditions over which we have little control?

Joseph Stalin might be seen as a psychopath or an extreme narcissist, but he was essentially driven by the same basic need we all have, namely the need to achieve an inner feeling of being in control of his situation. He had almost unlimited physical power, and in the pursuit of his sense of being in ultimate control, he was willing to kill 21 million people, including most of the people close to him. Yet despite his unlimited physical power, did he ever achieve this inner state of feeling secure, of feeling he had enough control? Of course he didn't! He became more and more paranoid until it ate up his entire life and attention. My conclusion is that no matter how much physical power to change the external world we might have, it will never be enough to give us the inner feeling we seek.

When we rise above the fear-based needs, we realize the futility of seeking to change our internal situation in the roundabout way of changing our external situation. We realize that what we actually want is not a set of ideal outer circumstances. In reality, our dream of having ideal outer conditions was based on a misunderstanding that this would give us the inner feeling we seek. As I said, the welfare society is based on the assumption that if society fulfills people's material needs, they will automatically become happy. As has been proven by millions of people, this is not the case. Money cannot buy happiness, only a temporary diversion from unhappiness.

When we rise to the self-actualization needs, we realize that if our goal is to produce an inner feeling, it is futile to seek to do this by changing external conditions. Instead, it is logical that we seek to produce the inner feeling we want by working directly with our internal conditions, our psyches. Self-actualization is all about rising above the compulsion to change the world and other people (factors over which we have little control) and instead working directly with our own psyches—a factor over which we have the potential to take complete control.

I know this last statement will go against what we were all told as we were growing up, namely that we have little or no control over our own psyches. I will later explain why we were told this, but the important point for now is that millions of spiritual people have proven that we can indeed take control over our psyches. And the development of democracy also proves that we can rise above the obsessive-compulsive need to change other people and instead focus on changing ourselves. Because a truly democratic society has, by its very nature, transcended the need to violently overthrow other societies, even the need to control people.

Why we must do unto others

I once imagined what would have happened if representatives from the Soviet Union met with representatives from Denmark and many other democratic nations. The representatives from the Soviet Union would have a paranoid fear that the modern democracies were plotting to overthrow the Soviet system. The democratic representatives would know that they had no such intention, but how could they ever convince the Soviets of their non-violent intent? There could be no negotiated peace because the Soviets were still trapped in fear and believed that everybody wanted to do to them what they wanted to do to others.

It was a big revelation for me to realize that this is the psychological reason behind the universal admonition to not do unto others what we don't want them to do to us. The simple psychological mechanism is that if you have a desire to control other people, you automatically think all other people want to control you. This means you think you are living in a world where everybody wants to control you, meaning you can never be at peace. During the cold war, the Americans were convinced that the Soviets wanted to take over America, and the Soviets were convinced that the Americans wanted to take over the Soviet Union. It doesn't really matter whether one or both of them were right because the psychological effect was that none of them could be at peace.

Democracy is actually based on the realization that there is a fundamental truth behind the statement to do unto others. In most modern democracies we attribute this statement to Jesus, but it is actually found in virtually every religion known to humanity. I have come to see that this is because it describes a universal principle, a natural law, if you will.

Again, we human beings are psychological beings. For thousands of years, the vast majority of people were trapped in the deficit needs and feared that other people would harm them in order to further their own interests. That is why we had such a long period of world history that was dominated by distrust and conflict. How did we ever start to get out of this distrust? Because some people gradually rose to the realization that changing themselves was more important than changing other people. They realized that if all people actually trusted each other and cooperated, we could achieve so much more by being united than we could ever achieve by being divided.

They realized that in order for us to move out of conflict, some people had to take the first step. Some people had to believe in the promise made by all religions, namely that if you treat other people as you want to be treated, they will (maybe not right away, but eventually) treat you the same way and then everybody will prosper. This is essentially a higher understanding of cause and effect.

We can see that while humankind was divided, relatively little progress was made. For over a thousand years during the so-called Dark Ages, Europe made only marginal progress in terms of the living conditions of the general population. Yet after the advent of democracy, the greater freedom and cooperation has led to incredible progress in the living conditions of the population. If the cause is *division,* the effect is *poverty.* If the cause is *cooperation,* the effect is *prosperity.* Yet as long as people are trapped in the deficit needs, they find it hard to cooperate. Only when they step up to the self-actualization needs, will they be able to cooperate in a way that leads to mutual progress, a win-win situation.

What really drives history

I have come to see that my history classes in school gave a very one-sided understanding of history. They were focused on outer events and therefore reinforced the fear-based view that the only way to change our life experience is to change our external conditions, meaning changing other people and taking control over nature.

I now see that the history of humankind cannot be understood without considering psychological conditions. All of the events we have seen in the pre-democratic world were driven by the obsessive-compulsive need to deal with fear, and the misunderstanding that the only way to overcome the inner fear was to control external conditions. Behind all of the outer, political and technological progress we have seen, there is a deeper cause. There has also been progress in our general level of consciousness. The existence of democratic societies based on the respect for universal rights proves that a critical mass of people have started to work on their self-actualization needs and are no longer dominated by fear and paranoia. This development has so far been largely unconscious. People have been going through the process without being consciously aware of what they have been doing.

Yet imagine the possibilities if more people could consciously embrace their self-actualization needs and begin to work on them? For starters, just imagine how this could impact the problem of mental illness. Self-actualization is all about taking command over our own psyches, and if we can deal with psychological conditions on our own, why would we need to use the public health care system? Of course, this would also have a tremendous impact on people's psychological well-being. It could move us from the welfare society to the wellbeing society.

Maslow's needs and modern democracies

The consequence of Maslow's pyramid of needs is that we can divide people into groups, based on which needs dominate their psyches. Let us relate this to modern democracies:

- Physiological needs. In the modern democracies, these needs do not dominate the lives of most people. People know that by holding a job or by taking advantage of the social safety net, these needs can be met. There are some exceptions, for example criminals who still feel the need to steal in order to meet these needs.

• Safety and security needs. Again, most people feel they live in societies where their safety is ensured. Criminals and conspiracy theorists are the exception.

• Love and belonging needs. Some people are primarily focused on belonging to a group and therefore doing whatever it takes to be accepted by the group. Yet in the modern democracies most people do not find it difficult to be accepted by their society and they do not find it restraining to conform to the normal culture. There are exceptions to this in the form of criminal gangs or radical religious or political groups.

• Esteem needs. Modern democracies have generally made progress in overcoming the class structure where some people were seen as an elite and the general population as belonging to a lower class. This has made it easier for most people to fill their esteem needs by living what is considered a normal life. More and more people are therefore moving into seeking self-esteem, meaning esteem that comes from inside the psyche. And this means they are now approaching the dividing line of working on the self-actualization needs. You cannot have true self-esteem by coming from a sense of deficit. You need to step up and start working on how you see yourself, what kind of being you think you are.

• Self-actualization needs. As Maslow said, the previous categories of needs are deficit needs, fear-based needs. When a person feels these needs are met to a critical degree, it is natural for the person to step up to the next level of needs and start working on self-actualization. And what modern democracies have achieved is to create societies where a large number of people have attention left over to focus on these higher needs.

The logical conclusion is that when a society makes it relatively easy for people to fill their deficit needs to a critical degree, that society has given people the foundation for working on the self-actualization needs. This means that in all of the modern democracies, it is to be expected that a higher and higher percentage of the population is ready to work on self-actualization needs. This is simply to be expected, and it brings us right back to the topic of why modern democracies are seeing an increase in mental illness.

I think what I will say here might go beyond Maslow, so I am not claiming this is his conclusion. In my experience, there is a critical dividing line between people who are driven by deficit needs and people who are focused on self-actualization needs. As long as we are driven by deficit needs, we perceive that the fulfillment of our needs depends on factors outside ourselves. We think that in order to produce the inner condition we desire (security, belonging, esteem) we have to get something from outside or change something outside ourselves. When we move into self-actualization needs, we realize that we do not need anything from outside ourselves. We have everything we need in order to actualize the self within the self. Meaning, we no longer have a need to change external conditions, including other people. Of course, this shift doesn't happen in one glorious epiphany, which is why we see so many spiritual people who go through a long phase of approaching self-actualization by thinking they need an external guru or teaching.

However, when we shift into self-actualization needs, we do begin to focus on changing our own psyches instead of changing the universe or other people. This means that our most important need now becomes to find some idea or teaching about how we can deal with our psyches. And this need is what is precisely *not* being met in the modern democracies. The reason being, as I have already explained, that the war between official Christianity and Materialism has prevented our societies from giving people a universal teaching about how to master our own psychological conditions.

What happens when people have become aware that the most important aspects of their lives is to change themselves but they have no knowledge of how to begin doing this? Well, is it any wonder that this can quickly develop into what we today call mental illness, such as a sense of hopelessness that can lead to depression? When you shift into self-actualization, living the good material life offered by your society will suddenly seem utterly pointless, or at least not enough to give you a sense of purpose in life. And if a person who is in self-actualization mode has no sense that life has a purpose, this can quickly become a serious psychological problem. In my view this explains a large part of the cases of depression seen in modern democracies.

I have heard psychologists say that many forms of more severe mental illness is a cry for help, an attempt to say: "Here I am and I have an urgent need that is not being met!" What if that urgent need is to learn how to actualize the self? Consider how much mental suffering is caused by this and then consider how utterly unnecessary it is. It is all caused by the fact that our modern societies have not been able to move out of the gridlock caused by the war between Christianity and Materialism.

When I first realized this, which happened at the age of 18, it was such a shock to me that my society could claim to be so sophisticated and yet be so utterly impotent to resolve this war of the world-views. And I am still shocked that in the past 44 years so little progress has been made. I mean, really, how much unnecessary suffering does it take before a critical mass of people wake up and realize this simply cannot continue and that we need to think beyond these two closed mental boxes?

6 | HOW DO WE KNOW WHAT IS REAL?

Of course, the question in the end of the last chapter is rhetorical, in the sense that I already know the answer. It is that our society is still dominated by people with closed minds. Their minds are closed because they are focused on the deficit needs, the fear-based needs. They have a domineering need for security, and they get a sense of security by adhering to a world-view that they think is complete, infallible, has ultimate authority and presents the one and only truth. They need this sense of having an ultimate thought system in order to be able to deal with the existential insecurity of human existence, and they cannot survive psychologically if their worldview is threatened. Therefore, they have to defend that view with all means they deem appropriate—it is simply a matter of what means they deem appropriate (violent or non-violent means). However, I think we can go to a deeper level of understanding.

One of the big explanation problems that I wrestled with as I was growing up was why two human beings can hold absolutely opposite and incompatible viewpoints and each of them is convinced that it is their viewpoint that is the only true one. The classical example would be a fundamentalist Christian who believes the Bible is the literal word of God and a fundamentalist materialist who believes what he or she cannot see (or what material instruments cannot detect) doesn't exist. If two people's viewpoints are incompatible, most people would say they can't both be right, as it seems so logical that there can be only one truth. It took me decades to be able to resolve this enigma, and the explanation has layers. So let us begin with the most universal.

The process of perception

I once worked in an open office setting in Utah with a group of very nice people. We had many discussions about spiritual topics, born from the fact that I was the only non-Mormon in the place and they really wanted to convert me. (My standard answer was that the Mormon Church is too old for me.)

One day, the manager of our department comes in and without warning blurts out: "How do we know what we know?" He was very serious, as he had just realized the epistemological problem that philosophers have wrestled with for centuries. I tried to say that we know what we know because it intuitively seems right to us, but that didn't satisfy him (nor myself for that matter). I often thought about his question later and it took me a long time to find what I consider a reasonable answer. Let me begin by talking about perception.

My father worked at a printing factory, and every year at Christmas they would publish a newsletter. One year it had the following illustration on the front cover:

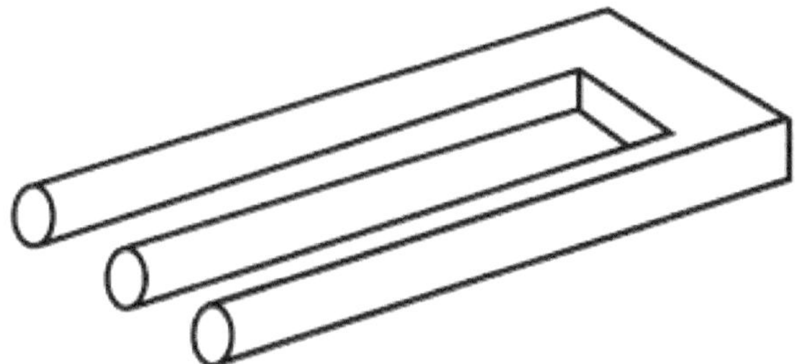

I saved that newsletter and over the years, I must have spent hours staring at that drawing. Today, it is easy to find more of these so-called optical illusions, including the classical drawing that looks like either an old woman with a big nose or a young girl with a feather in her hat. I was fascinated by the drawing because I intuitively sensed it could help me understand something important about how we look at life.

When we look only at the left side of the drawing (perhaps covering the right side), it looks like there are three separate round pegs. When we look quickly at the whole drawing, it looks like the three pegs are joined to a rectangular block. But when we look closely at the right side, we see that there are some lines missing so that the pegs are not fully connected to the block. It is an impossible object that could not actually be made in three dimensions. Now, most people call it an *optical* illusion because they say it cheats the eye. I say it cheats not only the brain but the mind, and it shows us something essential about how our subconscious minds influence how we look at life.

Naturally, we have all heard about Sigmund Freud, sometimes called the "father of psychology." Whatever we may think about him, he did make it clear that we have a subconscious part of the mind that can have a profound influence on our conscious behavior and choices. This also relates to how we see the world.

Let's say I am looking at an apple. Most people would say that my eyes are seeing the apple, but scientists have known for a long time that this is not correct. My eyes are not seeing an object and they are not calling it an apple or anything else. The eye is a complex apparatus, but all it does is to receive light rays (that bounce off the apple), convert them into electrical signals and send those signals to the brain.

When I was a child, the newspapers had only black-and-white photographs, which naturally showed a person as having various gray skin tones. It was fascinating to me when I learned in school that by looking at such a photograph through a magnifying glass, I could see that what seemed to be areas of varying tones of gray were actually made up of small black dots. The whole picture was made of black dots, and the more dots there were (the closer they were together), the darker of a tone of gray was produced. If you looked at such a picture from a very close distance, you could see only a pattern of black dots, you could not see that it formed the face of a person. When you pulled your eye back, you would suddenly see the whole picture.

Well, the human eye does not see any picture, it sees only what is the equivalent of the black dots that make up a newspaper photograph. The retina receives these light signals, but it does not send the light itself on to the brain. The eye converts the light rays into a form of electrical signal and then it sends that signal to the brain. This signal is received by the visual cortex. However, this part of the brain also does not see an apple. It simply displays an image of the signals it receives from the eye somewhere in the brain.

Let us compare this to a real-life situation. We have a city that has a lot of cameras placed at intersections. One camera is recording an image of a particular intersection and the image shows how much traffic there is. Take note that we would never say that the camera is seeing the intersection because we know the camera is a mechanical device without a mind of its own. Well, the eye is also a mechanical device without a mind and that is why the eye does not see anything. The eye does what the camera does: records a scene and sends the impulses on to somewhere else.

The traffic camera receives light rays that bounce off the objects in the intersection, converts them into digital signals and sends them on to a command room where a computer (comparable to the visual cortex in the brain) displays them on a screen. So far, this process is purely mechanical and no human element is involved. Inside the command room are some human beings and they are looking at the screens to evaluate how much traffic there is and what to do to make it flow more smoothly.

To me the interesting thing is that these traffic controllers are sitting inside a dark room, and they are not seeing the actual scene, only an image of it. Likewise, my brain is also inside a dark room (my skull) and it is not seeing my surroundings. In fact, the brain might think it sees light, but in reality, the brain has never experienced light directly. It has only seen the image that comes from the eyes and is displayed on a screen in the brain by the visual cortex.

My whole point for this long explanation is that when I am looking at an apple, my eyes are not seeing an apple. Even my visual cortex is not seeing an apple, it is simply displaying an image inside my brain. So what is it that calls this object an apple and attaches some kind of meaning or story to the image, perhaps even some kind of evaluation of whether it is good or bad? For some people an apple might be seen as something healthy to eat. For other people an apple might be the most dangerous object in human history, given that it caused Adam and Eve (and supposedly also the rest of us) to be kicked out of Paradise.

In other words, there is a genie inside my skull that takes every image recorded by my eyes and displayed by my brain and imposes some kind of interpretation upon the image and what it means for me. This genie is not simply observing. It is looking for patterns by comparing what we see to what we have seen before and what we think we know. The big question is whether the genie is *looking for* patterns or *creating* those patterns and *imposing* them upon the image in the brain? Do we see what the eyes see or what the subconscious genie wants us to see?

Pushing the panic button

So how do we know what we know? We know what we know because inside our minds is a process that takes every impulse we receive from the outside and imposes an interpretation upon it. The question is how this process works and how it influences the way we individually look at life. Let me give a practical example.

Say I wake up before dawn and go outside. It is summertime so the birds are singing and I enjoy the tranquil scene. After some time my eyes detect a light that grows gradually brighter. I then see that the light comes from a certain direction, and gradually a very bright spot appears. This spot moves higher and after a long time, it again disappears in the opposite direction and it is now dark again. What I have described here is what my eyes detect and what the image inside my brain shows. However, this is not what the genie in my subconscious mind sees. It would describe the event as follows: "The sun rose in the East, moved across the sky and set in the West."

At first thought, this might seem like a reasonable explanation. But take note that the eye is only seeing light so it is the genie that imposes the entire interpretation upon it and labels something as the sky, the sun and East and West. Also take note that the interpretation is completely out of touch with reality. What we label the sun is not actually moving across the sky. It is the earth that is moving relative to the sun. The earth is spinning on its axis, but our senses cannot perceive this movement. We cannot see that the earth is turning, and as we are moving around with the earth, we gradually move to the side of the earth that is turned towards the sun and that is why we can now see the sun. Take note that the earth actually does not spin in the direction we would assume based on sensory input. We are moving in the opposite direction of the sun, meaning we are moving from West to East, making it appear as if the sun moves from East to West.

Why is this significant? Because it shows us how easily we can impose an interpretation on the world that is out of touch with reality, and this might help us understand why we can't all get along. You take a fundamentalist Christian and a fundamentalist materialist and you give them the exact same information. This is the situation we have in the world where we all pretty much have access to the same general knowledge. The Christian is likely to still conclude that the Bible is the word of God and therefore correct in every detail. The materialist is likely to take the same information and interpret it as proof that the Bible is fake and there is no God. In my observation this is the root of all conflict, namely that two people can take the same input and inside their minds they reach completely opposite and incompatible conclusions.

Take note that we can relate this to the deficit and self-actualization needs. When we are trapped in the deficit needs, we cling to our perception and are completely closed to the possibility that our minds could impose an interpretation on what we think we know. We need to believe that what we know is reality, is truth. When we move into self-actualization, we gradually begin to question our perception until we begin to see beyond the interpretation of the subconscious genie. More on this later.

How do we explain that people can reach opposite conclusions based on the same input? I earlier said that we live in a world that presents us with a lot of uncertainty and this creates a psychological reaction that is difficult to live with. I was aware of this mechanism for many years, but I could not identify the exact psychological reaction caused by the external uncertainty. I since realized what it is: panic.

Psychologists are well aware that when people are pushed by violent or dramatic outer events, they can go into a state of panic where they cannot think clearly. We all know that in stressful situations, we might feel like we are losing control and we make shortsighted decisions. At the time, we cannot see how non-constructive these decisions are, although it becomes obvious to us when we are no longer in panic.

My conclusion is that we human beings are constantly living with the threat that something can happen that causes us to panic. Life on a planet like earth is simply so fraught with uncertainty that we must constantly fight off panic. In other words, life on earth is constantly pushing our panic buttons and we must push back. How do we do this? Well, for starters let us just say that we have created a genie in the subconscious mind and its task it to make sure we are not thrown into panic. How does the genie do this? The genie develops a sense of how the world works, which gives it a sense of being in control. We may think the genie (or ourselves) are in control of the world, but the genie is actually only in control (somewhat) of what happens in our minds. When the genie has set up a worldview that explains how the world works, and once we have accepted it with the conscious mind, it can push back the existential panic so we no longer feel it consciously. We can therefore live what we (rather ironically) call "normal lives." The moment the genie feels that its worldview is threatened by a new idea, it will send a very strong impulse to our conscious minds to reject the idea.

Our sense of what is real

What must our sense of how the world works be based on? Well, it must be based on a sense of reality, meaning we must feel that the explanation offered by our worldview is real. We might therefore say that another basic human need is the need for a sense of reality, the sense that something is real and can be relied upon. Something that is certain in a world of uncertainty.

One of the basic human needs is to push back panic, and we do so by adopting a thought system that explains how the world works. As we can all observe, throughout history we human beings have defined a large number of such thought systems. What then determines whether a person accepts this or that system? Well, the explanation of the world offered by the system must seem real to a person. Okay, so what determines whether Christianity or Materialism seems real to a particular person? Something in that person's subconscious mind. The genie evaluates both systems and determines that one of them is real. Let's look at a fundamentalist Christian and a scientific materialist. From a superficial viewpoint they seem to be very different, but when we look into the subconscious mind, we see the same psychological mechanism. They both have the exact same need to fight back panic, and they have chosen the exact same way to deal with the problem, namely to adopt a thought system and accept that it is real. The only difference is that they each have a different sense of what is real and that is why they have chosen different thought systems.

The fundamentalist Christian feels he has life and the universe under control because it is ultimately controlled by an all-mighty and good God who can be persuaded by various means to grant personal favors to the people who follow his commandments. This gives the person a sense of security (an illusion of being able to control God) that makes it possible to push the existential panic into the subconscious mind. The fundamentalist materialist feels he has the universe under control because it is *not* controlled by some personal God who might make arbitrary decisions and not grant him favors. Instead, the universe is controlled by laws of nature that absolutely never vary. This gives the materialist a sense of security (an illusion of being able to use the laws of nature) and again the panic can be pushed into the subconscious mind.

The problem for both is that the sense of security is inherently fragile. It is based on a thought system that comes from outside the person, and given the condition of the world, this thought system could potentially be proven wrong. It could even be threatened if another thought system was proven right. And if – and here is the big problem – a person's thought system was proven wrong, then the panic would escape its subconscious prison and take over the person's conscious mind. This would be unbearable and thus it is only a matter of what the person is willing to do in order to avoid this condition that is seen as threatening, potentially a life-and-death issue.

Why is it so threatening? Because when people are trapped in the fear-based deficit needs, they have an all-or-nothing approach. The typical example is a fundamentalist Christian who has pushed back panic by accepting that the Bible is the literal word of God. This view is very fragile because, if something is the word of God, it must be true in every detail. In other words, no detail, no statement in the Bible, could ever be proven wrong because if it was, the fundamentalist would have to reject the Bible in its entirety. This would be unbearable because it would throw him back into panic—as demonstrated by the many people who have lost faith in the Bible over the last couple of centuries.

The irony here is that most materialists can see how ridiculous the all-or-nothing approach is in the Christians. They fail to see that they have the same approach to Materialism. That is why they will not look at even scientific evidence that there is something beyond the material world or that there is a deeper understanding than what Materialism offers. My point being that these people have closed their minds to new ideas, and thus they have closed their minds to progress—which, as I said, happens as the result of a progressive expansion of our understanding. They don't want an expanded understanding, they want to cling to their fragile sense of security based on a worldview that they think does not need to be expanded.

They want their worldview to be the ultimate truth, and the ultimate truth obviously could not be replaced by a higher understanding. In other words, people dominated by security needs seek an ultimate truth. People dominated by self-actualization needs seek a higher understanding than what they have right now—and they continue to do so.

The scale of panic

We can define a scale that measures to what degree people are controlled by their fear of being thrown into panic by new ideas. The more they are trapped in fear (the more they are controlled by their subconscious genie), the more violent are the measures they will take in order to push back threats to their worldview.

The genie can be compared to a computer that has no moral or ethical awareness. It is not able to say that something is right or wrong. It only thinks about how it can accomplish its assigned task of keeping panic below the threshold of conscious awareness. If it evaluates that this can be done only by ridiculing or killing other people, then the genie cannot stop itself from doing whatever it takes. Only the conscious mind can stop the subconscious genie, but only if the conscious mind is making conscious decisions instead of allowing the genie to run its life. We could therefore say that self-actualization is all about learning to take back conscious control of our minds so we are no longer controlled by the subconscious genie.

We all see that world history before the advent of modern democracies is littered with examples of how far people will go to destroy a threat to their thought system. We see how many times people have used force, violence and war to spread their thought system or to avoid any potential threats to it. My point is that when a Christian goes on a mission to convert other people to join his religion, he is simply driven by his subconscious mechanism to fight back panic. And when a materialist (such as Richard Dawkins) goes on a crusade to prove the fallacy of religion, he is driven by the exact same psychological mechanism. They seem different, but only on the outer. Inside, they are psychological beings having to fight back the feeling of panic produced by an uncertain world.

I do think that as more and more people rise to the self-actualization level, we will see the public discourse change, as we have already started to see in the modern democracies. When we are no longer driven by the need to combat any threat to our worldview, we can have an entirely different form of communication. I think there is a huge potential if more people would become consciously aware of how our subconscious processes affect our perception. I think it could bring an incredible shift to the public discourse and we would be able to talk about things constructively instead of always being threatened by other viewpoints. After all, it was not the fundamentalist Christians, the fundamentalist Marxists or the fundamentalist materialists who brought the modern democracies to their present level. It was people who had moved into self-actualization without realizing it. So imagine what could happen if more people became consciously aware of their subconscious genies.

Why we – really – can't all get along

I have talked with fundamentalist Christians and religious and spiritual people of all persuasions. I have talked with scientific materialists. When I was young I even talked to some believing Marxists. And what I could not understand was how it was so utterly impossible to have a neutral conversation with them. It didn't take me that long to realize that there was absolutely nothing I could say that would have any impact on these people. Still, for most of my life I felt that there had to be a way to reach and talk to everybody and that it was part of my responsibility, even my mission in life, to find such a way. If I wasn't able to talk to all people, it must be because there was something wrong with me. I either wasn't good enough to relate to people, I didn't know enough or I had not discovered the ultimate argument that would convince all people.

It was of course my own need to fight back panic that wanted me to be able to get along with all people, and it meant that for most of my life I have had a deep inner frustration. I had a deep sense that human conflict is wrong because it leads to so much suffering—and I felt that suffering is also wrong. I had a deep inner desire to help people be free from suffering and overcome human conflict. I felt I was not here on earth just to live a normal life by focusing on myself and enjoying whatever pleasures people seek. I felt there had to be a purpose for my being on this planet, and it related to bringing a resolution to conflict. And I thought this could be done by finding some ultimate truth or argument that would replace all other thought systems and finally make all people see the one and only truth.

As I said, I have been consciously walking the path of self-actualization for 44 years, but for the first more than three decades, my striving was dominated by this frustration. I could not possibly have seen the cause of my frustration during those three decades. I don't think anyone could have made me see it because I simply had not matured to the point where I could take a look at myself and come to a very simple, yet profound realization. The conclusion is that I am a human being like everyone else and I had the same need to fight back panic as everyone else.

I have said that Christians and materialists have the same psychological mechanism. They want to avoid panic, and they do so by adopting an external thought system. Once they have done so, they gain a sense of security, but it could be taken away if their thought system was proven not to be real. There was a period of more than two decades where I had started seeing this in other people. I had started seeing how blind were the various fanatical groups, such as the Nazis, the communists, the fundamentalist Christians and Muslims and the more extreme materialists. Yet I had not seen that I myself had the exact same psychological mechanism.

I had the same existential panic as everyone else. I had also set up a subconscious mechanism to beat down the panic. The only difference was that my sense of security wasn't based on one of the traditional thought systems, such as Christianity, Islam, Marxism or Materialism. Instead, I had a more fragile worldview because it was based on a set of spiritual beliefs that were not as clearly defined or believed by as many people as the established systems. I was, in a sense, in search of the ultimate thought system, but I had not found one that seemed real to me.

I thought my mission was to find or develop such a system and I saw it as an unselfish attempt to finally bring peace to this troubled planet. In reality, my desire to find a way to overcome conflict and bring "peace on earth, good will towards men" was simply my way to overcome panic. And my desire to find the ultimate argument was not really directed at bringing peace, it was directed at giving myself a more solid sense of security. Or we might say that my efforts were not aimed at bringing peace *outside* myself, they were aimed at bringing peace *inside* myself. Yet I still thought that the only way to bring inner peace was to change something outside myself—and that was the cause of my frustration.

So what happened? Did I get over this frustration or is this book just another attempt to convert other people to my worldview? Well, that question is for the reader to decide, but what I can say is that over the past 44 years my worldview has changed so dramatically that my subconscious genie has had a hard time keeping up. Naturally, I today have a worldview that seems real to me, but I have transcended the need to feel that this is the highest possible truth. Instead, I have come to an inner resolution that I don't need an ultimate truth. I am constantly willing to raise my awareness, and there is nothing I know today that could not be replaced tomorrow by a higher understanding. That is a much less frustrating frame of mind to be in than when I started the path at age 18.

During the process of overcoming my aversion to questioning my worldview, I gradually came to a conclusion that would have been stunning to me when I was young. In order to explain my conclusion, I have to take a slight detour back to ancient Greece and a philosopher named Aristotle.

7 | IS THERE ONLY ONE TRUTH?

About 2,500 years ago, Athens was the primary city state in Greece and it had a functioning democracy, although by modern standards, it was rather limited (slaves, women and other unimportant people couldn't vote). There was also a golden age for philosophers, with the most famous being Socrates whom we know only from the writings of Plato. Plato's primary student was Aristotle, but he deviated in profound ways from his teacher, and this has had a major influence on western thinking.

Many consider Aristotle to be the father of modern science, but he is primarily the father of materialistic science. Plato said that there is a realm beyond the material world that influences how things are in this world. We cannot understand the material world without understanding the underlying causes in what Plato called the world of ideal forms. In his famous analogy of the cave, he likened our situation to a group of people who are chained inside a cave. Outside the cave were people walking around but those inside could not see them directly, only the shadows they cast on a wall in the cave. Thus, what we see with our physical senses is only the shadows of unseen causes.

Aristotle ignored Plato's analogy of the cave and claimed we can understand everything we need to know about the material world by looking only at the material world. He also said that we can understand a whole by breaking it down into its smallest components. Once we understand how the components (such as atoms) work, we will understand how the whole (such as a human being) works.

Aristotle also developed a system of logic, and it has influenced our thinking in a way I consider catastrophic, calamitous and disastrous (I'm trying to be diplomatic here). Aristotle's goal was to define the nature of reality in a way that was independent of the observer, meaning it was universally true. To this end, he defined logic in such a way that a statement must be either true or not true because it cannot be both at the same time. He called this the law of the excluded middle.

Now, when I learned about this in high school, I thought it was perfectly logical. It seemed both obvious and real to me that a statement cannot be true and untrue at the same time. The earth is either round or flat because it obviously cannot be both. Today, I realize that Aristotle's logic seemed logical to me because for 2,500 years it has dominated western thought. We think it is logical because we have been programmed to think it is logical. Furthermore, my own subconscious genie wanted it to be true that there is only one truth and that a statement must be either wholly true or wholly untrue. The reason being that if I have the one and only truth, it is the ultimate way to push back my panic.

The problem I see today is that Aristotle's logic is dualistic, meaning it operates with two opposite polarities with nothing in between. It is black-and-white thinking because it assumes that every aspect of how the world works can be reduced to, or at least expressed as, a polarity that has two options: one that is true and one that is untrue. In other words, every question can be formulated in such a way that it can be answered with a yes or a no.

The law of the excluded middle says that a statement is either true or untrue because it cannot be both true and untrue at the same time. This tends to give us a simplistic view of life. We seek to reduce every aspect of life to something that can be expressed as having two options, or perhaps even one option. But what if some aspects of life are so complex that they cannot be reduced to just two options or cannot be understood according to a logic that only operates with true and untrue? Let me give some examples.

According to Aristotle, we have only two options: A statement is either true or untrue. There are certain aspects of life where this logic works well. For example, a circle is round and a square is, well, square. Something cannot be round and square at the same time. We can mention numerous other examples. Something is either up or down, black or white, a cat or a dog. Aristotle would express this as what he called syllogisms, which are statements that lead to an indisputable conclusion. Here is the most famous one usually attributed to Aristotle (although it isn't found in his writings):

All men are mortal.
Socrates is a man.
Ergo, Socrates is mortal.

Using the example of a circle and a square, Aristotle himself would probably say:

> All circles are round.
> All squares are not round.
> Ergo, all squares are not circles.

A shape is either a square or a circle because it cannot be both at the same time. And while this seems reasonable enough, here is where we begin to see the potential dangers of seeking to reduce everything to statements with two polarities, two options. Someone who had not quite understood Aristotle's logic might conclude that the law of the excluded middle means that every aspect of life can be reduced to this dualistic view, to a simple all-or-nothing choice between two options. For example:

> All circles are round.
> All squares are not round.
> Ergo, all shapes that are not round are squares.

This person has then (by twisting Aristotle's use of logic in a way he would not agree with) created a simplistic view of life according to which all shapes are either circles or squares with nothing in between. Obviously, we know that when it comes to geometric shapes, circles and squares are not the only options. There are many other shapes, even many other shapes that we can call "round," such as ovals, ellipses or many of the more gentle curves found in nature and the human body. In other words, the statement that something is "round" or "square" might not be precise enough to deal with all shapes. In fact, a Danish philosopher has constructed a shape, called a "super-ellipse," which is mathematically a combination of a square and a circle.

Another example is colors. We can easily define two opposite colors, namely black and white. Yet we cannot say that black and white are the only options for defining colors because we know there are many nuances, even a mixture of black and white, called gray. So if we cannot reduce our knowledge of colors to two options, black and white, why do we sometimes think we can reduce human beliefs or opinions to two options, black or white, true or untrue?

The primary effect of Aristotle's logic on western thinking is that gradually, during the past 2,500 years, there emerged in western thought the idea that there can be only one truth. This idea was actually promoted by the Catholic church that considered (and still does) itself as the only true religion. For about a thousand years, the Catholic church suppressed the writings of Aristotle, but in the 1200s they were resurrected by Thomas Aquinas, and the church now used Aristotelian logic to cement its position as the only source of truth. Materialism claims to have freed us from the superstition of religion, but it has not freed us from the idea that there can be only one truth.

I consider this idea to be the single most dangerous idea in human history and it has led to more conflicts and atrocities than any other idea. This has caused some people to develop the following syllogism:

My worldview is the only truth.
Any worldview that contradicts the only truth is false.
Ergo, all worldviews that contradict my view are false.

And here is the more "advanced" version:

My worldview is the only truth.
It would be better for the world if my truth was
the only truth.
Ergo, it is better for the world to kill all people
who do not accept my truth.

There can be only one true religion

In fairness to Aristotle, the idea that there can be only one truth has been around for a long time and didn't originate with him. Yet he is still the one who is primarily responsible for putting this idea into western thinking. This is because his logic reduces everything to a polarity between statements that are true or untrue because they cannot be both and there are no other options. Here is how we can observe that this has played out in the field of religion.

Since the time of Aristotle, there has emerged a general awareness in the western world (and most of the world) that there can be only one truth. Many religious people have interpreted this to mean that there can be only one true religion, and we can all see how much conflict this has created, including wars, crusades and inquisitions. Many people will say that it is logical that there can be only one true religion, but do we say this because Aristotelian logic has programmed us to think in terms of two polarities (true and untrue) and an excluded middle? Why couldn't there be more than one true religion?

Well, according to Aristotle, it is possible to define a statement that is universally true (all men are mortal, all circles are round). And if this statement is true, it follows (according to Aristotelian logic) that any statement that contradicts it, or even differs from it, must be untrue. These are the only options in Aristotelian logic: true or untrue. But what if this isn't true?

Let's look at how most religious people reason. We live in a world with much suffering and where bad people do terrible things to other people. There are many ideas in the world, and many of them are obviously wrong because they contradict each other and they cannot all be true. How do we know what is true and not true? Well, we can know because beyond this world is another world, and in that world there is an all-mighty and all-knowing God, and this God has given us a religion through direct revelation that is therefore absolutely true.

Obviously, this all-knowing God knows what is true in an ultimate sense so when he gave us our religion, he gave us the ultimate truth. Since there is only one real God and since this God obviously would not contradict himself, it follows that he would not give any other religion to humanity. Because if he has already given us the one true religion, why give a different one to other people? Anything that is different from the absolute truth obviously cannot be true, and since this would only create confusion, God would never give us more than one true religion. God is all-good and therefore does not want us to be confused. Yet, this all-mighty God has an opposite, namely the devil, and he wants to confuse and deceive us, so it follows that any religion that contradicts ours (or even differs from ours) cannot come from God but must come from the devil. In Aristotelian logic, this can be expressed as follows:

> God is the source of truth, the devil is the source of lies.
> Christianity is true and given by God, so any religion that differs from Christianity is untrue.
> Therefore, any other religion comes from the devil.

Of course, this form of reasoning applies not only to religions but to political theories and any other aspect of human opinions and theories. It even applies to scientific Materialism, and here are some other examples of Aristotelian logic transferred to thought systems:

Communism is true.
Any political theory that differs from communism must be untrue.

Materialism is true.
Any theory that differs from Materialism must be untrue.

If you are a true believer of such a "one and only truth" thought system, you will see this as perfectly logical. There can be only one truth, yours is that one truth and thus anything different is false. But let me just present a simple alternative. The goal defined by most religions is to get us to heaven. Let us say that we have discovered a giant meteor heading straight for earth. We realize the planet will be obliterated so we construct a giant spaceship to take all people away from here. On the appointed day, all people head for the spaceport and get on board. Some arrive by private jet, some by train, some by car, some by bicycle, some ride on a donkey and some walk. Once the spaceship has blasted off and we have watched the earth disappear in a giant fireball, does it really matter how we got to the spaceship? So if the goal of religion really is to get us to heaven, why couldn't there be more than one way to get us there? And after we got there, would it really matter whether we arrived via this or that road?

Why we (desperately) want only one truth

Again, I am not trying to present Aristotle as the ultimate villain that screwed up civilization. Obviously, Aristotle's worldview became accepted only because it appeals to something in us, it fills a psychological need that we human beings have. So what is that need?

Let me reach back to what I said earlier about us being psychological beings who have a need to beat back panic and that we have a subconscious genie assigned to perform this task. The most common way for the genie to do its work is to use a thought system to define how the world works. It doesn't matter whether it's a religion, a political philosophy, a spiritual teaching or scientific Materialism. Yet in order for us to accept a given thought system, it has to seem real to us. And what can make it seem real? Well, that it has validity, authority and is true. Therefore, in order to give us the ultimate sense of security, the ultimate sense of being in control, we have a desire for there to be only one truth and for this truth to be absolutely true. And if something is absolutely true, meaning it is the only real way to look at or describe reality, it follows that all other ways of describing reality must be untrue.

Once we accept this bastard offspring of Aristotelian logic, we put ourselves in an irreconcilable, an existential, conflict with all people who do not accept the same "one and only truth." The very fact that they are not accepting our truth is a threat to our sense of security and it raises the specter that they might be right and we might be wrong. Thus, in order to beat back our sense of panic, we must seek to establish our truth as the only truth on earth, and that means seeking to eradicate all alternatives, either by proving them wrong, by converting people to our system or by eradicating the people who will not be converted. To me, the real cause of all religious wars, the war between Nazism and the rest of the world and the war between capitalism and communism, even the war between religion and science is a psychological mechanism. We humans seek to escape panic by adopting a thought system that promises us that we have control over our destiny. Yet this only helps us beat back panic as long as we can believe our system is absolutely true, and the existence of other systems (especially if accepted by many people) is a threat that we cannot ignore. Therefore, it seems justified that we must destroy all false thought systems or the people who will not abandon them.

Aristotle obviously didn't cause this condition. He simply defined a system of logic that appeals to our most basic psychological mechanism, and thereby he gave us a tool for justifying that we seek to force other people to accept our worldview. After all, if there really is only one truth, doesn't it follow that it's actually in the best interest of the world, of historical necessity, of God, of science and even of other people that we force all people to see the one and only truth?

What have we now created? A monster that can justify any human atrocity! The end can now justify the means—even means that violate the most basic rule for human behavior: Do unto others as you want them to do unto you. The subconscious genie cannot fathom this rule, it can only look at what might accomplish its defined task to beat back panic.

Do you want other people to seek to force their thought system upon you, even if they believe it's the absolute truth? Would you want others to force a thought system upon you even if it *was* the absolute truth? Wouldn't you want to be given the freedom to use your own sense of what is real to decide which thought system to follow? So, why wouldn't you give that same freedom to others? If you don't want to be forced to accept another thought system, why do you think it is justified to force others to accept *your* thought system? The answer depends on where you are at on Maslow's pyramid. The more you are focused on the lower needs (the more fear-based is your approach) the more you are willing to force others.

I have more to say about this epic mindset that makes people think there is some cosmic importance to forcing people to accept one thought system, but for now I want to stay with Aristotelian logic. This logic says that a statement cannot be true and untrue at the same time. Many people interpret this to mean that if two statements contradict each other, one must be true and the other untrue. Yet I see another possibility: They could both be untrue. I also see a third possibility: They could both be partially true, meaning based on a limited understanding—they could both be *incomplete*. The consequence would then be that there is a deeper or higher understanding to be obtained, and once we have it, we see that neither statement defined truth because there is much more to know about reality than what we could see through the filter of a closed-ended, one and only truth worldview.

My stunning conclusion

I have spent some time studying the history of science, and I am especially fascinated by physics. We probably all learned in school that there was a physicist named Isaac Newton who discovered the force of gravity because an apple fell on his head. He also formulated a set of laws about movement that are still valid today and can enable us to send a spaceship to Mars. There was a time when physicists believed that Newton had discovered the ultimate worldview, namely that the universe can be compared to a mechanical device, like a giant clock-work. This view said that the world is guided by invariable laws, meaning that if we knew the machine's starting point, we could use the laws of nature to predict all future events with absolute certainty. In other words, the universe was deterministic with no room for surprises. (This idea is appealing to the subconscious genie because it promises security—if only you know everything.)

As I said, there were physicists who believed this was the ultimate truth, and by the late 1800s one prominent scientist proclaimed that all of the basic laws had already been discovered, with only a few minor details left to explain. It seems rather obvious to me that the subconscious genie had been at work, giving these people a desire to find or define the ultimate truth, giving rise to ultimate security. Then, in 1905 an unknown physicist published an article that completely pulled the rug from under the deterministic universe. Naturally, this was Albert Einstein and his theory of relativity.

This didn't mean that Einstein invalidated Newtonian physics. What he proved was that Newton's laws were not universally valid, they only worked for certain phenomena or at a certain scale. In other words, Newton's laws were valid for a certain segment of the universe but they could not describe the workings of the entire universe. There was something outside the cave in which Newtonian physicists were chained. Einstein didn't actually say (as people often think) that everything is relative. He said that the observations we make are relative to the situation in which we are making them. In other words, in order to know whether our observations are valid, we need to consider how our method of observation influences what we see. I would say that in order to know whether our perception shows us reality, we need to know how our perception filter influences our observation.

In reading a biography of Einstein, I learned that what enabled him to develop his new theory was that he questioned the unquestionable assumptions on which Newtonian science is based. It was only by questioning what other physicists thought did not need to be questioned (because it was an absolute truth) that he saw something they had not seen.

Within a few years, other physicists had taken Einstein's theories and used them to develop a new branch of science that deals with the world of subatomic particles. One of these physicists, Walter Heisenberg, developed what he called the uncertainty principle, which says that there will always be something we cannot know. The outcome of this is that we cannot predict with certainty how the universe will evolve, meaning that the world is not deterministic. Ironically, Einstein could not accept this and to his death, he continued to fight quantum physics. The reason being that his own theory was also based on certain assumptions and Einstein was not willing to question them. Heisenberg, Niels Bohr and others were willing to question these assumptions, and thus they made a new discovery

Also very fascinating to me is that a mathematician named Kurt Gödel developed something he called the incompleteness theorem. Gödel proved mathematically that it is not possible to develop a system of mathematics that can explain every aspect of numbers. Any system that you can define will have certain inherent assumptions that will either limit what you can know or that will lead to contradictions. I know that many people will say that this applies only to mathematics, but when I read about such a discovery, my mind immediately makes one of these intuitive leaps and I see it applying to every aspect of how we attempt to explain reality. So here is the stunning conclusion that I have reached. Let me once again underscore that it took me a long time to reach this conclusion because for decades my subconscious genie (also called the ego) fought very hard to keep me believing that there could be only one truth. Naturally, my conclusion is that there is *not* only one truth.

Kim's theory of theories

Based on what I have described above, my conclusion is that we human beings need to create theories for various reasons. One is to give ourselves a sense of being in control in order to beat back panic. Another is to help us function in our everyday, practical situation by knowing how our environment works and how to create technology. So I am not saying we should throw away all theories and stop trying to create better theories. I am only saying we could benefit from throwing away the dream of creating an ultimate theory or a theory of everything.

My reasoning is that in our present state of consciousness (dominated by a sense of separation) we can only create a theory by defining a starting point, what scientists often call a paradigm. As an example, medieval astronomers based their study of the heavens on the paradigm that the earth was the center of the universe (coming from "infallible" Catholic doctrine). They still made observations of the movements of the heavenly bodies, but in order to explain them based on their paradigm, they had to create a very elaborate theory of epicycles. Only when Galileo and others were willing to question this paradigm, did they come up with a simpler theory that actually matched observations.

When we define a paradigm, we take a certain observation, or rather an assumption, and we elevate it to being absolutely true or self-evident, meaning that it does not need to be questioned. And precisely in doing this, we will limit the explanatory power of the theory. There will be certain things that the theory cannot explain because our basic assumption prevents us from asking certain questions. The theory can still be quite useful and lead to much progress. But there will come a point where the theory cannot take us further.

The only way to go further is to question the assumptions behind the theory, but then the paradigm can no longer be upheld. We must therefore develop new assumptions and this leads to a new theory, a new paradigm. This is explained in greater detail in a famous book by the philosopher Thomas Kuhn, called *The Structure of Scientific Revolutions*.

As an example of this process, Newton made certain assumptions and it clearly took science forward. However, Newtonian physics works only within a certain range of the universe. Science only made the next leap when Einstein questioned some of the basic assumptions and thereby developed a new theory with a different range. Newtonian physics is still valid so we do not need to say Newton was wrong. But he did not and could never give us the complete picture. So those physicists who believed that Newton's theory was the ultimate truth *were* indeed wrong.

I think that as a working theory we could propose that we will never develop a complete theory, at least as long as we are dominated by the black-and-white thinking that must operate with dualistic polarities. When I say there is no absolute truth, I can moderate the statement in two ways. One is to say that there is a truth but that we are not at a level of consciousness where we can discover it (Plato's cave). The other is that there is an absolute truth but that it cannot be expressed with the means of communication (language, mathematics, scientific measurements) we currently have available.

Actually, this conclusion is supported by several philosophers, including the famous Immanuel Kant. He said that there is an actual world out there, but that we cannot know it as it is (we cannot know the "thing in itself"). We can only know the world through our means of perception, which is what I have called the perception filter created by the subconscious ego.

Naturally, I am quite aware that saying there is no absolute truth is like waving a red flag in front of a bull. I will immediately attract the opposition of all people who are trapped in the deficit needs and have beaten back panic by defining thought systems based on the assumption that there is an absolute truth. Yet I don't expect such people to read this book. I have not written this book in an attempt to convert such people because I have overcome my need to convert them (or anyone else). I have written this book for people who are like myself, meaning they are ready to embrace self-actualization but they have grown up in a society that gave them no tools for doing this.

I can see today that if I had been able to embrace this conclusion 44 years ago, my path would have been a whole lot easier, and I would have avoided much frustration and even some serious blind alleys. In my experience, we gain a lot of advantages from scrapping the idea that in order to actualize ourselves, we need to find the one and only truth—the truth that no one else has found. I will talk more about this later because I want to summarize what I see as the human dilemma.

8 | THE DILEMMA OF HUMAN UNDERSTANDING

When I look at history, it is clear to me that there is a progression from a more primitive state towards a more sophisticated state. So much progress has happened between the stone age society and modern democracy. I also see that many civilizations have come and gone, and I see that some of these civilizations believed they were the most sophisticated civilization ever seen on earth (which could be true at the time) and even that they had reached some ultimate state of sophistication. This latter belief has always been proven wrong by the emergence of more sophisticated civilizations and it seems obvious to me that the same will happen to our civilization.

The basis for all of this progress is that we have increased our understanding and awareness. We have come to see and understand something that previous civilizations simply did not grasp. What is the basic mechanism that has brought about all of this progress? It is our willingness to question what we think we know and consider that there might be a deeper understanding than what we have right now. In other words, our current truth is not the final truth, what we currently see as real may not be ultimate reality.

Another tendency I see in history is that human progress has not been a smooth and ongoing process. We have seen some periods in which a particular civilization made no progress for centuries, and what was the cause of this stagnation? Well, on the outer, it was that the civilization had adopted a certain thought system or worldview, and people thought it was based on an ultimate truth. If you think you have the ultimate truth, then obviously it makes no sense to look for a higher understanding. What could be higher than the ultimate truth?

When I put this together with what I have said about our psychological need for security and how this drives us to seek for one ultimate truth, I see what I call the basic human dilemma. On the one hand, we seem to have a desire to know, to understand life. That is why so many people have thought deeply about life and come up with various explanations, from religions to philosophies and science. Yet our drive to understand can be restricted by our need to beat down panic by searching for a thought system that claims to offer us an ultimate truth. Once we think we have such a system, we close our minds to anything beyond it, and that is how an entire civilization can stagnate and make very little progress for centuries, such as the Roman empire, ancient China or Europe during the Dark Ages.

I see the history of human progress as a tug-of-war between these two forces in human psychology. There is the drive to know more, which is open-ended and perhaps never-ending. There is also the drive to define a one and only truth, which causes us to close our minds to progress.

So how have we actually made progress? Why haven't we developed a society that had an "ultimate truth" that enabled it to survive in the long run? Well, I see two options:

- Perhaps we haven't yet discovered the ultimate truth.

- Perhaps there is no ultimate truth, but only an ongoing raising of awareness.

When I was young and insecure I preferred the first one, today I prefer the second one. We can therefore say that what determines whether society makes progress or stagnates is whether it allows people in the deficit needs to shut down exploration, or whether it allows people in the self-actualization needs to look for a higher understanding.

Progress and thought systems

Back to the question of how progress happens. One way is what I call the School of Hard Knocks. Life is full of material, physical suffering and it is very hard to ignore. Thus, in an effort to escape or at least alleviate suffering, people have from time to time been willing to question what they thought they knew. This has led to a deeper understanding of some aspect of life that has alleviated suffering to some degree. In my view, the School of Hard Knocks is simply mandated by the second law of thermodynamics, and, as mentioned before, it basically states that a closed system will self-destruct.

To me it is clear that when we allow ourselves to think we have an ultimate truth, our minds become a closed system and we stagnate (on the personal level, on the level of one society and on the level of the human race). Our minds are closed systems and we will reject the very ideas that could bring us forward because our absolute truth has become a self-fulfilling prophecy, a self-referential system, an auto-validating system that sees only what it wants to see because the unconscious genie filters out anything different. How can we ever escape the suffering this causes, how can we discover the ideas that can help us progress? Our minds must become open again, and this means our worldview or our civilization must fall apart. Catholicism caused European society to progress very slowly for a thousand years, but after Catholicism lost its dominance, much more progress has happened. Yet perhaps we are today at another point where the dominant worldview is limiting our progress?

This brings up an irony in modern society. Over the past century we have seen more technological progress than in all of known history. We have seen how technology has alleviated much physical suffering, but not all. And technology has not alleviated psychological suffering. It is clear to me that the basis for developing new technology is to increase our understanding of how the world works. Therefore, one would think our society had thrown all restrictions to the wind and was willing to question everything we think we know, always reaching for that next insight.

I have met people who think that this is what science is doing but I have also met scientists who testify that there are very strict limitations to what scientists can actually investigate. Scientific thinking is currently dominated by the materialistic paradigm, and if you dare to research something that points beyond Materialism, you can quickly lose academic standing, research money or your job. If you doubt this, read the book *The Science Delusion* by Rupert Sheldrake. In other words,

Materialism is now a restriction to scientific inquiry on the same level as the Catholic doctrines that science supposedly freed us from. How do we explain this? Well, let me propose an Aristotelian syllogism of my own:

All humans are psychological beings.
All scientists are humans.
Ergo, all scientists are psychological beings.

Some scientists (perhaps a majority or at least a dominant minority) are still trapped in the deficit needs. They have the same need as everyone else for beating back panic, and they have adopted the most common solution, namely to define a thought system and proclaim it is based on absolute truth. If this thought system was to be proven wrong, they would again be thrown back into panic, and in order to avoid this, they are willing to hold back scientific progress by limiting research to areas that do not contradict or go beyond the two basic doctrines of their thought system:

- There is nothing beyond the material universe, as we can detect it with current instruments.

- Consciousness is a product of material conditions and therefore mind cannot influence matter. Matter creates mind.

Historically, what has held up progress in any civilization is that some people are trapped in the deficit needs. What has brought progress is that a few people have gone beyond these needs and gone into the self-actualization needs. In order to move from deficit needs to self-actualization needs, we must come to a simple realization: I have a higher potential than what I am manifesting right now. This leads to an equally simple question: Why am I not manifesting my highest potential but only my current condition? And the obvious answer is that there is something I do not know, understand, see or grasp. Therefore, I must seek this higher awareness, and I can do this only if I am willing to question what I think I know, to look beyond my current mental box, to penetrate my current perception filter.

The equation is simple. My current knowledge and understanding of life represents a certain mental box that separates what I think is real from everything else. The knowledge I need in order to manifest my highest potential cannot be found inside this box. If it could, I would already have manifested my higher potential. Therefore, I must look for knowledge outside my current mental box, and this means I must let go of the belief that says my current mental box contains the absolute truth and there is nothing beyond it.

We can express this another way. Any worldview that is closed will create certain problems. These problems will seem to have no solution, but the reason is that we are looking for the solution with the same perception filter that created the problem. As an example, the medieval Catholic worldview could not fully explain the movements of the stars in the sky. The reason was that it was based on the idea that the earth must be the center of the universe. Einstein once said: "We cannot solve a problem with the same state of consciousness that created the problem."

Human progress is determined by the balance between the need for security (that causes us to close our minds and cling to what we think we know) and the need for growth (which causes us to open our minds to something we cannot currently see).

Why we think something is real

Back to the question of how we know what is real. I have heard psychologist and materialists say that religion is based on superstition because it comes down to subjective belief. This is reinforced by many religious people who, when they feel any doubt, always tell themselves and each other to: "Have faith." In my eyes, religion has nothing to do with belief. It is based on the psychological mechanism that causes people to look for an ultimate thought system that can give them security.

What causes a person to accept a certain religion? It is a subconscious mechanism that causes the person to, not *believe* but actually *experience* that the claims made by that religion seem real. The religion gives the person an experience of reality, but it is not produced by the outer religion but by the person's internal perception filter. Of course, this is the same for any other thought system, including scientific Materialism. I know materialists will say that their system is based on scientific truth, but it is still the same psychological mechanism. Religious people also claim their system is based on an absolute truth (and they all say that their claim is true and all the other claims are false). Why should we continue to believe that one of these claims is the right one and all the others are false? What if we accepted that they are all limited?

Let me reach back to what I said about perception. I am looking at an object. Light rays bounce off the object, hit my retina and are converted into signals that are sent to my visual cortex. My brain displays an image inside itself and something then imposes an interpretation upon the object and says: "Oh, that's an apple." What is that something and how does it work? Or we could ask another question: "Is perception a passive or an active process?"

I was taught in school that perception is a passive process. If I open my eyes, light will enter them, and the image I see in my brain is corresponding exactly to the actual object that is out there. Now, I am not necessarily disputing this claim when it comes to seeing a physical object, such as an apple. There is an object, light does enter my retina, causes certain signals that my brain will process, and something in my mind makes the conclusion: "That's an apple." Yet my question is whether even something as simple as seeing a physical object is an entirely passive process?

For starters, who decided that apples should be called apples? If the first person to see an apple had attached the sound "orange" to the object, we would all be calling apples oranges and no one would think twice about it. There is no natural law that says that what we call an apple can only be called an apple. In Danish, it is called "æble," in Vietnamese "táo," in Chinese "Pínggu" and in Estonian "Oun." So at the very least, when my eyes detect an apple, something in my mind imposes the word "apple" upon the image in my brain.

That something may also impose other things, such as whether I like apples or whether I think they caused us to be kicked out of Paradise. There may be a whole personal, subjective story attached to apples because my mom used to bake wonderful apple pies for me as a child or because I fell out of an apple tree and hurt my leg. My conclusion is that there are two aspects of perception, namely what we see (the image displayed inside the brain) and what we do with it (the interpretation imposed upon it by something in our minds).

I will grant that scientist are probably right that when two people look at an apple, they have the same image displayed inside their brains (although some discuss whether I see the same color green as you do). But I think it is obvious that when it comes to the interpretation, there is room for a lot of individual, subjective criteria to be imposed by their minds. If we want to have any hope of overcoming human conflict, I think we need to understand how two people can see the same thing and impose vastly different interpretations upon it.

What makes two people look at the claim that the Christian religion is the only true religion, and one person accepts it and the other rejects it? I think it is far too simplistic to say that one person is naive and gullible and his acceptance is entirely subjective while the other is far more sophisticated and her rejection is entirely objective. I think we need to recognize that they both have an inner experience that seems completely real to them. We can then begin to consider what gives us this inner sense that something is real, and when we understand this, we can perhaps begin to develop a new approach to raising our awareness and knowledge. At least we might gain added motivation for questioning our existing understanding of the world.

Why we see what we see

Let me describe my favorite example of perception-based conflicts, even though I have used it in other writings and some readers will know it. Say I am taking a walk on a beach on a day where there is not a cloud in the sky. I am admiring the deep blue sky when I come upon two people who are in the middle of a heated argument. I hear one of them yelling: "Why do you keep insisting that the sky is purple, when I am seeing with my own eyes that it's green?" The other retorts: "Are you completely blind, anyone can see that the sky is purple." Given the ferocity of their exclamations, I do a quick check and the sky is still blue. I am stunned by this because here are two people arguing, and I can see with my own two eyes that they are both wrong. How can they both insist that they are right? As I come closer, I suddenly see the reason. The person who claims that the sky is green is wearing yellow glasses, and as we all learned in school, when yellow light combines with blue, we get green. The other person is wearing red glasses, which naturally makes the sky look purple.

I am now realizing what is the cause of their argument, and because I am such a nice guy who always wants to help people, I engage them and try to convince them that they are both wrong and that the sky really is blue. Yet none of my (to me) obvious and self-evident arguments have the slightest effect on them. Instead of coming around, they both insist that I am wrong and tell me to mind my own business (using some not very nice four-letter words).

The problem here is, of course, that the two people do not know that they are wearing colored glasses and therefore they think that their eyes are showing them reality as it really is. Now, think about all of the arguments that have taken place between people who adhered to different thought systems over the course of history. Could any argument ever settle the dispute between the two people wearing colored glasses? They see what they see and what they see seems completely real to them. They will continue arguing indefinitely because their individual process of perception gives them completely different sensations of what is real.

What could potentially break the stalemate between people with different perception filters? In my view, only that one or both of the two people became open to the idea that perhaps they are not seeing reality but are seeing it through a filter that distorts their perception. In other words, if they became open to the possibility that they were wearing colored glasses and then took off the glasses, the dispute could be dissolved. And this is what Maslow's pyramid of needs is all about. At the lower levels, our need for security is so strong that we cannot question our perception. Yet in order to move into self-actualization, we must indeed begin to question our perception and in my experience, we never overcome the need to do so. Self-actualization is an ongoing process of questioning our current perception because only by doing so do we reach a higher awareness.

Psychological perception

I have given a simple example relating to physical perception, but we also have a psychological form of perception, a perception of ideas. It is this process that determines how we look at life, including what thought systems we accept or reject. Back to my example of the Christian and the materialist. Let's say that both are presented with an idea that not directly contradicts but goes beyond each of their thought systems. How will they react to this?

Well, it depends on how strong is their need for security and their fear of losing the sense of being in control. Each of them has accepted a certain thought system and it has certain basic statements that the system claims cannot or should not be questioned (they are absolutely true, self-evident or you go to hell for questioning them). These statements have been installed in the people's subconscious minds where they form the equivalent of a database on a computer. A database is like an archive with file drawers that each contain certain information. Each database has a file folder with the label: "Do not question!"

So when a new idea enters our minds, there is a subconscious process that takes the idea and compares it to our subconscious database. The first task is to label the idea, to fit it into our existing knowledge so we can know what it is about.

This is equivalent to what happens when we look at an apple. We label it as an apple.

So far, I think this process is relatively neutral. Yet depending on what idea we are talking about, the next step will be a deeper evaluation process that seeks to compare the idea to other ideas (more complex than just labeling it) in order to evaluate it further. Once we have a more firm grasp of what the idea actually says, it will be compared to the contents of the "Do not question" folder. If it is found to contradict or question any of the beliefs that must not be questioned, it will immediately be rejected. The subconscious database operator (what I have called the genie or the ego) will then send the idea back to the conscious mind with the label "unreal," and we immediately reject the idea without consciously thinking about why we do so.

Even though we have not consciously thought about the idea (considered it with an open mind), we feel that the justification for rejecting it is valid because the evaluation from the subconscious mind seems completely real to the conscious mind. After all, the conscious mind has given authority to the subconscious mind in order to get relief from the sense of panic. The conscious mind has said to the subconscious ego: "You evaluate ideas so I don't have to think about them, because thinking opens me to doubt and that causes me panic." The subconscious mind is charged with holding back panic, and it has been given sole authority to reject any idea that threatens status quo. That is, if we are trapped in the fear-based needs.

My realization is that in our subconscious minds we each have a perception filter. It has the same effect as any other filter, namely to let through some ideas (that we then accept as real) and to hold back other ideas (that we then see as unreal). What happens when we move into the self-actualization needs is that we start a process (in the beginning without being aware of it) of reexamining our subconscious database. We start to question our perception filter and gradually let through more ideas, even ideas that go beyond what used to give us a sense of reality. We see a wider reality than our previous reality. In a sense we could say that we start to consciously think about ideas instead of allowing the ego to evaluate them.

It may take us some time to begin to question the beliefs in the "Do not question" folder, but if we persist on the path to self-actualization, we will eventually come to question *all* of the contents of our subconscious database. How long this will take depends on our willingness to confront our fear of going into panic. It depends on how much we are controlled by our egos and the fear of panic. Unfortunately, many people do not open their minds until some traumatic event forces them to question some existing belief. But it can also be done as a result of a conscious and voluntary process.

My working hypothesis is that we each have an individual perception filter, which means that the way we look at life is entirely subjective. The cause of most (if not all) human conflict is that most people do not acknowledge this. Thus, they think that their subjective perception is entirely objective. As a result, they think others should follow their subjective perception instead of following their own subjective perception. So we could say that if all of us would acknowledge that our perception is subjective, we could start making progress towards resolving conflict.

Obviously, I don't expect that this will happen anytime soon. Yet I think those people who are ready to consciously start the self-actualization process would benefit from making this shift. I have come to see the process of self-actualization (or the *spiritual path,* as I like to call it) as a gradual purification of our perception filters until we are able to look at everything without any filters, to look with neutral or naked awareness. In my view, this is the only way to attain happiness and peace of mind.

Our sense of reality

Over the past 44 years, I have had many interactions with people from various thought systems. When I was young I was very much affected by my need for security and I wanted to have other people validate my beliefs in order to maintain my sense of having some control over my life. After I found my first spiritual teaching at the age of 18, I had a period where I thought the one solution to all of the world's problems was to convert everyone to this spiritual teaching. Through some hard knocks, I eventually grew out of this, but I still kept wondering why we human beings do not see eye to eye. One of my insights is what I have described here, namely the subconscious process that imposes an interpretation, a reality filter, on every idea we encounter or every experience we have.

Take note that I am in no way excluding myself from this process. When I was young and naive (now, I am not young anymore) I thought that by finding a spiritual teaching that gave me a deeper understanding, I had taken off the glasses and could see the sky as it really is. This euphoria didn't last long, and I have now spent the last 44 years systematically, and often brutally, questioning the contents of my subconscious database, my perception filter. I am not claiming the process is complete, as I almost daily see new illusions or get new insights. Yet I can also see that compared to where I started, I have actually made some progress during those 44 years.

As I said, the cause of most human conflicts is a psychological mechanism. It is based on our need to beat back panic, but the central element of it is the idea that there can be only one truth. Given how much suffering this one idea has caused, I think it would be constructive to question it. We do not necessarily have to decide that there is not and cannot be only one truth. But it would be constructive to set it aside as an unproven conclusion and consider whether there might be another approach to the question of what is true or real.

As I said, for the first several decades of my personal path, I was driven by the need to find the ultimate truth, and it caused me a lot of mental anguish. I eventually came to a point where I realized that the important question is not: "Is there an ultimate truth?" The important question is: "Am I able to grasp ultimate truth? Would I know truth, if it bit me in the leg?"

Truth and our level of consciousness

I have spent a lot of time studying philosophy. One of the things that struck me is that western philosophers almost all make a fundamental assumption that only few of them question. They assume that we human beings, or at least themselves, are in a state of consciousness where we can use our current abilities and faculties (such as intellect and reason) to determine what is ultimately real, what is an ultimate truth. Yet in the East we find a different concept, namely that what is the most common state of consciousness (what we call normal human awareness) is not the ultimate state of awareness.

As I said, I was always searching for a higher understanding, but I didn't find anything during my childhood and teenage years. At the age of 18, I moved away from home to attend university. One day I was walking around town when I came across a used bookstore. Moved by an intuitive impulse, I went inside, found a shelf with spiritual books and suddenly my eyes focused on one book. I pulled it out, and the title was

Autobiography of a Yogi, written by a person with the strange name Paramahansa Yogananda. I opened the book and it had a lot of pictures of the author and also of various eastern yogis or spiritual adepts. Without any further thought, I bought the book even though it was a hardcover edition and beyond my student budget. I went straight home and spent the next two days devouring the book.

To say that reading this book was a life-changing experience is putting it mildly. Actually, the book itself didn't change anything. What it did was to put words on so many things that I had sensed intuitively during my childhood but that I could not articulate. The book brought to my conscious mind what I already knew at a deeper level.

The most important idea in the book was that we human beings have the potential to raise our consciousness to a distinctly higher level, a level that is beyond the fear-based black-and-white thinking that leads to conflict and suffering. And when we do raise our consciousness, we will be able to see and grasp something we cannot see now. We will gain an entirely different perspective on life that can resolve our doubts and give us true inner peace. This idea seemed instantly real to me, and I have spent the past 44 years pursuing this growth in consciousness (studying many teachings and practicing many techniques). I don't claim to have reached an ultimate level, but I experience daily that my awareness is very different from what it was when I was 18.

Ever since I read that book, I have grasped that we human beings are currently in a limited state of consciousness that gives us a distorted view of life (Plato's cave). We can free ourselves from this distorted view by systematically raising our consciousness. As we do so, we will gradually shed our perception filters and come to see things we cannot grasp today.

Thus, it is not constructive to assume that there is only one truth (or one way to express truth) and that we can see it at our present level of consciousness. In other words, it is an illusion to think that when we reach a higher state of consciousness, we will have the ultimate validation for our current beliefs. We will reach a higher state of consciousness only by looking beyond our current beliefs and then seeing something that we cannot grasp or even imagine right now.

We might say that there is a scale or ladder of human consciousness, leading from our present level to higher levels. It is like being in a dense forest and finding an observation tower. At the ground level, we can't see anything but the trees, we can't see the forest for the trees. We start by walking up a ladder and reach the first platform. We can now see more than we could see from the ground, but we are still not above the trees. As we continue climbing, we see more and more, and eventually we reach the top of the tower and are now above the treetops with a full view of the landscape. We can finally see the forest instead of being focused on one tree and thinking it is the one and only tree.

Given everything I have said about the subconscious mechanism that closes people's minds to new ideas, why am I writing this book? I obviously know that most people will not read it, and even if they did, they would reject most of what I have written. This book is not written with the hope of convincing people who are not ready for its ideas. As mentioned, it is written for people who are in a similar situation to my own. I was born as a person who was ready to pursue self-actualization but during my entire childhood and youth, nothing stimulated this drive. I know that if I had found a book like this at the age of 12, it would have been incredibly helpful for me. So I hope the book will find some people who are ready for it and help them raise their consciousness faster by learning from my experiences. After all, even though we have grown up in an anti-spiritual society, why should we each have to reinvent the wheel?

9 | PLAUSIBLE DENIABILITY AND PLAUSIBLE PLAUSIBILITY

Let me return to the question of why we can't all get along. I have now built up to the conclusion (self-evident to me, of course) that the reason is that we have different perception filters and therefore we look at ideas differently. We each have an individual sense of which ideas are real and which are not real. And this sense is based on the database that we each have in our subconscious minds.

If we step back and try to look at the forest instead of the trees, we might simply observe that we live in a world where there is no "one and only" truth that is defined for all people. If we had lived in such a world, then all people for all time should have known about and accepted the same truth. Since we can clearly observe from history that people have accepted many different things as "truth," it seems to me that we human beings have the ability to come up with an individual sense of reality, even though it obviously leads to much conflict and suffering. Now, I know this raises some questions about why the world is that way, but I will deliberately put them aside for later.

For now, I want to simply make the observation that we live in a world where there is what I call *plausible deniability* and *plausible plausibility*. In other words, whatever you want to believe or disbelieve, you can always find arguments that – when seen through a certain perception filter – seem to validate just about any viewpoint or theory. To me, this is simply the way the world is. Whatever you want to believe, you can find arguments to support it, and other people can find arguments to reject it. We might call it the psychological equivalent of a house of mirrors.

As just one example, take the existence of God. Some people have come up with elaborate arguments for why there must be a God, and to them they seem perfectly valid. Other people look at the same arguments and compare them to materialistic philosophy and reject the arguments as completely invalid. There is even a website that presents arguments for why we have all been fooled into thinking the earth is round, when it really is flat—and some people seem to believe this.

Historically, many people have dreamed of settling all conflict and creating peace. Among these are many intellectual and rational people who have attempted to overcome conflict by coming up with the ultimate rational argument. Obviously, this hasn't been successful since there is still conflict. I think the problem here is that intellectual people tend to think that everybody is as rational as they are. Or perhaps the problem is that intellectual people think they are rational and not subjective in their thinking. To me, this points to a limitation of the intellect.

The limitations of the intellect

In the western world we have been conditioned to use our intellects and rational thinking to determine what is true. We have a tendency to *glorify*, even *deify* the intellect. We have been conditioned to think that rational and intellectual thinking is superior to other forms of thinking. At this point, you might say: "What other forms of thinking," and that is precisely my point. We have been conditioned to think that there is no other way of thinking than intellectual analysis.

As I touched upon earlier, the intellect is an analytical faculty that works by comparing a new idea to what is already known. I have met many intellectual people who thought that they were entirely rational and not affected by subjective human emotions. Yet in my experience, the intellect works by comparing a new idea to the contents of its subconscious database, and in this database we find ideas with an emotional charge.

As I said, scientists are also human beings and thus psychological beings, meaning they also have feelings. If people are still focused on deficit needs, they will have a need for security, and this means they will have defined certain ideas as being absolutely true and therefore beyond questioning. A person may be very rational according to his or her conscious evaluation. Yet there may still be a belief in the subconscious database that is affected by the need for security. For example, a materialist may have a belief that there is nothing beyond the material world, and this is a belief that has a certain emotional charge. This may be caused by an experience where the person had an emotional reaction to religion, giving the person a subconscious belief that religion can't be true. This belief resides in the Do not question folder. As a more specific example, let me refer to Albert Einstein, who is often considered one of the most intelligent and rational people that ever lived. Yet to his dying day, Einstein had a very strong belief that the world had to be rational or ordered, and therefore the uncertainty of quantum mechanics could not be true. He expressed this in the often quoted remark that: "God does not play dice with the universe." To me, Einstein was generally a very rational man, which is especially evident in the way he dealt with his wives and children. Yet this particular belief was not based on rational thought but a strong desire to believe in an orderly universe. He may have thought it was entirely rational, but it was a belief that he thought could not be questioned.

What I am trying to say is that the intellect is an analytical faculty. The intellect has the ability to consider any issue from a variety of angles or perspectives. In other words, the intellect can take the arguments for the existence of God, and it can come up with reasons why they are true and reasons why they are not true. That is why one person can feel intellectually convinced that God exists and another can (based on the same argumentation) be equally convinced that there is no God.

The intellect can argue any issue from both sides, which means that to the intellect, there is no absolute truth or final argument. The intellect simply presents arguments for or against an issue. To the intellect all of the arguments have a similar validity, or perhaps they have no validity as they are simply arguments and not reality. There is a book by Gary Cox, called *The God Confusion*, which gives a very good description of the various arguments for or against God's existence. The author concludes that we can come up with good intellectual arguments for or against God's existence, and thus the only tenable position is to be an agnostic, meaning we think that we cannot know for sure. My point is that the intellect is good at presenting arguments, but not good at deciding which one is better than another. So who does decide, given that most people are not agnostics? In the language I have used here, it is the subconscious genie or the ego. The intellect present the arguments, but they are not evaluated neutrally. Because we have a file folder with certain beliefs that are beyond questioning, any argument that seems to question such an unassailable belief is labeled as being unreal by the subconscious genie. With the conscious mind we are not really considering the arguments presented by the intellect. Many people are not consciously thinking about a topic but are letting their subconscious genies decide what is real and unreal based on the sense of security and what beats back panic.

So what is it that makes one person say that the arguments *against* God's existence are real and the arguments *for* his existence are not real? Well, it is the belief in the subconscious Do not question folder—the belief that the person *feels* must not be questioned. This is what I call an intellectual holy cow, something that is untouchable. In other words, if a person has the belief or paradigm that there cannot be anything beyond the material world, then that person will not be able to consciously question this belief. And that is why the person will see the arguments against God's existence as being more real than the opposite arguments. Another person who has another subconscious belief, such as "The Bible is the Word of God," will come to the opposite conclusion because his ego will evaluate the arguments differently.

My point here is that the intellect can argue for or against any issue, but the outcome of the argumentation is not decided by the intellect. It is decided by what parameters the subconscious database sets for intellectual inquiry. Just take a look at the world and see how many times people have attempted to settle a conflict by using rational arguments. For example, militant atheists, such as Richard Dawkins, seem convinced that by presenting rational arguments against religion, it will be possible to convert all religious people to their atheism. And they are absolutely convinced that their arguments are entirely rational and objective, meaning they are not affected by any subjective beliefs. Yet when I read Dawkins' book, *The God Delusion,* it seemed obvious to me that his intellect is simply validating his subconscious belief that there is not and cannot be anything beyond the material world. He seems like a very subjective person to me. I am not thereby saying that I am objective. I am saying *we are all subjective.* More on this later.

Now, just consider how western philosophers and scientists have been using rational, intellectual argumentation for centuries. One would think that if an ultimate intellectual argument existed, someone would have found it by now. Yet what do we see in the world? There is no intellectual consensus, and I have come to see that this is because of the limitations of the intellect that I have described here. In other words, trying to overcome human conflict through intellectual reasoning is simply not going to work because there can be no final or ultimate intellectual argument.

My conclusion (reached after over 40 years of frustration) is that rational, linear, intellectual argumentation never settled any arguments. There simply is no ultimate argument that will convince all people, and trying to find such an argument (as I did for over 30 years) was a grand waste of my time. The reason being that no argument can make people see what they cannot see due to the subconscious perception filter.

An alternative approach to reality

After having spent 30 years trying to find the ultimate argument or theory, I finally realized it was impossible because our minds have a tendency to become closed systems, self-validating systems, self-fulfilling prophecies. There is a substantial amount of literature on the importance of positive thinking, starting with the book by Napoleon Hill, called *Think and Grow Rich*. The basic idea is that it is our attitude to life that determines whether we attract positive or negative circumstances to ourselves.

The way I eventually came to understand this is that our subconscious genie constructs a personal worldview. This is something that goes beyond an outer belief system, such as Christianity or Materialism. It is a very individual thing that has many subtle beliefs, which most of us are not aware of. For example, I once discovered that I had an attitude to money that said that as a spiritual person I should not have too much money, something many of the spiritual people I have met share. The point is that if we have such a subconscious belief, we will – without realizing it – push away or ignore opportunities for making money. So if we believe that we are not allowed to have money, we will reject opportunities for making money and thus we will seemingly confirm the belief that spiritual people should not or cannot have lots of money. Our attitude becomes a self-fulfilling prophecy. A materialist sees only arguments against religion so instead of being an objective and rational person, he is simply validating his unquestionable belief that all religion is subjective. He thinks this is an objective and rational conclusion because he is not conscious of the subjective belief that the subconscious genie gives an appearance of absolute reality. When I started seeing this, the question that became prominent in my mind was: "How do we get out of this closed system of our own minds? How do we become able to consciously see what our subconscious genie does not want us to see?" The answer that I found was that we can get somewhere by using the intellect because we can actually analyze our situation and see that our minds are closed or biased in a certain way. Or we can see inconsistencies in our beliefs. Yet we cannot reason our way out of the subconscious beliefs that must not be questioned because they have for so long been seen as absolutely real.

I then realized that the only way to overcome a belief that seems real is to encounter something that seems more real. For example, when people thought the earth was flat, they were afraid to sail too far out onto the ocean. Yet Columbus dared to do so, and when he spotted land, his experience was so real that it replaced any sense that the flat earth was real.

We can of course have a physical experience that gives us a sense of reality that is beyond our subconscious beliefs. But our minds have another faculty that gives us the ability to have experiences that are very real, and it is normally called intuition. When I realized that our minds become closed systems, I thought back to the concept I had learned when I was young, namely that the brain has two hemispheres. The left brain is the seat of intellectual, analytical thinking and the right brain is the seat of intuitive or big picture thinking. I don't actually believe this is confined to the brain, but nevertheless my point is that analytical thinking cannot get us out of the closed system of the mind because it cannot come up with an ultimate argument. The subconscious genie can always override an intellectual argument by pointing to the unquestionable belief that has a sense of reality. Of course, the subconscious genie cannot get us out of the closed system either because its role is to keep us inside the system it has created.

To me, the only way out is an intuitive experience whereby we suddenly see a larger picture, a broader view. This experience can be so real that it overrides the fear-based sense of reality in the subconscious database. So the alternative to intellectual thinking is intuitive thinking, or rather intuitive experience. The problem is that when we are stuck in the fear of going into panic, our egos can very easily close our minds to an intuitive experience. In order to have such an experience, we must be open to seeing something new, which basically means we have started going into the self-actualization phase.

The progression towards intuitive thinking

I have talked about a ladder of consciousness leading from lower to higher levels, as described in Maslow's pyramid. At the lower levels where people are focused on deficit needs, they are completely identified with their subconscious genies and they are convinced that their perception filters show them absolute reality. That is why they are so prone to feel threatened and get into arguments with people who have different perception filters. That is why they are sometimes willing to kill those people who threaten their one and only truth. They literally fear what will happen if their absolute truth was proven wrong, they fear going into panic.

As we move towards self-actualization, we gradually move away from being security addicts and become able to question what we previously did not dare to question. We begin to see that we have a perception filter and that it distorts how we look at the world. We become open to questioning the contents of our "Do not question" folder, and gradually we come to see that what we used to think was an absolute truth was only a small part of a much larger picture. Our "absolute" truth may not be wrong, but it is not the ultimate understanding of the issue.

Questioning our perception filter can indeed be done by using the intellect and rational thinking. The intellect is an analytical faculty, and it is therefore quite well-suited for comparing our different beliefs and spotting if two beliefs are incompatible. I know many spiritual people who went through a phase where they looked at the religious beliefs they were brought up with and they saw inconsistencies and incompatibilities. So the intellect can certainly play an important role in freeing us from our fear-based beliefs, partly because the intellect doesn't fear anything. To the intellect, everything is just an argument and no argument is inherently dangerous. The fear that you could go to hell for questioning the Bible simply doesn't compute to the intellect. It is willing to question anything, but only if it is allowed to do so and not confined by beliefs in the Do not question folder.

When I look at society, I see that centuries ago, our societies were dominated by fear. There was the fear of going to hell if you questioned God, meaning people were afraid to question the Bible, the church, the king or the noble class. How did we get out of this fear-based mental prison? In large part by using rational thinking to show the inconsistencies of fear-based beliefs. One effective way to overcome fear is to see that it is based on an irrational or contradictory belief. So I think it was necessary for us, given the thousand years of fear-based Catholic dominance, to go through a phase of focusing on intellectual and rational thinking. It was also necessary in order to create the technology that has made it easier for people to attain a lifestyle that gives us time to work on self-actualization rather than spending all of our energy on physical survival. Yet as we move into self-actualization, we also become more open to intuitive thinking. The theory of the two halves of the brain says that some people are more focused on analytical thinking and some people are more focused on intuitive thinking. Ever since early childhood, I have been a more intuitive thinker, and it was a relief for me to learn that this is perfectly natural. In fact, based on Maslow, I think that as we move into the self-actualization process, we shift from analytical to intuitive thinking. I have certainly met many spiritual people who are more intuitive than analytical, which is one reason we are looked at as crazy people by people who are strictly intellectual. Our rational societies have not yet learned to appreciate people who do not think analytically, but I think it will come.

So to me the obvious alternative to intellectual thinking is an intuitive experience. The right brain does not analyze, and thus doesn't really think according to an intellectual definition of thinking. Intuition is not about presenting an argument that is based on analyzing the separate components of an issue. It is based on looking at the whole, the big picture, seeing the forest instead of the trees.

Incidentally, it was a major epiphany to me when I, as a young child, heard the concept that we can't see the forest for the trees. It revolutionized my whole outlook on life because I realized that I am a holistic thinker. I am always stepping back from the details and looking for the big picture, the overall vision. I have since come to make peace with this and not feel bad about the fact that I am not as intellectual as some people. As a child, I wanted to be intelligent and it bothered me if I could not live up to the standard definition of an intelligent person. Today, it just doesn't matter to me anymore. I am at peace with the fact that I am no Einstein and that I am not suited for an intellectual, academic environment.

Intuition, Plato, Aristotle and Zeno

In order to present a different perspective on intuition and intellect, let me go back to Plato and Aristotle. To me, Plato's idea of the cave actually describes that our minds become self-fulfilling prophecies. He realized that we are trapped in our outer or subconscious minds, chained by our unquestionable beliefs, by our subconscious genies. We see only what makes it through our perception filters—we see only shadows. He realized that there is a way to look beyond our filters, but it is not through intellectual analysis but through intuitive experience. It is by connecting to something that is beyond the physical world and our outer minds. And it is our intuition that gives us the potential to make such a connection.

It seems to me that Aristotle did not grasp this point. He was the more analytical person, and that is why he became the spokesperson for the idea that we can understand the world through analytical thinking. One aspect of analytical thinking is that we analyze a topic, meaning that we break a big and hard to understand whole into smaller components that are easier to deal with. We then study the components, and according to Aristotle, when we fully understand the components that make up the whole, we will also understand the whole.

This idea has dominated western thinking at least since the emergence of science, and we might say it is the foundation for what we normally call the classical or hard sciences, such as physics and mathematics. I know many scientists and intellectuals are completely convinced that this is the ultimate approach to knowledge and their minds are completely closed to questioning it. Yet obviously they are not going to read this book, and in my experience spiritual people are indeed open to questioning whether intellectual analysis can give us all of the knowledge we need.

As one example of what I mean, let us again look at mental illness. Materialism makes two assumptions that come from Aristotle. One is that we can understand everything in the material world by looking only at the material world, and the other is that we can understand a whole by breaking it down to its most basic components. Thus, materialists assume that human psychology can be understood as a material phenomenon, and they assume we can understand the psyche by understanding the chemical and electromagnetic components of the brain. If we break down the material brain to its most basic material components, we can understand everything there is to know about the human psyche. So how is that working out for people?

It should be obvious by now that in my observation, a materialistic approach to psychology has failed to solve our psychological issues and cure mental illness. In my view, this is because of two problems. One is that we are not entirely materialistic beings, but the other is that we are not entirely rational beings and thus our psyches cannot be understood by reducing them to a set of basic materialistic components. Why is this obvious to me? I believe we can actually come to see the shortcomings of modern psychology through an intellectual analysis, but for me personally, my conclusion is a result of intuitive thinking. I know intuitively that I, as a person, as a human being, am not a collection of separate components. I am an entire person, and although my psyche has certain components, it can only be fully understood by looking at the whole.

Fortunately, I did not have an abusive childhood, but I have met many spiritual people who did. Many of them sought help from traditional psychology but they did not overcome their issues. So they turned to spiritual teachings in an attempt to find healing. I have talked at length with such people and studied the issue of trauma. According to a materialist, reductionist approach, when a person is exposed to a traumatic situation, there is a part of the brain that is affected by this experience. So if we can find that physical part and fix it, we should be able to cure the trauma. Yet no one has been able to find it, and many psychologists have become open to a more holistic approach to healing people's traumas. To me, the obvious problem is that when we are exposed to trauma, it is not components in our brains that react to the situation. We experience the situation as an entire being and we react to it as an entire being. Thus, what we have experienced as an entire being simply cannot be fixed by dealing with individual parts, certainly not material parts in the brain. Of course, this is obvious to me because I see a human being as a mind that is more than the brain. I have this view because of an intuitive experience, and I freely admit I have no ultimate intellectual argument for it.

I also have no ultimate argument against the reductionist approach, but I do have an observation. I think what has caused western thinking to accept the analytical approach of Aristotle is that we have not paid attention to another ancient Greek philosopher, named Zeno of Elea. Zeno is famous for presenting a paradox (even described by Aristotle), and here is a simplified version. The question is whether Achilles (who was the fastest runner) could actually make it all the way from Piraeus to Athens, a distance of about 12 kilometers. In Zeno's paradox, it is said that he would first have to cover half the distance, which was easy. He would then have to cover half the remaining distance, and he would have to continually cover half of the remaining distance. Since the distance could be divided into halves indefinitely, Achilles could never actually make it all the way to Athens. He would be caught in an infinite loop of covering half the remaining distance. This is pure math, as we can divide the "distance" between the number one and the number two into smaller components indefinitely. There is always a smaller division and it never ends.

How my mind works is that I make an intuitive leap that says Zeno's paradox proves that we will never fully understand a whole by breaking it down into smaller components. Why? Because in order to gain a full understanding of the whole, we would have to find the smallest possible component, and as Zeno's paradox and pure math proves, there is no smallest possible component. We can divide a whole into smaller parts indefinitely.

This doesn't mean I think it is non-constructive to look at smaller parts and seek to understand them. We can indeed, as science has proven, gain much knowledge by looking at the smaller components. The problem is when we think that understanding the components will give us an ultimate understanding of the whole. We think we can understand the whole without looking at the whole but looking only at its components. In my view, if we want to understand a whole, such as a human being, we have to look at the whole, as some scientists have indeed started doing. Yet these scientists are still considered marginal by mainstream science, which is firmly invested in the reductionist approach.

In Switzerland there is a scientific facility called CERN, and it has built the world's largest and most expensive machine, named the Large Hadron Collider. The purpose is to accelerate subatomic particles close to the speed of light and then smash them together, supposedly causing them to split into smaller components. I am not saying this isn't a worthy pursuit (although I think ending world hunger could be a more immediate scientific goal), but when I hear scientists say that this will give us the ultimate understanding of the universe, my intuition tells me there is something missing here. The physical reality is that according to Einstein's theories of relativity, nothing in the material universe can go beyond the speed of light. In order to accelerate a subatomic particle to near the speed of light, an enormous amount of energy is needed. That is why scientists want to built ever-more powerful accelerators. Yet the fact is that accelerating a particle to the speed of light will take an almost infinite amount of energy, so in reality the ultimate accelerator could not be built.

And what if it is all a futile pursuit? What if we will never find the ultimate subatomic particle? In the early 1900s scientists thought there were only three subatomic particles. Since then they have discovered an entire zoo of particles, and what if we can simply continue to split subatomic particles indefinitely, just as we can divide numbers indefinitely? What if the reductionist approach can never give us ultimate truth because there can never be an ultimate division into the smallest possible component? What if we can never understand the world by breaking it down into smaller components but only by looking at the whole? And what if our way to understand the whole is not intellectual analysis but an intuitive leap? What if analysis leads to an infinite loop of plausible deniability and plausible plausibility? What if we can only find a way out of this loop by using our intuitive faculties to connect to something that is beyond the infinite loop of our own minds?

How to increase our intuition

I have said that our subconscious genie gives us a sense of security by creating an explanation of how the world works and then projecting at us that it is based on reality. I have also said that an intuitive experience gives us a sense of reality. So why should intuition be better than the sense of reality from the subconscious genie? For starters, the subconscious genie is driven by fear, but intuition is beyond fear. The subconscious genie always projects that if we question its unquestionable belief, there is a risk or penalty. The classical example is a Christian who believes that questioning the Bible will land him in hell. So the subconscious genie or ego is always seeking to scare us into staying within the mental box it has created and it projects that it is dangerous to go outside of it. Intuition doesn't do this, it simply gives us an experience that is beyond intellectual argumentation, and then it allows us to do with it what we want. We might say that the ego has an intent to control us, whereas intuition simply presents us with an alternative to our current mental box.

In fact, one of the most common experiences is that we have an intuitive experience and then our egos immediately start arguing why it cannot be true or accurate. I have met people who think they never have an intuitive experience, but I think the reason is that their subconscious genies are so good at invalidating it that the conscious mind never realizes what the experience is. Interestingly, many prominent scientists, such as Einstein and Bohr, recognized the validity of intuition. Some scientists have intuitively seen a new idea and then later used their rational minds to describe this as a scientific theory.

In my view, most spiritual people have a well-developed intuition, but we can still have problems dealing with the mechanism where the ego seeks to override and invalidate our intuitive experiences. It was very helpful to me when I realized what I have described here, namely that there is something in the subconscious mind that resists growth. While we are trapped in the deficit needs, we have such a strong need for security that we cling to our present worldview, thereby resisting the intuitive experiences that show us there is something beyond our mental box. Once I saw this, I became better at seeing when my ego would override my intuition and thus consciously deciding to follow my intuition rather than my fear-based ego.

It was also very helpful to realize that intuition cannot and should not follow intellectual reasoning and argumentation. An intuitive experience is not an intellectual argumentation, but if we allow it, our egos will use intellectual argumentation against our intuition. As just one example among many, some years ago, I had a small boat with an outboard motor. I one day took a short trip in the boat, and as I was coming in, I had the intuitive sense that this would be my last trip with the boat unless I took the motor home. Since it was a hassle to take the motor home, I allowed my ego to rationalize why it wasn't necessary to do so. Two days later, the motor was stolen and I never again sailed in that boat as I ended up selling it. Let me describe this problem from another angle.

Doubting my intuition

Because our western societies have been dominated by intellectual, analytical thinking for so long, we have all been brought up to ignore or even deny our intuition. During my childhood I was often using my intuition to evaluate ideas. As I already mentioned, when they told me I descended from Adam and Eve and when they told me I descended from the apes, I knew this wasn't real. This wasn't a fear-based sense of reality because I didn't feel threatened by these ideas. I didn't go into a process of arguing against them or trying to disprove them. My sense that they were not real was not based on any analytical arguments, it was based on a quiet inner knowing: "Oh, that's not how it is." I am not saying my intuition was always clear. I often had a sense that some idea was not true, but I was not able to come up with any analytical argument for why it wasn't true. This became a source of distress as I grew older because in school I was constantly indoctrinated with the idea that I should be able to support everything I thought or said by these intellectual, linear arguments. If I could not come up with such arguments, I would often remain silent.

I also gradually came to doubt some aspects of my intuitive knowing because of the massive pressure to accept the form of thinking that dominated my society. The message that was projected at me (and everyone else) with great force was twofold:

- I do not have the ability to know truth on my own. Instead, I should accept that I live in a society where only the authority figures know what is true. I do not have the ability to know truth inside myself. I am deficient and therefore I need to believe what the experts tell me and only accept what comes from an external authority.

- I cannot simply say that something is true because I know it is. I have to be able to give a rational, linear argument, and if I can't, I will be rejected and possibly ridiculed so I better keep quiet.

I am not saying this was done deliberately or maliciously, as Denmark during the 1970s was not the Soviet Union, but it was clearly done and the pressure to accept the "rule of experts" and linear thinking was massive. This was part of the reason why I at some point came to doubt my intuition, but there is more to it.

At the age of 18, I found my first spiritual movement. For the purpose of this discussion, it doesn't matter which one it was. The point is that I felt a very strong intuitive sense that I needed to join this movement, so I did. In the beginning I was very enthusiastic, but after a couple of years, several experiences caused me to realize this was not the kind of movement I wanted to be in. So I left the movement, and my ego immediately started using this to argue that because I was intuitively led to join the movement, my intuition must have been wrong. Therefore, I should never trust my intuition again and instead obey what the ego told me so I would never make a mistake again.

For the next couple of years, I had no spiritual movement and no coherent teaching to study, and in retrospect I have to say that I was in a state of depression. There is really no other word for it, as I felt a huge emptiness inside. The emptiness was caused by a very specific psychological reaction. I had felt a clear intuitive guidance prompting me to join the movement. Yet now my rational, linear mind reasoned that I had been fooled. Adding to the pain was that after finding the movement I had felt a great sense of having been proven right, meaning that my growing up in an anti-spiritual family and society had given me certain wounds, including a sense of inferiority. My society was very good at making people feel that if they were not like the majority, then it was them and not the majority that were wrong. After finding a spiritual teaching, I felt it had been proven that I had been right all along and that there really is a spiritual side to life. This sense had now been shattered and although I still felt there was a spiritual side to life, I wasn't sure there was any reliable teaching about it. I vowed never again to join a spiritual movement.

The problem was that since I had been intuitively led to join what I now considered a false movement, I wasn't sure I could trust my intuition. So far I had felt my intuition was always right and that it would not lead me astray. Now, I felt that it had indeed led me astray, leaving me to doubt if there was anything in this world I could trust and rely upon. This was incredibly distressing to me, and it was truly a psychological trauma. I think it is comparable to what many people experience in a divorce where they doubt that they can ever trust another person again. There was also an element of hurt pride since I was feeling: "How could I have been so stupid." I didn't feel like telling my family about it, as they had been very negative about me joining a spiritual movement, almost as if I had done the worst thing they could imagine.

I have met many spiritual people who have gone through a similar experience with their first spiritual movement. Some abandoned the spiritual path forever (or at least indefinitely). Some went into depression like I did. Others threw themselves into another spiritual movement (when you fall off a horse, you have to get right back on) while others went into denial, pushed away their doubts and used their outer minds to reason that their first spiritual movement was right after all.

All of the pain I experienced was completely unnecessary *if* I had only been aware of something really, really simple. This so-called simple realization has several parts:

- My experience with the movement came in the mid-70s, which was just the beginning stages of the awakening of spiritual interest in the modern democracies. We had all grown up in societies that denied the spiritual side of life so we were the pioneers who had to experiment with what it means to be a spiritual person in a modern, materialistic society. How could we possibly have the experience necessary to evaluate a spiritual movement or guru and get it right the first time? We had to try out what was available until we got enough experience to make better evaluations. I feel this relates to intuition. The more knowledge and experience we have with an area, the clearer our intuition can be.

•   Spiritual growth is a life-long process that has many stages. I can see today that my first movement was exactly what I needed at the time. There was also the practical reality that there was a much smaller selection at the time so from a practical viewpoint, it was what was available to me.

•   As spiritual people we are following what I like to call the spiritual path, and the most important realization one can come to about this path is that it has stages. These stages build upon each other. My first stage was this movement. My problem was that due to my lack of experience, I thought the movement was the final spiritual teaching and movement I would find. Had I only realized this was the beginning, it would have been much easier for me. I could have been at peace with the fact that this movement gave me the exact experience I needed in order to reach the next stage and find my next spiritual teaching.

•   Had I known this, I would not have felt that my intuition had betrayed me. I would have realized that it was indeed part of my spiritual path that I should join this movement because I needed that experience. I would also have been able to avoid thinking that my first pair of pants should be able to fit me for the rest of my life. I would have seen the movement as the beginning lesson instead of thinking I had found the ultimate spiritual teaching. So my intuition had been accurate because it was indeed part of my path to get experience with this movement.

As it was, it took me about 20 years before I reached that conclusion and was able to fully make peace with my experience and fully trust my intuition again. This did not mean I stopped listening to my intuition because after a couple of years with no spiritual teaching, I found another teaching and joined another movement. But it did take me those couple of decades to fully trust my intuition, and it really didn't need to take that long. That being said, fully trusting my intuition did not mean I thought it would always be right in every detail. This was because I had gained a deeper understanding of the spiritual path.

Intuition depends on our level of consciousness

The most important insight I eventually came to is that our rational societies have conditioned us to think that intuition should live up to the same criteria as rational, linear, analytical knowledge. In other words, intuitive guidance should be absolutely true or it is worthless. It is all or nothing.

Today, I see intuition as a guidance from a higher part of our minds (I will describe it later), and it is not always true from a linear perspective. In other words, an intuitive insight may be valid, but it may not be the final insight about the topic. As my long explanation about perception filters is meant to illustrate, we start out our individual path by wearing many layers of colored glasses. These glasses distort our vision, and we can say that as we walk the spiritual path, we gradually take off some of the colored layers so we come to see more clearly. When we are seeing everything through these colored glasses, there is a limit to what kind of intuitive guidance we can receive. Because our outer minds are closed to certain ideas, our intuition cannot give us guidance that is too far beyond the outer beliefs that we cling to as a result of the ego's fear. So our intuition faces a very delicate task.

The goal of our intuitive guidance is to set us free from all illusions. Yet if it gave us an insight that was too far beyond our outer beliefs, we either could not accept it or we simply could not grasp it. We wouldn't even see it. Therefore, our intuition must guide us one small step at a time. It must give us an insight or direction that takes us one small step up the staircase of the observation tower in the forest. As we gradually climb one small step at a time, we eventually reach a plateau from where we can see more.

The secret to being successful on the path of self-actualization is to realize that no matter where we are on the staircase, and how much higher we feel we have climbed from our starting point, we must never believe the ego's claim that we have reached the final step. It is my clear conclusion after 44 years on the path that as long as we are in embodiment on earth, we will not have reached the final step on the staircase. There will always be another step, there will always be another illusion to see through and another insight or revelation to be gained. If we think we have reached the final step, we simply will not see this, and thus we will stop at that level instead of going further. Our minds will become closed systems. That is why I at some point adopted the motto: "From this point forward—from *any* point, forward."

In my view, a spiritual person is one who listens to his or her intuition. Our intuition can give us an inner knowing that is always valid, but not the final or ultimate insight. I can see today that my intuition was always valid, but it was never ultimate—according to the intellectual, linear perspective. In the beginning, I would often get intuitive insights while studying a spiritual teaching. My intuition would tell me that a certain statement was valid. However, I have so many times experienced that later (often years later) I would receive another insight that showed that there was so much more to understand. In other words, my first insight was valid enough based on my level of consciousness and what I could see at the time. Yet it was only a small part of a larger picture, and when I saw that larger picture, my previous insight was put into an entirely new context and often took on a different meaning.

My conclusion is that as spiritual people, we need to follow our intuition because there is always some meaning behind our inner directions. It may not be what our outer minds think it is. In fact, it was important for me to realize that my outer mind always superimposes its own interpretation on my intuitive insight. For example, my intuition told me to join my first spiritual movement. Yet the entire idea that this was supposed to be the final or ultimate spiritual teaching was imposed by my ego.

It might take some time before we have cleaned the perception filter enough that we can see the real reason our intuition sent us in a certain direction. In that respect, it is very important to realize that the spiritual path is not always comfortable. I have met some people who think everything should always be pleasant, easy and comfortable. Yet we sometimes need a certain experience in order to shed a particular illusion held by the ego. And when that illusion is shattered, the ego will always experience this as very uncomfortable, and it will often try to make us believe that there must be something wrong with this.

The spiritual path is neither the Via Dolorosa nor a walk in the park. It can be downright hard work because we are often led to confront the very illusions upon which our egos have built their sense of security, their sense that they have the universe under control. I have seen people who came to a point where they faced a particular illusion that they were not willing to question, and that became the end of their progress, at least for the time being.

What happened when I entered my first movement was that I followed my intuition, but my outer mind or subconscious genie immediately started putting an overlay upon the experience. My genie wanted the movement to be the ultimate spiritual teaching because it would give it a sense of security. So when I realized the movement was not the ultimate teaching, my ego told me my intuition had been wrong—because the ego can never admit that it has been wrong.

I earlier said that human progress is a tug-of-war between two forces in our psyches. One is the ego that pulls us to close our minds to new ideas, the other is our intuition, which pulls us to open our minds to new ideas. When we do open our minds to a new idea, the ego is threatened, but if it cannot stop us, it attempts to impose an interpretation on what we are doing. In my case, my ego projected that the movement should be the ultimate spiritual teaching. My intuition had never said this, but I was not mature enough to realize this. I thought that my intuition had guided me to the movement because it was the ultimate teaching. So when I realized it was not the ultimate teaching, I believed my ego's projection that my intuition had been wrong, and from now on I should only listen to the ego and forget about intuition. It took me a couple of years to get out of this blind alley, but at least I didn't stay in it for the rest of this lifetime.

What really helps us escape our perception filters

Now, in one sense we could say that what can help us escape our perception filters is our intuition, the ability to look beyond the details and see the bigger picture. As I said, the perception filter can have a very strong emotional component, but the mechanics or how the filter works are quite analytical. Analysis is a process whereby we compare something new to what is already known. As modern technology proves, this is both a necessary, valid and quite useful process.

However, as the rise in mental illness proves, it cannot solve all of our problems, and the reason is that feelings cannot be reduced to rational arguments. The intellect wants to take any problem and break it down into its smaller components, studying the details in order to then reason how the whole works. The problem is that when it comes to human psychology, seeking to reduce it to electrochemical processes in the brain (or other details) causes us to lose sight of the whole, namely that there is a real human being here who has a problem that is not caused by details but by an experience that impacted the person as a whole.

Our perception filters work as the colored glasses I talked about previously. While we have the perception filter, we cannot see certain things because the filter filters them out. So within the parameters of the filter, we cannot reason that the filter is wrong because we cannot even see, or see the validity of, the arguments that might contradict the filter. Our experience is that only what the filter allows through is real and has validity.

What is the way out? It is to become aware that there is another way to look at a given issue than the one presented to us by our own subconscious minds. We must come to actually experience that there is something outside the perception filter, we must acquire a frame of reference from outside the filter. As an example, imagine that while you were asleep, someone put yellow contact lenses on your eyes. As you woke up, you would see the sky as green, but because you remember that the sky really is blue, you would not believe your own eyes. You have a frame of reference for questioning your direct perception. Now imagine someone had put yellow contact lenses on the eyes of a baby. That child would grow up with no frame of reference for questioning its direct experience that the sky is green. Well, our so-called free democratic societies have still put certain worldviews into our subconscious perception filters and they do not want us to question them.

Does the mind have the ability to mentally step outside our perception filter, outside our normal state of consciousness and have an experience that is as real (or more real) than what we normally experience? Yes it does, and this has been documented by millions of people throughout history. Materialistic science has largely ignored this because it doesn't validate its paradigm, and that is in my view the most severe way in which Materialism limits us as human beings and even limits science and our progress as a society.

We can call such experiences intuitive experiences, but they have also been called mystical experiences. I have had such experiences throughout my life, as have most of the people who are open to the spiritual side of life. I am convinced that many people have had such experiences without realizing what they were or what to do with them. This is in large part because our rational societies cannot help children deal with such experiences and therefore can only tell us to deny them, to rationalize them away. I think many people have had these experiences but have denied them, and that is why they are not openly spiritual.

The first such experience that I remember came at the age of 3 or 4. My mother was taking me to my grandmother on a sunny day with a blue sky. We were passing a field with yellow grass, and the sun was shining on the grass, giving it a golden hue. As I spontaneously looked at the grass, it was as if the whole world filled up with golden light, and I was literally transported out of my body. There was nothing disturbing to me about the experience, as it felt completely familiar. I felt so at home in this golden light that it seemed much more real and natural to me than being in my physical body and experiencing the world through my senses and outer mind.

During my childhood I had many experiences of feeling like something shifted in a situation and I was like a silent witness, watching it from somewhere outside my body. I sometimes felt as if time stood still and I was outside a situation. This did not happen in dramatic or traumatic situations but in ordinary day-to-day situations.

Such experiences seemed so real and so familiar to me that it was always self-evident that my mind is far more than my physical body, is not limited to the body and not trapped in the body. I have had more dramatic experiences that I will describe later. Obviously, as a child I had no awareness of subconscious perception filters, but the net effect of these experiences was that I never fully identified myself with my physical body or my outer mind. I always knew I am a non-material being who is temporarily residing in a material body. I was using the body and the outer mind to interact with the world and other people, but I was far more than the body and the outer mind.

This doesn't mean I was completely dis-identified from the outer mind. I had many situations that would trigger me to go into a reactionary pattern where I was pulled into a situation and could not look at it from the outside. I was pulled into my outer mind and was now trapped in responding to the situation through my subconscious perception filter and reactionary patterns. Yet no matter how difficult my situation would get, I always had some moments where I could step outside of it. This gave me a frame of reference for knowing that there is more to me than the outer mind, and it is precisely because of this that I have gradually been able to free myself from more and more of my psychological limitations.

I can look back at my father and see that if he had such experiences, they didn't have the same impact on him. During my first 18 years, I did not have any outer stimulation that helped me get started on the path of freeing myself from my psychological limitations. Yet I was still able to pull myself onto this path and eventually find outer teachings that helped me, and the main reason was that I had these experiences that gave me something to pull on. My father was not able to pull himself onto the path, but I cannot help but wonder if he – and millions of people like him – could have done so with a little bit of guidance from the society that claims to be so sophisticated. In my view, all people have intuitive experiences. Those who become spiritual are those who acknowledge the experiences instead of using the rational, analytical, linear mind to deny them.

10 | WHAT'S THE PURPOSE OF LIFE

Another explanation problem of my society was the purpose of life. We have a concept of "crimes against humanity" and it is normally connected to physical atrocities, such as the Holocaust. I think we need a psychological parallel that defines psychological crimes against humanity. One of these crimes is the fact that due to the war between religion and science, several generations of young people in the modern democracies (the supposedly most sophisticated societies ever seen on earth) have been brought up without having any sense that their lives have a purpose beyond accumulating and consuming material goods.

I think that's a crime against humanity because for me one of the deepest needs that followed me from infancy was the need to feel that life has a general purpose and that my life has an individual purpose. I am not saying all people are consciously aware of this need, but all people who are beginning to move into self-actualization do need a sense of purpose. If we don't have one, it can lead to all kinds of self-destructive behavior, from depression to substance abuse and other forms of escapism to mental illness. So what then *is* the purpose of life?

Traditional views on the purpose of life

Quite frankly, I am not sure what Christianity defines as the purpose of life. I suppose one could say that it is to be saved after this lifetime so I can avoid going to hell where I will suffer horribly for all eternity. Of course, in order to be saved, I have to be a member of the one and only Christian church and I have to follow its outer rules so I can please God and make him want to take me into heaven. Obviously, this never was a motivating factor for me, and I think it's the same for most spiritual people. The reason for this is simple, yet mainstream Christianity hasn't gotten the message.

I think there is a universal side to this and it all begins with what I have talked about before, namely that in democratic nations we don't fear our leaders. So for now over a century, people have gradually moved out of a fear-based state of mind. Yet Christianity is still promoting the same fear-based message of avoiding hell, while the priests cannot understand that they are preaching to empty churches. Well, if people have lost their fear and your message is based on fear, is it any wonder they don't feel your message is relevant to them?

There is also a more specific side in that spiritual people have started to move out of the deficit needs and into self-actualization needs. The deficit needs are fear-based whereas the self-actualization needs are love-based. So what kind of message do you need when you are in self-actualization mode? Well, definitely not what you hear from Christian pulpits all over the world. Now, let's look at what scientific Materialism has to say about the purpose of life. That's easy because it has *nothing* to say. According to materialists, we live in a universe that started and evolved as a result of a completely random process. There are certain laws of nature that guide this process (how can there be rules in randomness?), but they are completely unconscious and impersonal. The point is that in a random, unconscious universe there can be no meaning to life.

Furthermore, our consciousness is just a product of material processes in the brain. The specific make-up of my brain is the product of my genes, and genetic mutations are completely random. So our brains do not have a mind of their own and there is no point in thinking there is any purpose to our lives. The idea of a purpose implies a direction towards some goal, but given that our minds will supposedly be extinguished when the brain dies, there is no point in thinking about where we might go after death. If we need a purpose to life, our longing isn't based on anything real, it's just a result of some unfortunate genetic mutation.

The only purpose to life could be to have the maximum enjoyment while you are alive. In other words, eat, drink and be merry, for tomorrow we die. Is it any wonder that an entire generation threw itself at consumerism and lived as if there is no tomorrow for themselves or the planet, mindlessly consuming resources without thinking about any long-term consequences? Why think about the future when there is no future to think about? Is it any wonder that Materialism has caused as many human atrocities as religion? After all, the Soviet Union and Mao's China were entirely materialistic societies and after having lived in a former Soviet republic, I can guarantee you that it defined no long-term purpose for life, causing many people to live in a constant state of depression. Is it any wonder that modern materialistic societies have led to various forms of self-destructive behavior from alcoholism, to drug abuse or even crime, rape and the like.

The simple fact is that people trapped in the deficit needs do respond to fear. If they fear going to hell, they might moderate their behavior in order to avoid this. If they have no fear of any consequences, and Materialism doesn't define any consequences beyond this lifetime, then what is to stop them from doing whatever they want regardless of the consequences it has for others? Take note that I am not here talking about whether or not there is a hell. I am only talking about the fact that for some people the fear of hell did have an effect on their actions towards others. Materialism defines no such restraints, and that could be why we see a rise in destructive behavior, such as the incredible crime surrounding illegal drugs, drugs that there should be no market for if people had a sense of purpose.

Incidentally, I once met a Danish woman who had lived for a time in Cuba. She and her husband went there as flaming Marxists and were looking forward to experiencing this Marxist Utopia first-hand. It became the disappointment of a lifetime, and she claimed that 90% of the Cuban population were on anti-depressants and that was the only reason Marxism could survive.

So what is the purpose of life?

As long as we are in the deficit needs, we need some external authority to define for us what is (or is not) the purpose of life. Once we start moving into self-actualization, we begin to see an internal purpose. That purpose is in its broadest sense to actualize ourselves. However, what exactly does that mean to us? Well, because we have grown up in anti-spiritual societies, we really have no idea. I remember even as a child having a very strong sense that my life had a purpose, but I could not put words on what it was, and this caused me a lot of confusion and frustration.

For several years in my early teens I had a newspaper route and every day after school I would distribute newspapers in an upper middle class neighborhood. I remember watching these very nice new houses with their new cars in the garage and the people and their children and dogs who all seemed to have perfect lives. I was doing well in school and I knew that by applying myself, I could get an education and have all that these people had. I could buy a nice house and live in it for forty years, watching the children grow up and the trees grow into a jungle.

Yet over those years, a very clear feeling grew inside of me that this simply wasn't enough for me. I knew I could have this life that was far better materially than what my grandparents' generation dared to dream about. I also knew that it simply wasn't enough for me and that I needed something more in life. Yet what exactly that more was I could not fathom and it was very frustrating to me because I felt like I was wasting time that could have been used better. I knew what *was not* my way of life, but I had no idea what *was* so I felt a deep inner emptiness.

My point is that we all have to start somewhere. If we had been given a spiritual upbringing, we might have had a clear sense of our individual life purpose by the time we turned 18. As it was, we have had to find our life's purpose the hard way by experimenting with pursuing self-actualization as we could see it when we first realized there is more to life than what our parents and society called life.

For me, I always had a sense that it was possible to deliberately change myself, meaning changing my psychology. By watching my father, it became clear to me that we are all victims of our personal psychology. My father's life was set on a track by the reactionary patterns in his psyche, and I was very determined to rise above my own patterns so I would not live the kind of life my father had lived. I have met many spiritual people who have had very difficult childhoods, often being exposed to various forms of abuse. Compared to them, my childhood was easy. Such people are often interested in spiritual teachings because they hope this can help them heal and overcome their psychological traumas. And in my experience, it can indeed work for people even though there are some pitfalls, as I will describe later. To sum up, for many spiritual people the first purpose we see for our lives is to heal our psychological wounds and patterns so we can attain a greater degree of psychological freedom.

After I read Yogananda's book, I realized there is an even higher purpose, and it is to raise our consciousness beyond what our societies call normal human awareness. This also has an appeal to many other spiritual people. The idea is that the vast majority of human beings are trapped in a certain state of illusion or ignorance, or what I have called our perception filters. This idea was first introduced by the Buddha some 2500 years ago, when he said most people live in Maya or illusion, yet it has had little impact in the West. When I first read about the existence of higher states of consciousness, it was immediately obvious to me that this is a real possibility. I had experienced glimpses of such higher states during my childhood and youth so it was not a matter of believing something. It was simply that my personal experiences had now been explained more clearly and put into a larger context. I realized that I did not have to passively wait for such experiences to happen (or not happen) spontaneously. I could engage in a systematic, active process to produce such experiences and raise my general level of consciousness. So at that point, raising my consciousness became my main purpose in life.

I know this might seem like a vague goal, but that is because we have not been brought up with the concept that there are higher states of consciousness than what we call normal in our anti-spiritual societies. I will later talk more about what it means to raise consciousness. For now, I want to try to describe the incredible contrast I experienced between life as I had been brought up to see it and how I saw it after I realized there is a spiritual path and a spiritual teaching.

11 | THE BIG CONTRAST

Let's imagine that we create an institution that can keep the people inside of it isolated from the rest of society. We now take a group of infants and place them inside. We then tie one hand of each infant behind its back. Obviously, we need some adults to take care of the children, and they also have one hand tied behind their backs. So we now have a group of children who grow up thinking that the normal condition for human beings is to have one hand tied behind your back. After all, they have never seen anything else.

How will the children react to this? Some will no doubt accept that this is normal and never question it. They might not even feel it is a restriction to have one hand tied behind their backs as they have never experienced an alternative—they have no frame of reference to question their condition. Yet at least some of the children will feel that their movements are being restricted and they will sense that this is not natural. They might long to have freedom of movement. Some will wonder why they have two hands when one of them is not being used.

Now, imagine that we take this second group of children outside the institution and we untie their arms. How are they going to feel? Are they not going to experience an incredible contrast between having one hand tied behind their backs and having freedom of movement? Is it not going to be such a stark contrast that it has a truly profound, even revolutionary, effect on how these children look at life?

Some of these children might develop a desire to go back into the institution to set the rest of the children free as well. And they will indeed be allowed to go back in, but not with their hands untied. They can only go back in with one hand tied behind their backs, meaning that the children inside cannot directly see that it is possible to have both hands free. In other words, the children coming in can only tell the children inside that it is possible to become free of the bonds. They can only use words, not direct demonstration.

Consider the task faced by these incoming children and how they might be received by the children inside. The contrast between life inside the institution and life outside is so huge that it is very difficult to describe it with words, especially because the children inside do not have a frame of reference, do not even have a vocabulary, for relating to life outside the institution. Many will refuse to believe that there is a world outside the institution. Many will refuse to believe that it is possible to untie a hand and move freely. Some will question why you would even want to do so when life works just fine with one hand. Some will say it is dangerous to untie one hand, and they will come up with all kinds of reasons for avoiding this like the plague. Some will want the incoming children to stop talking or even go away, perhaps even becoming aggressive towards them. The simple reason being that the incoming children are threatening the sense of security of those inside. My point being that our sophisticated societies are bringing up all people to be psychologically crippled, as if we were wearing the mental equivalent of a straitjacket. Some people go through an awakening process and realize there is a world outside the mental institution we call earth. The contrast between that world and the world inside the institution is so huge that it causes a revolutionary shift in these people's minds. And that means it suddenly becomes very difficult for such people to communicate with those who still think wearing the mental straitjacket is the normal, natural or only state possible for a human being.

This has often led spiritual people to have conflicts or become alienated from their families and old friends, even alienated from society. And the reason is that our societies have for so long been anti-spiritual that it is virtually impossible to communicate openly and neutrally about any topics that are defined as "Don't even think about this" by either Christianity or Materialism. Let me describe just one such experience.

Losing my family

When I was 18, I moved away from my home town to attend university. Here, I had my awakening to the fact that life has a spiritual side, and I met a group of people who were into a spiritual movement promoting meditation. I learned this meditation technique and joined the movement. I cannot remember how I told my parents about this, but I must have done so or they would not otherwise have known about it. Some time later, there was a birthday party at my parents' house, and there were about 20 people from the closest family.

I must admit that I am sometimes very naive about the intentions of other people, and at first I didn't sense any tension at the party. Of course, I had a certain inner tension because in my youthful exuberance I wanted to tell people about the wonders of meditation. After all, these were my family members so why wouldn't I want to share with them something that was so important to me?

For a time, the conversation was normal, meaning people talked about other people they knew and the latest political events. Then, one of my aunts started talking about how her migraine was getting worse, and the doctors didn't know what to do about it. Immediately, my clever mind saw this as the opening I had been waiting for, and I (causally, I thought) mentioned that scientific studies had shown that meditation could help people overcome migraine.

As I said the word "meditation," there was a stunned silence in the room. Everyone stopped their movements, some with a spoon or glass halfway to their mouths, and turned to stare at me. Then, I felt as if a pack of ravening wolves threw themselves at me in order to rip me apart.

For the next two hours, the only topic of conversation was how I could be so stupid to join something as crazy as meditation, which was clearly some religious nonsense and just out to get my money. From the very first reaction, I immediately realized I had made a mistake by bringing up the topic, so I backed down and tried to turn the conversation to something else. Yet I soon realized the entire family had been talking about this behind my back, and they had been looking for an opportunity to confront me, make me see the error of my ways and get me to come back into the fold that defined how people in our family should and should not behave.

Especially shocking to me was that one of my uncles became aggressive in a way I had never expected from him. He was normally a very gentle person, and he would often let people take advantage of him. Yet here he was so angry that I was letting this meditation movement take advantage of me that he simply could not let the topic go. He got unusually drunk and wouldn't stop talking about it. I tried to just calm the waters, but he apparently saw that as me being arrogant and overbearing and he barely talked to me for the rest of his life. He even made a bet with me that before five years had passed, I would have forgotten all about this spiritual nonsense.

After I went to bed that night, I was literally in shock. I felt psychologically traumatized and really didn't know how to react to the situation, lying awake for several hours. In retrospect, what I really couldn't deal with was that I felt I had lost my family because they had rejected me. One might say that they had only rejected my beliefs, but what I felt was that they had rejected me as the person I really was. During my entire childhood, I had been a good boy and had lived my life within the parameters of how my family defined life. Yet now I had taken one step outside those parameters, and immediately they threw themselves at me and literally attempted to destroy me psychologically in order to bring me back into the fold so I would conform to their norm for how one is supposed to live one's life. And I can honestly say that not one of them tried to understand why this was so important to me (and none of them have done so to this day).

At the time, I didn't know anything about perception filters and deficit needs that give people a need for security and how they attain it by building a certain view of life that must not be threatened. Had I known this, I might have realized they were simply acting out their psychological hang-ups and not felt so rejected. Instead, I experienced this as a complete shock and the reason is that at the time I had a very naive view of life.

My experience had been that all of my childhood I had been longing to find a deeper understanding of life. I had assumed that everyone else felt the same, that everyone else had realized they had one hand tied behind their backs and wanted to be free. For 18 years I had not found anything that pointed me towards that greater understanding, and I had assumed that was because it just wasn't readily available. Yet when I did find it, I immediately embraced it, meaning not that I embraced meditation only but the very idea that one can escape psychological limitations. I assumed everyone else was aware that they were boxed in by their psychological limitations and wanted a way out. So I expected that when I told other people that there is a way out, they would embrace it as I had done. This was of course hopelessly naive on my part, and it was part of what caused my shock that evening.

However, the main part of the shock was that I had honestly expected that I would be able to talk to my own family about something that was so revolutionarily important to me. Even beyond any hope that they would accept it, I had expected I would be able to talk about it. Yet what I realized was that my own family members only accepted me as long as I stayed within the parameters of what they had defined as acceptable behavior. As soon as I strayed outside the fold, all I met from them was rejection.

And it wasn't just that they reacted to meditation and the specifics of that movement. On a deeper level, that I am sure they were not aware of, they rejected the entire idea that one can take command over one's life and free oneself from one's psychological limitations. They clearly thought it was dangerous to have that one hand untied.

Perhaps a more mature person would have been able to avoid feeling rejected. But for me, I was so new in my awakening to the spiritual side of life that it was clear to me that I was never, ever going to give up the spiritual path. And since my family's rejection had been so total, I couldn't see how I could ever reconcile what was the most important aspect of my life with my own family. So I never again talked to anyone in my family about what is so important to me. It wasn't that there was any open break with them, and I have later had a cordial relationship to my family members. Yet is has been entirely on their premises, meaning we only talk about things they feel safe talking about.

How do we talk about deeper questions?

What I have tried to portray here is that because our societies have been trapped in this fight between religion and Materialism, they have become so anti-spiritual that it is virtually impossible to have an open and neutral conversation about the deeper aspects of life, the so-called fundamental questions of life. I think this is what prevents us from dealing more effectively with the rise in mental illness. I think it is what prevents us from moving from material welfare to psychological well-being. I think it creates enormous conflicts between people, both in families and among groups on a world scale (such as between Muslims and Westerners). And I think it creates untold suffering on the individual level because people have psychological needs that they can't even articulate and that no institution of society knows what to do with.

How do we overcome this impasse? The rise in mental illness is the only way I can see. As more and more people come to the system with mental problems, there will come a point where some people will realize that either the system breaks under the strain or it will have to find a different paradigm, a paradigm that can help people take care of some mental issues themselves. When will that happen and how much individual suffering will it take to get society to that breaking point? Well, the answer my friend, is blowing in the wind, the answer is blowing in the wind.

12 | DEATH, THE ULTIMATE EXPLANATION PROBLEM?

In America they have this wonderful expression that there is a 300 pound gorilla in the room. For those who are not familiar with it, the idea is that there is a group of people who are in a room talking, and there is a 300 pound gorilla in the room but the people are ignoring it, talking about everything else. Well, I think the 300 *ton* gorilla in modern democracies is the topic of death. Of course, if we can't talk about any other sensitive issues, how could be possibly have a meaningful conversation about death?

I described the evening where I felt I lost my family. Well, most of my family members from my parents' generation have since died, but did we ever have a conversation about death? Nope. A person gets ill and dies, we go to the funeral but we are not talking about what it means that someone has died. There is a cone of silence about it, and I see the same at the level of society.

In 2014 I moved back to Denmark because my mother had fallen ill with cancer and needed some help. She died five months later, and during those last months I several times asked her if there was something she wanted to talk about. But there wasn't and I think it was partly because she never knew how to talk about personal feelings but also because she believed death was just like a long sleep. In other words, you seize to exist. Now, my mother wasn't particularly afraid of this and perhaps even welcomed it in some way. Yet I have met many other people who are extremely afraid of death. As I see it, the fear of death has historically had an enormous impact on people and caused tremendous anxiety and suffering.

If we look at the history of the Catholic church, we can see how it used the fear of death to control people. This was caused primarily by the idea of original sin, meaning we are all sinners by birth. If we do not receive salvation, then we will burn for all eternity in a very unpleasant place, called hell. Of course, the only way to receive salvation is through the Catholic church, thereby automatically giving the church enormous power over those who believe this. It never, ever made sense to me that my salvation – a process of entering a realm that is beyond the material world – should depend on an institution in this world. But 1,3 billion Catholics have a different perception filter.

Just consider for a moment how much suffering has been caused by this fear of burning in hell. How many people have lived their entire lives being psychologically crippled by this fear? How much manipulation has been carried out by the church and its clergy because the fear of death made people afraid to protest what the church was doing? I was profoundly shocked when I (as a child) learned about the crusades, the witch hunts and the Inquisition. Here is an institution that claims to represent Christ, but it is performing actions that clearly are out of alignment with the teachings of Christ, such as "do unto others" and "turn the other cheek." Why didn't people object? Because the fear of hell was so strong that they were willing to endure all kinds of abuse in this world in order to get a better life or avoid a worse fate in the next world.

Consider medieval society in which the primary resource was agricultural land. There was only a limited amount of land and you would get it by inheriting it from your father. In other words, the most important duty of a father was to take care of his sons (or at least the oldest) by passing on the land to them. Yet in this culture, the Catholic church managed to become the single largest landowner in all of Europe. The church didn't buy most of the land, so how did they get it? Well, imagine a farmer who is nearing death. He calls the Catholic priest and "confesses his sins," as the church requires. He can see that it doesn't look all rosy for him, but the priest offers him a way out. If he donates a part of his land to the church, then his sins can be absolved. Suddenly, the fear of hell can outweigh the need to take care of his children.

Of course, we aren't really any better off in our materialistic societies, even though we have supposedly overcome all religious superstition. What does Materialism – this supposedly most sophisticated worldview ever developed by man – have to say about death? Well, as little as it has to say about the purpose of life: *nothing*. At least the church gave people the hope of some kind of life after death, but Materialism offers nothing at all.

All that you are as a conscious being is a product of the processes in your physical brain, and when those processes stop, it will be lights out and there is nothing of you left. As I said, I was always aware that I have self-awareness, and I have come to see it as the greatest gift of all. In a way, my deepest desire is to express myself as the unique individual I am. Obviously, I don't think I am the only one who feels this way.

I think most people have a sense that life is worth something. They may not have a clear sense of purpose, but they have a sense that life has value.

When you look at mass murderers, such as Hitler, Stalin and Mao, you see that they had no sense of the value of life—at least for other people. I think the only thing that prevents us from wholesale slaughter is that most people have a sense that life has value, and thus you cannot just kill other people. Of course, this sense of the value of life cannot come from a materialistic view of life, according to which the most fit have a right to devour the less fit.

The sense of loss

The flip side of this sense that life has value is that your own life has value. And this means there will be a sense of loss associated with the cessation of your life. When we talk about the fear of death, it has two aspects. One is that many people fear the way we die. They fear a painful death, either through violence or illness. Yet behind this, I recognize in myself a deeper fear of the loss of my existence as a self-aware individual being. I think all people have this although many may not be consciously aware of it or able to articulate it.

This brings up a question that materialists have no answer to: "How can we have the sense that life has some kind of enduring value?" If the materialists are right, then where is the mechanism that gives us this sense? It cannot be created by the material brain since the molecules and synapses have no awareness. And Materialism must by definition deny the concept of a soul. So why do we have it, if it is out of touch with reality and gives no evolutionary advantage? My answer is that we have it because our self-awareness is not the product of the physical brain. One of the huge explanation problems of Materialism is how the matter of the brain, which is unconscious and has no self-awareness, can produce consciousness and give us self-awareness. This is one 300 pound gorilla that materialists always ignore, except in calling it the "hard problem of consciousness," as if that explains anything.

I am more than my body

To me, the way out of the enigma of death is the experiences I have had since childhood, experiences that made it very real to me that I am more than my physical body and that my mind is not limited to or dependent upon the body. I have had so many of these experiences, and they have been so real to me that since my early childhood I have not really been afraid to die. I did at times identify a certain fear of death in me, but this clearly came from the culture in which I grew up. I have not personally been afraid to die because I have always known that what I truly am, a self-aware being, will survive the death of my physical body. Let me just describe one such experience.

After I had turned 19, I participated in a month-long course arranged by the meditation movement in Denmark. It was the first time I had ever spent such a long time focusing on spiritual teachings and practicing spiritual techniques, and it definitely raised my consciousness. After I came home, I one day laid down on my bed to rest. Suddenly, I started hearing this loud, high-pitched noise that oscillated. I spontaneously focused on this vibration, and I suddenly found myself outside my body. I had the distinct sensation of moving in a tunnel, but the actual sense was that of falling—only I was going in an upward direction. I literally felt as if I was in a free-fall, but I was falling *up*.

After a short time, I could see a faint light far ahead of me in the tunnel. As I continued to fall up towards it, the light grew bigger and took on a golden yellow hue. I then plunged into the golden light and it felt very familiar and at home to me.

Now, I used to wish that I had retained the memory of what happened while I was in that light. Perhaps I had some stunning insight or otherworldly experience? However, the next thing I was aware of was that I was falling again, and this time I was going down. I then entered my body, and it literally happened with such force that by body bounced 2-3 times on the mattress (which had metal springs). I tried, but I could not recreate this bouncing while lying flat on my back.

The experience was extremely real to me, and I had no doubt whatsoever that my mind had left my body. The experience was as real or even more real than my everyday experience. That is why I was not really surprised when I learned that many people (perhaps millions) have had similar experiences. In the United States some psychologists have documented such experiences, and they are called out-of-body experiences.

Near-death-experiences

Naturally, as with everything else, there is divided opinions about how to interpret such experiences. Materialists generally tend to deny them or push them aside as entirely subjective. Yet to me the reason for this is simple. They have never had such an experience themselves and therefore they have no awareness of how real it feels. For them, this phenomenon is not based on experience, meaning it is something that can be interpreted and thus believed or not believed.

Imagine that you are walking through a busy marketplace and you meet a friend who says: "Hey, you know, over there is a booth where they sell this amazing new fruit that has been discovered in the Amazon rain forest, it's like a mixture between an apple, a pineapple and a banana." At this point, the existence of this new fruit is for you not based on experience. You have only heard your friend talk about it, and you can choose to believe or not believe what he is saying. You can continue to stay in this frame of mind by refusing to go to the other side of the marketplace. In that case, you can remain in your present belief system and believe what you want to believe.

Yet, you do have the option to walk over there and see for yourself. The moment you stand in front of the booth, see the fruit on the table, pick it up and take a bite, the existence of the fruit is not a matter of belief or disbelief. The bubble of belief has been punctured by the arrow of direct experience. You have, as quantum physicists say, made a measurement and collapsed the waveform.

I have experienced that it is possible for me to leave my physical body and still be conscious. It feels so real to me that there is no need or room for interpretation. It is not a matter of believing or not believing. For people who have not had the same experience, it is naturally still a matter of belief of not belief, and I am in no way wanting anyone to believe what I am saying. I am only pointing out that it is possible for a human being to have the experience that some part of you leaves the physical body and has self-awareness outside of the body. And as long as you have not had that experience yourself, it will always be a matter of belief or disbelief. And this of course is what materialists say is subjective. Naturally, materialists will say that my experience is subjective, but at least I am having an experience and for them it's only theory. So who is the more subjective?

Now, I know that most people will never have an out-of-body experience, but it is not the same with death. All people will eventually have the experience of dying. If the materialists are right and there is no awareness after death, they will never know that they are right. They cannot know until they die, and after they die there is no awareness so they still can't know. If there is nothing, they won't be aware that they are not aware. Only if the materialists are not right (and there is consciousness after the death of the physical body), can we actually know.

Of course, there is another phenomenon that is quite well-documented in the United States and it is that of near-death-experiences. These are experiences where people have actually died and been declared dead by doctors, only to later awaken again and report that they had conscious experiences while their bodies were clinically dead. These experiences are not as well-known in Europe, but in America there are a number of books about them. It is estimated that 8% of the population have had such experiences. Naturally, the phenomenon is being vigorously denied by materialists who are seeking to come up with a material explanation about the brain playing tricks on people. The problem with this explanation is that the brain would then be playing tricks on itself and that begs the question: "Why?"

How do you explain that a person can be declared brain-dead by competent doctors and yet wake up later and report that she had conscious experiences while there were no brain processes that (according to materialists) can produce such experiences? How do we explain that normally, if a person is not breathing for four minutes, there is permanent brain damage. Yet some people have been clinically dead for 2-3 days and had no brain damage upon waking up.

To me, the explanation is self-evident. Based on my personal experiences, there is a part of my mind (call it a soul, if you will) that is not produced by my brain. This part of me did not come into existence when my body was born or conceived. It existed before my parents ever had sex.

This part of my mind is only using my physical body as a vehicle for interacting with and expressing itself in the material world. As such, my sense of self-awareness can be affected by my physical body and brain. I have never taken any kind of recreational drugs and never been drunk, but I have no doubt that my state of mind can be affected by my brain chemistry. I did have my tonsils removed, and the anesthetic made me unconscious for hours. So I am not denying that our brains can affect our state of mind, but I do not see this as proof that our brains have created the entirety of our consciousness.

I see consciousness as a movie projector. Self-awareness is the white light that shines through the projector. My physical brain and subconscious mind is like the filmstrip, and the light is naturally colored by the images of the filmstrip as it moves through. Yet the light is not produced by or dependent upon the filmstrip. The movie screen is like my conscious awareness. Normally, I am focused on the images on the filmstrip. But it is possible to realize that they are just that: images and that the light comes from beyond them. It is possible (as millions of practitioners of various spiritual techniques have proven) to go beyond the contents of the mind and experience self-awareness in its pure form. I have had many experiences of awareness without any content in the mind, what I call pure awareness.

I have never had any doubt that I, as a conscious being, will survive after the death of my physical body, and the result is that I have never actually been afraid of death. What is there to be afraid of when the worst thing I could imagine was the loss of self-awareness and when I have experienced that this does not depend on my fragile physical body? I really don't see any other way for people to overcome the fear of death than to increase their awareness of what kind of beings they are and that they do not die when the body dies.

Are all our experiences subjective?

Of course, a materialist will say that the experiences I have personally had, no matter how real they seemed to me, were just subjective. Yet millions of people have had near-death or out-of-body experiences and many of them have written about it. They have all experienced the same sense of reality and they have all overcome their fear of death. So if many people have the same experience, can we just push it aside by saying that it's all subjective and thus not scientific? Doesn't there come a point where a dedicated scientist says that here is a phenomenon that science needs to investigate (as some scientists are doing)? And doesn't there come a point where a democratic society says that if there is a way to help people overcome the fear of death, shouldn't we at least take a look at it in order to help our own citizens and minimize our health-care cost?

I know of course that when people are trapped in the deficit needs and driven by their quest for security, they must reject any idea that threatens their sense of security without even thinking about it. So I understand why materialists will reject all personal experiences as subjective. Yet I can't help but wonder why these self-proclaimed rational people never take the logical consequence of their own theories. If my out-of-body experience is entirely subjective and simply a trick that my brain played on me, why isn't *their* experience just as subjective? If *all* of our mental experiences are the products of our brains, why isn't their belief in Materialism a product of their brains? How can you on the one hand claim that the world is entirely materialistic and produced by chance and at the same time claim that any aspect of human consciousness is objective? How can you claim that *your* mental experience is objective because you accept Materialism, while the mental experience of those who do not accept Materialism is entirely subjective. Once again, why should I believe in their theory when they apparently don't believe in it themselves? If they did believe in it, they would not claim that I am *subjective* and they are *objective* when our brains work the same way. Or do they actually believe that their brains work differently from mine and that is why they are superior to me and know best?

Now, I am not trying to say that materialists are entirely wrong. I think many scientists are driven by an inner knowing that it is possible for us human beings to go beyond subjective experience and gain some objective knowledge. Yet that inner knowing is based on an intuitive experience that there is more to us than the outer, subjective mind. If Materialism was correct that there is nothing more to our minds than the material processes in our brains, then objective knowledge simply would not be possible.

Science is proof to me that we can gain objective knowledge, but given that science has been hijacked by Materialism, there is currently a limit to what kind of knowledge we can get. Obviously, if science is not allowed to investigate anything beyond the borders defined by Materialism, then science can never find objective knowledge about a level of reality beyond the material world. Perhaps science cannot give us this knowledge? Perhaps our only way to get such knowledge is to use our intuition and say that if many people have the same intuitive experiences, then they must have some level of objectivity? Anyway, to me the claims of Materialism really are no more objective than the claims of medieval Catholicism.

In summary, the fear of death has caused incalculable suffering, and to me it is all completely and utterly unnecessary because part of us will not die. Of course, this raises the question of what exactly survives after death and what happens to that part of us when the body – when *one* body – dies?

13 | LIFE: ONE-SHOT DEAL OR ONGOING PROCESS?

In our modern democracies we would like to think that people are becoming more and more equal, that society is becoming more egalitarian with everyone having the same opportunities in life. Yet we can observe that this is not the case, and this presents a massive explanation problem.

Why are some children born in rich and privileged families with a silver spoon in their mouths while other children are born in the slums of Calcutta with a slim chance of surviving to adulthood? Why are some children born with a debilitating illness that puts their entire lives on a track while others are born with normal health? Why are some people born with a psychological make-up that predisposes them for success in life while others are born with a psychology that predisposes them to become criminals or unable to take care of themselves? Why are some people born with such a lack of empathy for others that they become either career criminals, politicians, serial killers or dictators like Hitler or Stalin? Why are some people born with a psychological knot (like my father) that makes it impossible for them to get along with others?

Christianity has struggled with this question for 1700 years and has failed to come up with an explanation that seems real to me. The best they can do is talk about God's will, but they cannot explain why a supposedly all-powerful and all-good God would want one child to be born with a crippling disease and another healthy. Materialism isn't much better. All it can talk about is the differences in our genetic make-up. I grant that when it comes to physical differences, such as me being born with blue eyes, this can be explained by genes. But the major differences between people are found in the psychology, and despite their frantic efforts, geneticists have found no genes that can account for psychological traits. In fact, we human beings, as incredibly complicated as we are both in terms of physical bodies and psychology, have almost the same number of genes as the common fruit fly.

I was in my early thirties when I started realizing that I had been brought up with a highly distorted view of genes. This started when I read a college textbook stat stated matter-of-factly that our genes only and exclusively contain information that tells the cells how to make proteins. This started a process that made me realize I had been brought up to think that genes can explain every aspect of my life, from my blue eyes to the fact that I prefer strawberry over vanilla ice cream.

I was brought up to think that my genes contain an almost unlimited amount of information, but the reality is that they only contain information on how to make proteins. Now, proteins are the building blocks of the cells, but nothing more. Imagine that you took a group of builders and only gave them information on how to make bricks, planks and nails. Would they, with only the information about how to make the raw materials, be able to build an entire house? So how can our cells, based on only the information on how to make proteins, build an entire structure as complex as the human body? How can 37.2 trillion individual cells, each of which only has instructions for how to build proteins, build a whole as complex as the body? And how can instructions for building proteins account for my psychological make-up, which is even more complex than my physical body? This would be the equivalent of the bricks of a house containing information about what the inhabitants of the house will have for dinner tonight. And if you studied those bricks in the minutest details, you would be able to predict what the family will choose to have for dinner tomorrow.

There is a concept found in philosophy of a "black box." The idea is that when people have a strong emotional attachment to a given thought system and then come across something that cannot be explained by the system, they invent a black box. This is something that we human beings cannot look inside. So we cannot explain exactly why the black box produces the results that it produces, but by labeling events as the outcome of the black box, we still gain that fragile sense of having control because we can uphold the system instead of looking beyond it.

When it comes to explaining why people are born with such clearly unjust differences, Christians invented a black box called "God's will." Materialists have invented a black box called "Genes." In both cases, the black box does not explain why children are born with such huge differences. It simply gives the people who believe the black box is real an excuse for not questioning why their system cannot explain the phenomenon. Yet an explanation for the differences between our birth circumstances and psychological make-up is readily available to anyone willing to look beyond the black boxes and closed boxes of Christianity and Materialism.

What if we have lived before?

I was brought up to think that there was a large and fundamental difference between religion and science and that they presented opposite and mutually exclusive views of life. Yet the more I learn, the more I become aware that there are also some similarities between the views of life presented by Christianity and Materialism. Sure, when you look at the specific design, there is a huge difference between an iron sword and a nuclear bomb. Yet when you step back and look at the bigger picture, they are both weapons designed to kill human beings (and the iron sword has so far killed many more people than nuclear bombs—although that could change in 15 minutes).

I have come to see that Christianity and Materialism are both weapons designed to deceive and control human beings. I am basing this on the fact that both systems are dis-empowering by presenting us as limited beings who have no real power to change our destiny. Historically speaking, the only reason to create a thought system that limits the population is so that a small elite can control the rest of us. A neutral look at history shows how a small elite of Catholic clergy, kings and noblemen controlled the general population of Europe for over a thousand years. You might have to look a little harder to see that a small elite of scientists and academics have an enormous influence on our democratic societies and have managed to almost entirely control the public debate.

It is amusing to me that a person like Richard Dawkins is constantly criticizing religious people while failing to see that he, and the academic system he claims to represent, is exactly the same elitist society as Catholic clergy. It is a closed club where only those who have sworn allegiance to the system may enter. How do you become a member of this exclusive club? By taking a vow never to question the basic paradigm upon which the system is based. In order to enter the Catholic club, you must never question papal infallibility, and in order to enter the materialist club, you must never question the infallibility of Materialism.

As with Catholic clergy, the materialists clearly see themselves as an elite who know better than the population what is true. Thus, they are entitled, even obligated by their place in evolutionary history, to tell the rest of us what to believe about ourselves and our abilities. They clearly believe that the general population simply does not have the intelligence to decide what is true in life. It's like medieval clergy believing the population should not be allowed to read the Bible.

Another similarity between Christianity and Materialism is that they both vehemently deny the idea that can explain why one child is born rich and gifted and another is born poor and crippled. Why do they deny this idea? Well, officially for different reasons, but unofficially because it has the potential to empower people to take command over their lives and change what is so often called fate. The concept of fate is often taken to mean something over which we have no control. Things just happen because they are fated, and there is nothing we can do about it. Yet when you accept the simple idea I am talking about, you can actually begin to change your fate and avoid the inevitable and make the impossible possible. (Why both Christianity and Materialism do not want to empower the people is a topic I will talk more about later.)

There is a scientific concept called "Occam's Razor." The basic idea is that we human beings have a tendency to create a thought system and claim that it can explain everything. Inevitably, we will run into things that the system finds it difficult to explain, and in trying to come up with explanations within the system, we often end up creating more and more complex theories (that still don't explain the problem). Yet a medieval philosopher, called William of Occam, claimed that the simplest and most elegant explanation is usually the right one. Meaning that if the explanations that adhere to the parameters of the system become too complicated, we need to look for a simpler explanation, even if it goes beyond the system or questions the system.

Another similarity between Christianity and Materialism is that they both claim that life is a one-shot deal. You only have this one lifetime and then you will either go to heaven or hell or disappear into oblivion. Yet think about all of the differences between the birth circumstances of children. If we have absolutely no influence over the circumstances into which we are born, then we obviously have no power to change them. Yet what if we could actually gain influence, not only over our birth circumstances but also over how they affect us for the rest of our lives? How might we get such power to change our lives? Well, what is the one ability we have that can change our lives? It is the ability to make choices. So how do we gain influence on our birth circumstances? Well, we cannot do so within a thought system that denies that our power to choose can influence those circumstances. The alternative, obviously, is a thought system that presents our circumstances in life as the result of choices we have made. If something is not the result of a choice I made, there is not much I can do about it. But if something is the result of a choice I made, there is the possibility that I can change it by making a more aware choice.

Okay, so how can the situation into which I was born be the result of my choices? How did I make a choice before I was born? Did I sin in my mother's womb as some Christian theologians claim? Of course not, the simple explanation (which Occam would have liked if he had not been a Catholic monk) is that I made those choices in a previous existence, a previous lifetime, a previous incarnation. If we have lived perhaps many lifetimes before this one, then the choices we made in those lifetimes can account for the circumstances we were born into in this lifetime, even the psychological make-up we were born with. We did not become the complex psychological beings we are at conception nor during childhood but through a long series of choices made in previous lifetimes. And that means we have the power to become aware of these choices and consciously and systematically change them so we heal the traumas and overcome the hangups built in past lifetimes.

The idea of reincarnation is a simple and elegant idea that can help us overcome the explanation problem that we have struggled with since the Catholic church banned the concept of reincarnation as heresy in the year 553, a ban that has been reinforced by Materialism. Why was reincarnation banned as heresy? Well, that's actually an interesting story.

Why Christianity denied reincarnation

Two-thirds of the world's population accept reincarnation, as it has been taught by Vedic teachers for over 10,000 years and Buddhist teachers for 2,500 years. So why have we never heard about it in the West? Well, because some powerful Catholic theologians did not want us to hear about it, and the materialist theologians apparently feel the same way.

There is a concept that "the winners write history," and from the year 381 to well into the 1500s the big winner was the Catholic church, and it wrote the history of Christianity to make itself look good. I have met many Christians, even many ministers, who have virtually no knowledge of how the Catholic church has falsified the history of Christianity. As a result of this, they have no idea how much the Catholic church distorted the original teachings of Jesus. This is a topic I have published several books about, so I will just present one simple idea here.

If we take the Christian scriptures at face value, it was the leaders of the Jewish religion who wanted Jesus to be executed. There can be only one reason for this. The Jewish society at Jesus' time was a highly elitist society where a small elite of priests had enormous power over the population. The Jews believed that unless their sins were forgiven, they would go to hell, and they believed only the priests of the Jewish religion had the power to forgive their sins. In other words, the only road to heaven went through the Jewish priesthood. Then, Jesus appears, and what he actually does with his teachings is to threaten the monopoly on salvation claimed by the priesthood. Jesus gives his disciples the power to forgive sins, but even worse, he claims that people do not need an external institution and its priesthood in order to be saved because "the kingdom of God is within you."

The Jewish religion was dis-empowering to the people whereas Jesus' original teachings were empowering by giving people the power to change their lives and their destiny. The result was that the priests felt threatened, and they did what a power elite always does: They executed the person who personified the threat. The point being that Jesus came to free the population from a small elite and empower them to take command over their own destiny and salvation. Jesus was anti-elitist and anti-establishment, he was a spiritual revolutionary.

For the first centuries, Christianity was nothing like the coherent religion we have come to see it as. There were many individual sects and their interpretation of Jesus' teachings varied greatly. In other words, there was no Christian establishment, no elite claiming to have the power to say what was true and not true about Jesus' teachings. There was no one and only church. This gradually changed with the emergence of a church that thought it was necessary to create a more uniform religion, including a set of official scriptures. Yet this movement had little traction until an event occurred that changed western civilization in a fundamental way that is not generally understood (because the winners do not want us to know what actually happened).

This event took place in the year 325 when the Roman emperor Constantine created the Catholic church. He did this for purely political reasons because he was in danger of losing control over the Roman Empire. He thought he might reverse his fortunes by creating a new religion that could unify the people and make it easier for him to control them. To this end, he took a group of Christians who had been severely persecuted by previous emperors, and he offered them the chance to become the leaders of the new official state religion. They took him up on the offer, but what few people have understood is that the price they had to pay was that they had to create the kind of religion that Constantine was looking for.

Without going into too many details, let us just look at what is the central message of the Catholic church. It is that the only road to salvation is through Jesus and that the Catholic church is the only true church, the only church that represents Jesus and can guarantee your salvation. Now compare this to what I said earlier. The Catholic church was from its inception the exact same type of religion as the Jewish religion that had Jesus killed. The Jewish religion claimed that the only road to heaven was through its priesthood and the Catholic church has made the exact same claim from 325 to this day. In other words, the Catholic church was the same dis-empowering religion as the religion that had Jesus executed in order to prevent him from liberating the population from a small elite. The Jesus who came to set people free from the elite had now been turned into the primary tool that another elite has used for 1700 years to control the population. The spiritual revolutionary became the opposite of what he wanted to be. Instead of being seen as an example that all of us could follow to a higher state of consciousness, he now became the exception that none of us can emulate. The Jewish power elite killed Jesus and the Catholic power elite killed his example.

Take note of what happened here. Christians always claim that Jesus' statements represent a higher truth. Yet when you take a neutral look at the history of the Catholic church, you see that truth didn't matter at all. What mattered was what could help the church and the secular authority control the people. The teachings of Jesus could be dis-interpreted to fit that end.

Again, there is much more to say about this, as I have done in books and websites, but I want to focus on reincarnation. At Jesus' time, reincarnation was an idea that was known in society. The Pharisees taught reincarnation as did many of the so-called mystery religions that existed at the time. These religions taught an individual path for raising your consciousness until you had qualified for salvation, exactly what Jesus actually did. Some of the early Christian sects also taught reincarnation.

The idea was even part of early Catholic theology, not in terms of the official church, but several prominent theologians, such as Origen of Alexandria, openly taught reincarnation. This came to an abrupt end in 553 when a church convent in Constantinople officially banned reincarnation as heresy, a ban that was heavily enforced over the following centuries until the entire idea had largely been obliterated from western thought.

Why was the church so intent on banning reincarnation? Because the key to the church having power over people was that they could secure their salvation only through the church and not in any individual way. If you think you have more than one lifetime to secure your salvation through an individual process, you don't feel the same pressure to obey the church in order to be saved after this lifetime. When correctly understood, reincarnation says that it is your state of consciousness that determines whether you are ready to leave earth behind and enter a higher realm. If you are not ready, you can have one or more lifetimes on earth according to your own choice. This is an empowering idea, as opposed to the dis-empowering idea that you have only one lifetime and thus must submit completely to the church.

Why Materialism denies reincarnation

From a superficial viewpoint, Materialism suppresses the idea of reincarnation because its official doctrine is that the human mind is the product of the physical brain. If there is a part of the mind (call it soul or something else) that was not created by the brain, then this contradicts the "absolute" doctrine of Materialism that there is nothing beyond the material universe.

Materialism claims to have freed humanity from the superstition of religion. To me, it is obvious that Materialism has merely replaced one type of superstition with another one. How has Materialism proven that there is nothing beyond the material universe? From a logical viewpoint, you cannot actually prove that something does not exist. All you can say is that we have not found it so far. Yet science has actually pointed to the existence of something beyond the material universe, at least as it is defined by Materialism. I have spent a lot of time reading about physics, and I have been especially fascinated by quantum physics. This branch of physics deals with the smallest building blocks of matter, called subatomic particles.

So many of the findings of quantum physics go beyond the materialistic worldview. For example, it has been observed that a subatomic particle can appear where there was nothing before, divide itself into two particles that then collide and disappear again. This has caused some scientists to theorize that there must be something we cannot currently detect, and they talk about a quantum field or a vacuum state.

The most amazing finding of quantum mechanics is the one that invalidates the Holy Grail of Materialism, namely the dream of the neutral observer. The main claim to authority made by materialists is that any observation that involves the human mind is unreliable and subjective. Only when we conduct measurements that are not affected by the mind of the scientist, can we make a reliable, objective observation (of course, measurement in one thing, interpretation another and it is not necessarily objective). Quantum physics has proven that at the level of subatomic particles, it is impossible to make an observation that is *not* affected by the mind of the scientist. When a quantum physicist makes a measurement, the result is a product of the entire measurement situation, meaning the phenomenon being observed, the measuring device (particle accelerator) *and* the mind of the scientist. At the most fundamental level of matter, there is no neutral observer. The physicist is not simply observing a phenomenon that exists independently. What the physicist sees is in part produced by his or her consciousness. The act of observation creates the observed.

Naturally, hard-core materialists have done everything they can to suppress the logical and philosophical consequences of this indisputable discovery. So what is the consequence? Well, after Materialism emerged, it claimed that because the human mind is so subjective, there is no point in science investigating the human mind. That is why so few resources have been dedicated to investigating the human psyche or consciousness. Yet when it has been known (since the 1920s) that at the fundamental level of matter, our consciousness influences everything we observe, how can we uphold this refusal to research consciousness? If the consciousness of the scientist is part of the entire measurement situation, it seems logical to me that science should make an all-out effort to investigate what consciousness is and how it can possibly interact with the basic building blocks of matter.

There is a very old idea floating around in the world that mind is separate from matter and thus cannot influence matter. This can be traced back to Aristotle but probably beyond, as it is based on our normal, sensory experience. We normally experience that we cannot deliberately change matter by our thoughts. Yet the findings of quantum physics leave us with some interesting options:

- Consciousness can indeed influence the separate substance of matter.

- Consciousness is not separated from matter.

- There is a form of consciousness present at the subatomic level, and human consciousness can interact with this form of consciousness.

- Matter is not the fundamental reality. Consciousness is the fundamental reality. What we call matter is created out of a form of consciousness and that is why a scientist can co-create the subatomic "particle" being observed.

Of course, any and all of these options go beyond Materialism, which to me means that since the 1920s, Materialism has been dead in the water. In my view, there is already so many scientific findings that point beyond Materialism that it is possible to build an entirely solid proof that there must be something beyond the material world. Of course, given the principle of plausible deniability, it is also possible to find other scientific findings that seem to uphold Materialism. Again, I am not trying to come up with an inconvertible proof because I realize this will depend entirely on people's perception filters over which I have no control. I am only seeking to describe how I look at the phenomenon, and my purpose is to describe how I have used the idea of reincarnation to empower myself to take command over my life and my destiny.

Reincarnation is not fatalistic to me

I am not sure when I first heard about the concept of previous lifetimes, but it would have been in early childhood. My father was a passionate hunter (his ersatz career was duck hunting) and he would sometimes remark: "When I was a big-game hunter in Africa in a past life." For him, it was just a joke as he claimed he did not believe in reincarnation. Even though I don't remember the specific event, I know that when I first heard about reincarnation, it was instantly obvious to me that it's real. I don't remember ever doubting this, and as I grew older, it became obvious to me that there are certain things we can only explain by considering that we human beings have lived before and that what we did in past lifetimes has set the stage for certain conditions we experience in this lifetime. Yet beyond the explanatory power, I always knew that I am a very old being who has existed for a very long time.

I think most spiritual people have experienced awakening to the realization that there is so much more to know about life than what we were told growing up. And as part of this awakening, most spiritual people have come to accept reincarnation. The reason for this is simple. The essence of being a spiritual person is that you no longer see yourself as a helpless victim of circumstances beyond your control—otherwise you cannot actualize yourself. Instead, you begin to see yourself as a being who has at least some potential to change your life. When we awaken to seeing ourselves as spiritual people, we begin to take a higher degree of responsibility for our own situation than the average person.

Incidentally, in my observation, most of the people who deny reincarnation do so because they are not willing to take responsibility for themselves. They want to retain the belief that certain circumstances in life are beyond their power to change because they are not the result of their own choices in a past lifetime. Incidentally, the Catholic ban on reincarnation was reinforced in the 7th century on the initiative of Theodora, the wife of the emperor Justinian. She did not like the idea that she could be punished in a future life for what she had done in this life—again an unwillingness to take responsibility for your actions.

As a result of the Catholic and materialist campaign against reincarnation, most spiritual people in the West have heard about reincarnation through eastern teachings. This is a little unfortunate because some eastern teachings about reincarnation are quite fatalistic and can actually have the effect of people not taking responsibility for themselves. Some eastern teachings say that everything that happens in your life is the result of karma you made in a past life, and thus there is nothing you can do to change it. You must accept that this is the way your life is. As an extreme example, some Hindus say that if you see a person who is drowning in a river, saving him will interfere with his karma, and thus you are responsible for taking care of him for the rest of his life. I have never for a second subscribed to this version of reincarnation, and I once heard an Indian guru say: "What if it was only his karma to get his shirt wet?" My understanding of reincarnation is not fatalistic, although it may seem so at first. Eastern teachings tend to see karma as a form of punishment for something you did in a past life. If you killed someone in a past life, your karma mandates that you be killed in this lifetime. I do not see karma as punishment because my view is that the purpose of life is our growth in consciousness. Life is a schoolroom and every aspect of our lives is a teaching device, including our so-called karma from past lifetimes. Every physical circumstance is meant to teach us something about our state of consciousness so that we can free ourselves from our psychological limitations. Let me make this less abstract by describing how I see my own situation.

How I see my own life

To me, planet earth is an educational institution. We learn by making choices and experiencing the consequences of those choices. The choices I make are based on my psychological make-up that causes me to take certain actions. The material world is a kind of feed-back machine and when I take a certain action, the result is a physical circumstance. This gives me the option to evaluate if I want to experience more of this kind of circumstance or if I want to experience another type of circumstance. For example, if I am aggressive towards others, I am subconsciously saying that I want to experience an environment in which people fight with each other.

If I want more of the same, I can continue to make choices based on my current psychological make-up, my current state of consciousness. If I want a different circumstance, I need to change my state of consciousness so I can make different choices and thereby take different actions. When I do change my consciousness, I will no longer embody in an environment where people fight but in one where they cooperate with each other. So if I still want aggression, I will embody in the Middle East, and if I no longer want aggression, I will embody in Scandinavia.

I see a direct connection between the actions I take and the physical circumstances I encounter in life. However, this is not some external process. It is true that a physical action releases a physical consequence, but the action is based on a choice I make and that choice depends on my psychology, including how I see myself, how I see life and what kind of emotional scars or reactionary mechanisms I have in my subconscious mind. If I encountered an unpleasant consequence, this is not the punishment of an angry God in the sky, but the result of an impersonal natural law that makes me reap what I have sown. The purpose is to give me an opportunity to evaluate my state of consciousness and change it so I can make choices that produce different consequences.

When I was young, I still had a need for security so I needed a relatively simple view of reincarnation and karma. I thought that if you killed somebody in one lifetime, you would have to be killed in a future lifetime in order to learn the lesson that killing is not what you want to do. I now have a more nuanced view where I see life as much more complex, especially when you look at humankind as a whole.

We can make a simple observation, namely that we live in a universe where our actions have consequences, but they are often delayed. In other words, if I kill someone, I will not be struck dead immediately by a bolt of lightning from the sky. Why is that? By delaying the consequence, I have the opportunity to change my state of consciousness before there is a physical consequence. If I have changed my consciousness, I do not need to experience the physical consequence. To make it simple, say I killed someone in a past life. According to the eastern view of karma, I have thereby created a completely impersonal impulse, a wave of energy, that goes into the total energy system of our world. It moves through the layers of this system, until it again comes back to the material realm where it manifests as me being killed, likely in a future lifetime. This is the traditional view of karma. In my view, there is the potential that I can change my consciousness before the energy impulse comes all the way back to the physical level. If I have truly transcended the state of consciousness that caused me to kill someone in that past life, then I will not have to be killed in my present life. I have learned the lesson and thus do not need to experience the physical consequence. The universe is a *learning* facility, not a *correctional* facility based on inevitable punishment.

I have a sense that I am a very old being, meaning I have had many lifetimes on this planet. In those lifetimes, I have made just about all of the mistakes that a human being can make. I have created plenty of karma, but if I had to reap all of that karma at the physical level, my life would have been very miserable this time around. Why was I born into fairly easy circumstances in this lifetime? Because in my most recent past lives, I had transcended some of the lower or more selfish state of consciousness. Thus, I did not need these harsh physical circumstances in this life, as I had already stepped onto the path of taking responsibility for myself and being willing to look at my psychology and change myself. This was a process I started in past lives and that is why I was born with a higher degree of awareness about the importance of psychology than most people. It is not that I am somehow more advanced, I have just had a longer time to learn from my mistakes, and I have become willing to change myself.

The inner path versus the outer path

To me, there are two ways we can learn our lessons on earth. One is the School of Hard Knocks in which we refuse to consider that there is a connection between our state of consciousness and our physical circumstances. Therefore, we stay in the same state of consciousness, or we may even reinforce it over several lifetimes. This means that our karma becomes our teacher. We continue to do the same thing and as a result of a completely impersonal law, we reap the same consequences. Albert Einstein said: "If you continue to do the same thing and expect different results, you are insane." In other words, it is insane to expect that you can stay in the same state of consciousness and perform the same type of actions, and you will not reap the same consequences lifetime after lifetime.

The other way of learning is the path of conscious learning. We can also call it the path of self-actualization or the spiritual path. It is a path where we come to the most important conclusion one can come to as a human being: My outer circumstances are a reflection of my inner circumstances.

My consciousness produces my physical circumstances so the only way to change my physical circumstances is to change my consciousness. If you are willing to go way beyond Materialism, this is actually what has been shown by quantum physics in the connection between subatomic particles and the consciousness of the scientist. We are all scientists and our minds are constantly interacting with the most fundamental level of matter. As our consciousness interacts with the subatomic level, we are gradually building a set of physical circumstances and we will experience them either in this life or in a future lifetime.

In my view, this is the path taught by Jesus, the Buddha and many other spiritual teachers. In contrast to this is what I call the outer path, meaning the promise that we can be "saved" without looking at our consciousness, without looking at the beam in our own eye. This is the path taught by the Jewish religion that had Jesus killed, and it is the path that has been taught by the Catholic church from 381 to the present day. The promise is that by being members of an outer church, believing its doctrines, following its rituals and submitting to its clergy, we will be admitted to heaven after this lifetime. I have never (in this lifetime) believed in this promise and consider it entirely false. I have always known that it is my state of consciousness that determines where I will go after this lifetime.

I once had a conversation with an American man who had grown up with a father who was a fundamentalist preacher with his own television station. We were talking about what it takes to be saved, and he gave me the standard fundamentalist view that all we have to do in order to be saved is to declare that Jesus Christ is our Lord and Savior. Without having thought about this beforehand, I suddenly said: "So you are telling me that if Adolph Hitler on his deathbed had sincerely confessed Christ and declared Jesus to be his Lord and Savior, Hitler would have gone to heaven?"

There was a stunned silence as the man looked like I had hit him between the eyes with a hammer. He then said: "Well, based on everything I was brought up to believe, I would have to say that is true." Yet his tone of voice clearly revealed that this made no sense to him. What made Hitler Hitler? There is no genetic history of mass murderers in Hitler's family and his childhood was not any more difficult than many people I have met who did not become mass murderers. Materialism has no answer to where people with this magnitude of evil came from, and Christianity has little answer either because the consequence of Christian doctrines is that God must have created Hitler the way he was. Hitler may have been influenced by the devil, but God must have created him in the first place, and why would a good God create a person with such a propensity for evil?

To me, the answer is simple. Hitler originated as all human beings originated and was not created with or predisposed to be evil. He did what we all did, namely make choices over many lifetimes. Over those many incarnations, Hitler continued to make selfish choices, and as a result he gradually became more and more enveloped in a selfish, narcissistic, psychopathic state of mind. In his incarnation as Hitler, this culminated with him having no sensitivity for the lives of other people, being willing to sacrifice others in order to further what he saw as his epic goal but which was only a delusional fantasy. Hitler was not created as Hitler but *chose* to become Hitler. He may have been influenced by some evil force, but that was because he chose to open his mind to that influence in order to gain power (more on this later).

In other words, there is no way a person like Hitler can enter a higher realm. That is, until he has completely transcended the state of consciousness that made him Hitler. I see that as a possibility, although it will likely take many lifetimes for such a being to overcome all of its illusions and learn to make unselfish choices, as it took many lifetimes to enter such severe delusion.

The explanatory potential of reincarnation

Why are some children born with a silver spoon and others with ashes in their mouths? Because of choices they made in past lives, choices that brought them to a certain state of consciousness just before this incarnation. This may seem harsh, but it is far more empowering than the views of Christianity and Materialism.

Again, this is not the punishment of an angry God but the result of an impersonal law. Most of the people in the world are still in the School of Hard Knocks and because they refuse to change their consciousness, they continue to take the same kind of selfish actions lifetime after lifetime, meaning they are reborn into much the same circumstances in this lifetime.

How have we made any progress as a race? Because some people have been willing to look at their state of consciousness and deliberately move away from selfishness and into self-actualization. They have started performing actions that were not selfish and this has gradually set the stage for the emergence of societies that are not ruled by selfishness. The modern democracies are to me examples of such societies.

If we look at the world as it is today, one of the obvious questions to me is: "What kind of people are being born into democratic societies?" Based on my understanding of reincarnation, I think that democratic societies attract a large number of people who are beginning to move away from the fear-based deficit needs and into the self-actualization needs. These people have a clear desire to improve themselves and raise their consciousness, but because of the war between science and religion, our societies cannot offer them any guidance. And this leads to many of them becoming frustrated, developing mental illness or going into substance abuse or other forms of escapism. This is an enormous human potential that is going to waste, to the detriment of the people themselves and the growth of our societies.

This phenomenon of self-actualizing people embodying in democratic nations can to some degree explain the rise in mental illness in those nations. Yet I don't see it as the full explanation because I also see another factor at play. Consider the recent past of the modern democracies. The big thing that stands out is the two world wars in which millions of soldiers were killed, millions of civilians were killed and millions more saw their homes, cities and way of life bombed to dust.

Reincarnation makes it clear that when people experience such events, they receive deep traumas that create wounds and reactionary patterns in their subconscious minds, and this means they will come into their next embodiment with those wounds already there. To me, this explains the rise in mental illness seen in the societies that have already achieved material welfare. If you had been severely wounded in your past life-time, where would you want to embody in this lifetime? Would you want to embody in Africa where people struggle to maintain a living and have no attention left over for psychological healing? Or would you want to embody in an affluent nation where you might have the free time to pursue psychological healing? Furthermore, since it was *our* nations that exposed our citizens to the atrocities of war, does it not stand to reason that we would be responsible for healing them so they can move on and not be traumatized by their past? To me, this is patently self-evident, and there is a huge opportunity for truly doing some good for the collective progress of humanity by healing people of these deep traumas at the individual level.

Why groups of people fight each other

Another thing that reincarnation can explain is why certain groups of people refuse to change and why some of them are so aggressive. It was quite a shock to me when I visited Israel. I already knew that the Middle East is an area where people are living in a way that is far behind the modern democracies and where people are very aggressive and warring. Yet until I actually experienced the collective consciousness of the people, I simply could not imagine that these people are in a state of consciousness that is so different from what I had encountered in the democratic world.

There was one day when I was trying to visit the Muslim Mosque, called the Dome of the Rock, built on top of the Temple Mount in Jerusalem. It proved to be impossible because the Israeli Riot Police had cordoned off the area. The reason being that in the morning, some Jewish Zealots had blocked the entry so the Muslims could not get to morning prayers. The Muslims had fought back and soon the Riot Police came and arrested some of the Muslims and told the Jews to go home. But there was still a very obvious tension in the streets with groups of people standing around with ominous looks.

I ended up in a juice bar talking to a Palestinian man who worked as a tourist guide. He was a very nice man and seemed very kind, the type of person you would say couldn't hurt a fly. At one point I asked him: "So what would happen if the Jews destroyed the Dome of the Rock?" Spontaneously he exclaimed: "It would be World War III!" So here is this peaceful person, yet when it comes to someone destroying what he considers his most important religious symbol, he is willing to unleash a world war that would kill millions of people. Meaning, that his personal worldview is more important to him than millions of lives. This is an attitude I have not met in the modern democracies as it is of course completely against everything democracy stands for.

My point for this long story is that reincarnation can actually help explain why some people can't get along. In many parts of the world people in the same state of consciousness have gravitated together and they have reincarnated with each other over many lifetimes. They have created a spiral of conflict that has gradually become so strong that it overpowers individuality and makes people conform to the group think. If you are an Arab, you grow up to hate Jews and vice versa. The irony being that although a soul might embody in the same area over many lifetimes, it will not always be on the same side. It might be a Jew in one embodiment and an Arab in the next, meaning it is now fighting against the group that it was fighting for in its previous lifetime. Yet the fighting mindset is the same and it doesn't matter what the target is as long as there is an outlet for the anger.

Reincarnation also explains many conflicts at the personal level. For example, in some families, people with the same mindset have incarnated with each other for a long time so they have built an ongoing spiral of conflict. How is it possible that two brothers can be fighting each other from birth? Well, because they have been fighting each other for many lifetimes.

Why we are the way we are

To me, one of the most important things that reincarnation explains is why we are the way we are in a psychological sense. Even as a child I was aware that I am a complex being, and the more I have worked on my personal psychology, the more I have seen how many layers there are in the subconscious mind. I have uncovered deep traumas in my subconscious, and there is absolutely no way to explain them with the safe and secure lower middle class upbringing I had in this lifetime. I simply didn't have any major traumas during my childhood that can account for the incredible complexity I have uncovered in my psyche.

On a personal level, this has been very important to me because it has given me a different perspective on my personal growth. When I found the spiritual path at age 18, I was naturally all fired up by my youthful exuberance and wanted to attain a higher state of consciousness in five minutes. Yet I soon realized that, given that I have lived many lifetimes before this one, it is naive to think I can have the instant gratification on the spiritual path that our consumer culture promises us in other areas of life. The spiritual path is not a quick-fix but a lifelong commitment. This has caused me to develop a certain patience with myself so I don't get disappointed (as I have seen in many spiritual people) when I don't get instant results. There may be instant coffee and instant oatmeal, but instant enlightenment is a fantasy.

This has also given me greater patience with other spiritual people so I don't (any more) make demands on their growth. It has allowed me to realize that people who are not spiritual are simply growing at a different pace than I am, and it is not my business to tell them what path they should follow.

Your child's psychology is not your fault

One important aspect of reincarnation is that all children come into the world with a certain baggage from past lives, and this is not the responsibility of their parents in this lifetime. I see today in Danish society how the younger generation have a greater sense of responsibility for their children than my parents' generation. My parents thought that if they gave me good material conditions, then my psychological development would take care of itself. Today, parents feel much more responsible for their children being happy, and in my observation it puts enormous pressure on parents.

The materialistic culture says that a child is a product of its inheritance (genes) and the environment in which it grew up.

In other words, if a child is not functioning psychologically, it must the parents' fault—what else could it be? To me, this is an unjust and unnecessary pressure to put on people because when we recognize reincarnation, we recognize that some children come in with such severe psychological traumas from past lives that it definitely is not the parents' fault. In fact, if society recognized reincarnation, parents might be offered help to heal the psychological wounds of their children and this could spare both children and parents from enormous suffering and guilt. There simply is no way to avoid this in the present paradigm that effectively blames parents for everything that goes wrong with their children (while society wonders why the birth rate is falling).

It would in my view be constructive if children learned at an early age that they could have psychological wounds from a past life and then were given help to heal them. We might consider that, given that we are psychological beings, a major priority for society could be to help children heal their wounds so they could start adulthood with as wholesome of a psychology as possible. In my vision, this could avoid an incredible amount of suffering for individuals and avoid a huge expense for society.

Why we know what we know

I have said many times that there were certain things I simply knew at an early age. To me, the obvious explanation is that I came into this lifetime not only with a certain psychology but also with a certain knowledge. When we learn something through experience in one lifetime, it can be stored in the subconscious mind and brought with us into our next lifetime. We are born with a certain knowledge that we take for granted and often think we don't need to question. This can be both a blessing and a curse—and for me it has been both.

As an example, take a person who in this lifetime is very angry with the Christian religion and is convinced it is unreal and that there is no God. Why does the person have this, we cannot really say *opinion* because it goes much deeper? It is a conviction that the person feels doesn't need to be questioned. The explanation could be that this person has had several lifetimes where it grew up in a Christian society. It was told that if it was a good Christian, it would go to heaven after that life. So the person dies, and its soul finds out that instead of going to heaven, it will have to go back to earth for another lifetime. After perhaps several lifetimes of this, the person retains a memory based on its experience and is therefore born into its next lifetime with a deep conviction that the main Christian promise is a lie. It might even have a deep anger against Christianity because of this. Of course, a person could also have been exposed to potentially severe abuse by the Christian religion, for example through the witch hunts, the crusades or the Inquisition. To me, this explains why so many atheists have this deep anger against Christianity and seemingly want revenge over the Christian religion by making people stop believing in it.

On the one hand, this memory that the Christian promise of heaven is a lie is a step towards a greater understanding, but it is not the whole story. Instead of rejecting all spirituality because of a false promise, a soul can eventually come to the deeper experience that there are other forms of spirituality. To me, it seems obvious that the millions of people who do reject mainstream religion but not all spirituality (we are spiritual but not religious) have had experiences in past lifetimes that there is a different form of spirituality than mainstream religion.

That is why we are born with this deep desire to find something—we are born as seekers and we will not stop seeking.

Now, obviously when we are born with a deep conviction that is based on experiences in past lives, this does not mean that our conviction is the highest way to look at a certain issue or life in general. Many people could have had very negative experiences of poverty and abuse from past lifetimes and they might be born with a deep conviction that they are no good or that life always passes them by. Given the dark history of the last couple of centuries, I think we all have limiting beliefs. For example, I had a deep inner conviction that if I dared to stand out from the crowd and challenge the powers that be, I would just be killed and thus another lifetime would come to naught. It took me quite a bit of healing work to overcome this conviction to where I dared to publish my first book.

Yet even though we might have these limiting convictions from past lives, knowing that we have had past lifetimes, and that they could have been very difficult, can help us question our convictions. I have many examples from myself of how I have come to see these very subtle beliefs that were limiting what I think I can and cannot do, even limiting how I feel about myself and life on this planet. But let me not get ahead of myself as I will talk more about this later.

Of course, reincarnation answers some questions but raises others. For example, how can karma from a past life come back to us in this lifetime and what is the mechanism that allows us to carry traumas from one lifetime to another? Answering these questions will require us to rebuild our worldview based on the findings of Einstein and quantum physicists.

14 | EVERYTHING IS ENERGY- AND SO WHAT?

As I described, it was very profound to me when I learned that there was a time when people believed the earth was flat. As a child, I wondered how people could ever have believed something like that, but I have since gained a deeper understanding. As I said earlier, we all have a need to know what kind of environment we live in and how it functions. In order to function psychologically, we need to have a worldview. Once we have accepted a certain worldview, it gives us a sense of security, a sense of having some degree of control over our lives because we know how the world works. And that is why we are so reluctant to change our worldview—it threatens our sense of security.

While having a worldview is necessary, we can see from history that we human beings have had many different worldviews and that they have all eventually been replaced by another view. We can hope that we are gradually moving towards worldviews that are more aligned with how the world actually functions. Of course, many civilizations have believed they had the ultimate worldview, but all previous civilizations have been proven wrong. Ours is the only civilization that has not been proven wrong, but is that because we are right or because we are the latest so our worldview has not had time to be proven wrong?

Actually, I would argue that *our* worldview has already been proven wrong, it is simply that most people, including the opinion makers of society, have not acknowledged this. We are now in the same situation as when the astronomers had already proven that the earth is not the center of the universe, but the Catholic clergy and their followers had refused to acknowledge it. What is it that has proven our current worldview wrong? Well, it started with this little formula: $E=mc^2$. What does it actually say about what the world is made of?

Our current worldview is a mixture of many influences. A big part of it is our sensory experience that causes us to experience that the world is made of a solid substance that we call matter. This view can be traced back to some ancient Greek philosophers who claimed that the world is made from very small particles that could not be divided. They called them atoms, and we call these philosophers the atomists. We also have a certain Christian influence that portrays everything as being made from matter, such as: "From dust thou hast come and to dust thou shalt return," even portraying matter as being somehow sinful (the temptations of the flesh). Then, we have the materialist influence, which says that not only is the world made from matter, but there is nothing besides matter, there is nothing beyond matter. Well, there is also energy, but energy is simply something that operates in the matter world, for example, sunlight is produced by the sun.

So our senses, Christianity and Materialism tell us that the primary substance out of which the world is made is solid matter. This view starts with our sensory experience. We can see and touch billiard balls, and Materialism basically says that the world is made up of microscopic billiard balls that are constantly moving and bouncing off each other. Einstein's formula says that although there is something we call matter, it is not the primary substance out of which the world is made. The primary substance is what we call energy. The logical and philosophical consequence of Einstein's theory is that the world is made of ever-moving energy, not solid matter.

Even what our senses detect as solid matter is actually energy that has been captured into a stationary form. By splitting the atom, we can break the matrix that holds the energy stationary and thereby release it. This is what happens in a nuclear reactor or a nuclear bomb—we break the bonds that hold the energy in the form of what we call matter and release it to flow as energy again. This proves that the basic building blocks of the world is not solid billiard balls but vibrating energy waves. So why is that important? Well, for starters because we need to move some boundaries.

An energetic worldview is open-ended

I have said that every civilization has created its own worldview. When I look at history, I see that so far all civilizations have created closed-ended worldviews. They have defined certain boundaries or parameters that they did not question. They might have thought they were self-evident or that these "truths" had some superior authority that made it unnecessary or even dangerous to question them. In the end, it was precisely these boundaries that caused the system to fail. It became apparent that the system had certain limitations, and in order to explain what the system could not explain, people had to look beyond the boundaries defined by the system.

This is simply how progress happens, and we are not above it. The materialist worldview is obviously closed-ended because it defines an impenetrable boundary. There is nothing beyond the material universe as it is currently defined by science, and thus it is "forbidden" for scientists to investigate anything that points beyond this boundary. In order to illustrate what Materialism has done, let me give an analogy. Say a young man has grown up in a small fishing village by the sea. For generations, people have been going out in their boats, and they have always been going with the tide. Yet despite the tide being so important to them, no one has tried to explain what causes the tide. The young man decides that he will make it his life goal to explain the cause of the tide, yet he also decides that since the tide is a phenomenon that takes place in the sea, he will not look outside the sea for the cause of the tide. So he spends his entire life investigating water, from its molecular structure to the ocean currents. Will he be successful? Can you explain the cause of the tide by looking only at the sea?

Materialists have defined a closed boundary around our worldview, but this is not sustainable and it was proven by Einstein and further proven by quantum physicists. The reason is that we now know that the world is made of energy. What is energy? Scientists have a hard time explaining what energy is, but they generally say it is a form of vibration that moves like a wave. Based on this, I draw a conclusion that seems obvious to me.

I learned in school that there are many forms of light. What sets one form of light apart from the others is its vibration, such as wavelength, amplitude and frequency. There is something called visible light, and it is visible because it vibrates within a certain range or spectrum that can be detected by our physical eyes. So to our eyes, there is no light beyond what they can see. Yet there are many forms of light that are not visible to our eyes, but they are just as real as visible light. They simply vibrate outside the spectrum of what our eyes can detect but we can measure them with certain instruments. Based on this, we can set up a spectrum that shows light based on its vibration. Some light rays vibrate at lower frequencies than visible light, such as infrared. Some vibrate at higher frequencies, such as ultraviolet, and we can go quite high above what our eyes can see.

Despite this, science currently operates with a highest frequency based on what we have detected with the instruments we currently have available. They say there are no energy waves beyond what we can detect—there is nothing beyond the material universe. In my mind, this makes no sense at all. If we go back 100 years, scientists had far more primitive instruments than we have today. If we go forward 100 years, I am convinced they will have better instruments than we have today, meaning they will be able to detect what we cannot detect right now. To me it is obvious that there could very well be a range of energy waves that is beyond what we can currently detect. There could be a level of the world that is beyond what we today define as the material universe. Why on earth would we want to close our minds, and scientific inquiry, to this possibility? Oh yes, it is because we cling to the security of the materialist worldview.

Scientists have actually made discoveries that point to the existence of a realm of energy beyond the material. I already mentioned that quantum physicists have detected subatomic "particles" that appear out of nowhere and disappear back into nowhere. This *nowhere* is to me *somewhere,* and there are theories to explain it as a level of the world that is beyond the material universe. Scientists also theorize that there is something called "dark matter," which they say makes up the majority of the matter in the universe, but it is invisible to current instruments. So no one has actually detected dark matter, yet materialists still believe in it. Hm, that reminds me of something . . .

On the other end of the scale, cosmologists have discovered that the entire universe is expanding, and it is even expanding at an accelerated rate. Our current worldview is that everything started with the Big Bang. This is portrayed as a giant explosion in which all of the energy that exists (there was no matter at the time) was hurled outward from a central point, something called a singularity that no one can define. Yet this would mean that at the start of the universe, there was only a finite amount of energy available. When you think of an explosion, it is driven by a release of energy, but the energy eventually dissipates and the outward movement stops. In our universe, the outward movement has not stopped after 13 billion years, and it is even accelerating. Given that every movement must be driven by energy, where does this energy come from? It cannot come from inside what we call the material universe, so since it is there, it must come from outside, meaning there must be something outside. Some physicists say there is something called dark energy because it is undetectable by current instruments. So isn't it possible that it is this dark energy that streams into the material frequency spectrum and drives the expansion of the universe? The dark energy normally vibrates at frequencies that are above those found in the material universe. Yet some of the dark energy is lowered in vibration until it becomes visible energy, and this drives the expansion of the universe

In my mind, Materialism has been proven as limited as Catholic doctrine. My conclusion is simple. We need a new worldview based on the discovery that energy is the basic substance of the universe. Naturally, we could try to revise the materialistic view and move the boundaries of the material universe to encompass a new form of energy. Yet why not throw away the entire attempt to create the ultimate closed worldview? Why not adopt an open-ended worldview where we accept that there is something outside the material world and then start investigating what that is and how it might help us improve our lives? I have been in the process of developing an energetic world for over 40 years. I started out when I was much more driven by my psychological need for security, the need to have a final explanation of how the world works. Today, I have a much more sophisticated worldview than I had 40 years ago, but I have also largely overcome the need to feel it is the final or ultimate view. I am open to receiving a higher understanding than what I have right now. So let me give a brief description of my growth process and how an energetic worldview has helped me fulfill my goals in life.

An energetic worldview and mastering the psyche

The first effect of an energetic worldview was the realization that beyond visible matter is a realm where there is no matter particles but only energy waves. This means that what we see in the matter world actually originates in this realm of pure energy. The matter world is like the tip of an iceberg where 90% of it is below the surface and invisible to our physical senses. This applies to the world as a whole, but in the beginning I could understand this most easily by relating it to the body. There are some very old teachings in the East that say the physical body has an energy field around it. Acupuncture is based on the existence of such an energy body, or aura, that has a number of energy centers (chakras) and lines through which the energy flows (meridians). Acupuncture has survived for 4,000 years and in Denmark it has gained some acceptance when normal anesthetic doesn't work.

It seemed obvious to me that we have an energy body beyond the physical body and that it can have an influence on our health. It also seemed obvious to me that this energy body can explain a lot about the mind or psyche. One of the consequences of an energetic worldview is that everything is an energy field. Energy moves as a wave, but taken together, energy waves can form a field. We have probably all seen a teacher in school hold a magnet underneath a sheet of paper and spread iron filings on top, whereby they magically organized themselves to form lines around the magnet. This leads to a conclusion that has many ramifications: The mind or psyche is an energy field.

If everything is energy and energy is made of waves, that means any organized structure is made up of many energy waves that have been combined into a field. Energy waves normally move, but they can be captured into a stationary form by becoming part of an energy field. A subatomic particle is not a solid billiard ball, but is a combination of energy waves that have been organized into a field. So is planet earth, my physical body and also my mind. My body is made from energy waves that vibrate within a certain spectrum that makes them detectable to the senses, which are calibrated to detect vibrations within that range. My mind is made from energy waves of a higher vibration that cannot be detected by the physical senses, but can (naturally) be detected by the mind itself.

The philosopher René Descartes is famous for saying "I think, therefore I am." What he meant was that he had doubted everything that could possibly be doubted, but the one thing he could not doubt was that he was conscious (proven by the fact that he was thinking). He could not deny that "he" existed. What was it that was conscious and could not deny its own existence? It was his mind. What allows the mind to be conscious of its own existence? It is that the mind has the ability to detect energy waves that the physical senses cannot detect. After all, if everything is energy, then thoughts and feelings are also forms of energy. How could we be aware of our thoughts unless our minds had the ability to detect those types of energy waves? I have mentioned that at an early age, it became my goal in life to avoid being a victim of my own psychology, as was my father. This means I have to master my mind, and how can I possibly hope to achieve this unless I understand what the mind is and how it works? So if everything is energy, my mind must be energy and that means I have to understand how my mind is affected by energy. If I don't know how invisible energy can affect my mind, how can I hope to achieve mastery over my mind? It would be equivalent to not knowing how my physical body is affected by invisible bacteria, viruses, vitamins or minerals.

I talked about how reincarnation says there is something that can move from one body to another. That something is the energy body. There is also something that stores the traumas we receive in one lifetime and carries them over to future lifetimes. Again, to me that something is the energy body.

The concept of an energy body tells me that there is an energetic component to a psychological trauma. Let us say a person was killed in a brutal way during World War II. As this happened, the person obviously went into a state of fear or panic. What is fear? It is a form of emotional energy. So why would that energy disappear when a person dies? To me, it is obvious that the energy does not disappear, it is stored in the energy body and carried over to the next lifetime. This is parallel to how toxins can be stored in the physical body and carried over when the cells are replaced by new cells. The trauma also left an imprint on the energy body, possibly in the form of certain beliefs. This imprint can also be carried over to a later lifetime.

So we now have a child who is born with a pool of intense fear-based energy in its subconscious mind or energy field. How does that affect the person in this lifetime? Well, gravity is explained as a force that causes matter to attract other matter, that is why dropping an object causes it to fall to earth. Yet since matter is really energy, it seems logical to me that energy can also attract other forms of energy; like attracts like.

We now have a person who has two aspects of the mind, the conscious and the subconscious. As we know, our conscious mind is centered around our attention, which is something quite restless that can be pulled in many different directions. If a person has a large pool of fear-based energy in the subconscious mind, it seems obvious to me that this energy has a magnetic or gravitational force that can pull on the person's conscious attention. This might give the person a high level of anxiety or fear for the future.

The person does not consciously remember what happened in its past life, but the energy in the subconscious mind pulls the conscious mind into fearing that some disaster could happen at any time. The imprint left in the energy body might cause the person to have a certain distrust of the matter world. This might cause the person to be more open to believing in a religion or theory that portrays the world as a dangerous and unpredictable place. Or it might make the person more open to a belief system that offers an appearance of being able to explain the world in absolute terms.

Consider that if this is true, it can explain why many children feel more fear than is warranted based on what they experience in their present embodiments. A child might react more strongly to certain situations, and this might cause adults to see the child's reactions as irrational and try to just ignore them. I remember as a young child going to my mother in tears and saying I was afraid of war. I understand that she found this difficult to deal with so she sought to push it aside by telling me there would be no war in Denmark. Yet imagine that she had instead recognized that my strong fear might be because I had experienced war in a past life. First of all, she would not have had to push my fear aside, and that would have been important to me. Moreover, she might have even shown me a way to dissipate the energy and thus overcome the pull of the fear. Imagine that we could help our children with this instead of trying to belittle or even ridicule a child's feelings and fears. It is our own insecurity, or rather our need to uphold our illusion of security, that causes us to deny the experiences of our own children. These experiences are very real to them and that is why it is very hurtful when they are pushed aside, denied or even ridiculed.

What to do about energy in the subconscious mind

To me, it was quite frankly revolutionary to realize that I have an energy body that can store all kinds of energy from past lives (and this life), energy that can pull on my thoughts and emotions (how I see myself and feel about life). The most powerful aspect was the realization that I can do something about this energy instead of being a passive victim of my past. Science tells us that an energy wave has a certain vibration and that it will keep it indefinitely unless something changes it.

What can change one energy wave is that it collides with another energy wave. When two energy waves collide, they create an interference pattern and the result can be a different wave. In other words, both energy waves are changed into something else. The conclusion being that we can change one energy wave by directing another energy wave at it. For example, an energy wave created by fear has a certain low vibration, but if it collides with a wave of a higher vibration, the fear energy is raised in vibration. This means that if we can find a way to direct higher frequency emotional energy at the fear-based energy in our energy fields, we can transform the fear and remove its pull on our minds. This seems obvious to me, and there is quite a number of techniques available for producing high frequency energy and directing it at low-frequency energy. I have used such techniques for more than 40 years, and I have experienced that they made a tremendous difference in my life. I will later talk more about specific techniques, but for now I want to go further with the energetic worldview.

Matter is not solid

When I first heard about our energy field or aura, it was presented as a field of energy that surrounds the physical body. I think most spiritual people start out seeing this as an energy field produced by the body, as we are told that the field around the magnet is produced by the magnet itself. It took me some time to wrap my mind around a more expansive view.

We are brought up with a certain view of cause and effect. For example, the sun is emitting light, which is clearly energy waves. Yet we are brought up to think these energy waves are produced by material processes in the sun. In other words, matter is cause and energy is effect. The logical consequence of quantum physics is that our understanding of cause and effect is backwards. Energy is the underlying reality, meaning energy is the cause and matter is the effect. What we see in the matter world is produced by invisible causes at the level of pure energy, pretty much as Plato said 2,500 years ago. A matter phenomenon starts at the level of pure energy. This level is much more fluid, but then the energy is lowered in vibration and captured into a stationary matrix that we perceive as solid matter. Science has already proven that there is no such thing as solid matter. Although it is a bit dated, I learned in school that the atom is like a miniature solar system with a core and electrons orbiting around it. There is obviously a space between the electrons and the core, and it is proportionally bigger than the distance between the earth and the sun. So matter is really made up mostly by space. Why do we perceive matter as solid? Because our senses are calibrated to detect only energy that vibrates within a certain spectrum, as our eyes can see only some forms of light. I am not saying there is anything wrong with this. Naturally, we have physical bodies, and our senses need to be calibrated so we can do things through those bodies, meaning we don't need to be able to see inside the atom.

However, it is a problem when we deny that there is anything beyond what our senses can detect. It would be helpful if we could see beyond the material level and see that all matter is created from energy. This might help us see causes that are now hidden to us, and that could open up entirely new opportunities for changing our physical circumstances. To make this simple, let me focus on health.

Amazing implications for improving health

If matter is not solid, it follows that our bodies are not solid. Quantum physics has proven that if we go to the level of what scientists have so far called subatomic particles, we find a very strange phenomenon, called the wave-particle duality. It demonstrates that when we try to measure a subatomic entity, it will sometimes behave like a particle (found in a particular location in space) and sometimes as a wave (that extends through space). Materialists find it difficult to explain this so they largely ignore it. To me, the explanation is simple. There is a threshold where the pure energy that is the underlying cause of all matter phenomena crosses over into the physical vibrational spectrum. The wave becomes something we can see, and we call it a particle. The energy takes on the form of what we call solid matter.

This means that every matter phenomenon starts in a realm of pure energy. Something in that realm sets the stage or creates a matrix, and at some point the energy crosses the threshold and becomes matter. Quantum physics has proven that our consciousness can influence this process, which opens up amazing possibilities for improving health and healthcare. Our physical bodies do not produce our energy fields, it is our energy fields that produce our physical bodies. The physical body is the most dense part of a larger energy "body." This means a disease can start at the level of the energy field and then gradually make its way to the physical body (I am not talking about breaking a leg or ingesting poison but more complex illnesses). It also means that disease can potentially be healed by using energy to change the energy body because the level of pure energy is easier to change by using the mind. Many very competent and creative researchers and healers have accepted this idea for decades and they have done some amazing research into energy healing. I consider this the greatest potential for healing and I am sure the next decades will bring some groundbreaking discoveries.

Let me go back to the example of a person who was killed in World War II and received a deep trauma. This trauma created a certain fear-based matrix in the person's energy field, and it also generated a pool of fear-based energy that is stored in the field. The person comes into its next embodiment with this matrix. Let us now say that the person receives no outside help to dissipate the energy and also has no internal awareness of how to do this. The person is born with a certain fear, and it gradually becomes worse because the person sees the world as a dangerous place and focuses on what validates this worldview. The person also accumulates more fear-based energy instead of overcoming it.

Is it really that hard to imagine that the energy will eventually reach a certain intensity that can cause it to influence the person's physical cells? Some biologists, such as Bruce Lipton, have shown that our cells are incredibly complex structures that have a mechanism that can respond to our state of consciousness. Doctors have for a long time known that most illnesses are psychosomatic, meaning they have their cause in the psyche. To me, it is obvious that the condition of our energy bodies can affect our physical bodies.

It is also obvious that matter is more solid, meaning more difficult to change, than our energy bodies. So it is far easier to change a matrix in the energy body than to change an illness that has become physical. I have seen digital cameras hooked up to a computer that can record an image of our energy fields and display it on the screen. I believe that before too long, we will have something similar to a CAT scanner that can display images of the human energy field. These machines can show accumulations of energy that can be linked to specific physical diseases. This can show that a person is prone to get a certain disease before it actually manifests in the physical body. This opens up the potential that we can do something to heal the energy body and thereby prevent the disease from becoming physical.

I think this will lead to amazing new possibilities. We could use various techniques for dissipating the fear-based energy. But I also think it will be necessary to combine this with new forms of psychological therapies to help people consciously look at and resolve the traumas in the subconscious mind.

Such therapies have already been developed by forward think-ing psychologists and I have used some of them with profound effects. I am sure many more will be developed as people become more open to the potential. I think the time where doctors can only treat their patients with pills or surgery will soon come to an end.

Four levels of our energy field

It was very important to me to learn that my personal energy field has four levels. This is easy to understand when we look at what we know about visible light and other forms of light. We can set up a scale for light, ranging from lower vibrations to higher vibrations. Likewise, we can set up a scale where the physical body has the lowest vibrations and the energy body vibrates at a higher level. Thus, within the energy body itself, we can talk about several levels (that can be compared to the octaves on the tonal scale). This gives us four levels:

- The physical body is the lowest level of vibration.

- The next level up is the emotional level or the emo-tional body. This is where our feelings take place. It is also where emotional energy is stored. This level also contains certain beliefs about feelings, for example, we might believe that in certain situations, it is not only justified that we become angry, it is the only way to react. An accumulation of fear-based energy in the emotional body could also be a major factor in causing depression or other mental illnesses.

- The next level is the mental level, the level of thoughts. At this level our mental energy is stored (it has a higher vibration than emotional energy). It is also here that we find certain beliefs, especially beliefs about how things work and how we can do certain things. We also find beliefs about what we cannot do, meaning things we believe are impossible. The mental level is the seat of the intellect, which (as mentioned before) is an analytical faculty that compares everything new to something known. This is where we have a subconscious database with folders, such as "Do not question" and "This is truth." The mental level is very linear and concrete, which means it can be very practical and good at solving a certain type of problems (relating to the matter world). It is also the level where we can find arguments for or against any topic, meaning we cannot find an ultimate argument although we can decide that something is the ultimate argument and refuse to think further.

- The highest level of the energy field is the identity level. This is where our deepest beliefs about ourselves, the world we live in and how we can interact with the world are stored. This is what gives us a sense of who we are—at least who we are in relation to this planet and the material world. It also contains a subconscious database, but it contains deeper beliefs than those found at the mental level. For example, my father had certain beliefs about people (causing him to not get along with most people) that were not based on any intellectual reasoning. You could not reason with him about these beliefs because they were beyond intellectual argumentation. Another example is a person who identifies himself as a Christian. This means his identity body will limit his ability to intellectually analyze arguments against God's existence. Such arguments will be labeled as unreal at the level of the identity body and the mental body cannot override this. Naturally, we can learn to question and dissolve such beliefs, but it is a more difficult process than changing a mental belief.

So why was this so important to me? For many reasons, but for starters because it helped me protect myself from being so easily affected by the emotional energy of other people.

Being a highly sensitive person

Within recent decades, psychologists have started talking about a specific type of people who are very sensitive to other people's feelings. They are called Highly Sensitive People or empaths. Well, that description fits me, at least before I learned how to protect my energy field. Even as a young child, I was very sensitive to the suffering of other people and I was very willing to help them by taking on their worries or fears. For example, I was sensitive to my father being in a bad mood or to my classmates in school feeling bad. And while it might have been a relief for other people that I took on their emotional energy, it didn't really help them in the long run. They soon found something else to react to, and I was left with a burden of fear-based energy that I had not produced myself.

I especially remember seeing images on TV about children in Africa starving and feeling so bad for the fact that they had to experience this situation and that no one was helping them.

I also remember at the age of 6 sitting with my mother on the couch and watching TV. It was a live broadcast showing President Kennedy driving through the streets of Dallas, Texas. We literally sat there and saw him get shot, and I remember the intense feeling of fear. Why would I, a six-year-old living in Denmark, feel that way about the president of a far-away country being shot? It was because I took in the fear-based energy that came out of the television screen as the world reacted with shock.

There were so many situations during my childhood and youth where I reacted to the suffering of others and it caused me a lot of burdens. Quite frankly, I don't remember very often feeling bad on my own, I mostly remember reacting to other people's feelings. Maybe that is because as an empath I didn't recognize my own feelings, thinking other people's feelings were more important than my own? Anyway, taking in emotional energy was a real problem for me during my childhood. Do I need to say that none of the adults around me could give me any help in dealing with this problem?

Another aspect of this was that I had very strong reactions to certain phenomena or places. When I was eight my family went on an outing, and among other places, we visited an old monastery that was torn down after the Reformation and later excavated. They had an entire room filled with skulls, and some of them showed signs of having survived brain surgery (trepanation). They also had open graves in which skeletons were lying. I am sure none of my family members felt this, but I sensed a very intense fear-based energy in that place, a vibration of death. And because I didn't know better, I took it in and it affected me for years. I later met a spiritual person who had the exact same reaction to visiting that monastery as a young girl. I also remember watching an animated movie about skeletons jumping out of the graves and running into the camera so it seemed like their empty mouths were swallowing me up. All in all, such experiences gave me an intense fear of skeletons that burdened me during most of my childhood (until I cured myself through shock therapy).

I also had an intense fear of ghosts or supernatural spirits. Nothing could give me greater fear than the thought (promoted by some movies) that an invisible spirit could take over my mind and make me do things I didn't want to do. I had an intense fear of losing control over my mind and actions, which is probably the reason I have never used alcohol or drugs.

Of course, the adults around me could only seek to help me overcome this fear by ridiculing it and making me think it wasn't real. I understand that this is how their parents had treated them, and it is based on the materialistic view that all such supernatural phenomena are unreal and the result of superstition. But was I simply afraid of something that wasn't there? Or was I more sensitive than most people and therefore able to sense energies that most people cannot feel and that science (currently) cannot measure?

I have said we have an energy field around our physical bodies. I have said that energy is cause and matter is effect. It is obvious to me that there is also an energy field around the entire planet. This field has the four levels, meaning there is a planetary or collective emotional body. We human beings live on planet earth and what happens to some of the emotional energy we produce? To me, it is obvious that it goes into the collective emotional body and is stored there. When I take a look at human history, it is clear that we have produced an enormous amount of fear-based energy, and since energy cannot be destroyed, it must be stored in the collective emotional body where is has accumulated for millennia, creating very intense pools of specific types of energy. Is it really so far-fetched that some people can sense such energy and that all people can be affected by it? It is obvious to me that as a child I was very sensitive to this emotional energy. I sensed that there are certain accumulations of energy that have become so intense that they can actually overpower people's feelings, and this can be what people throughout the ages have sensed as dark spirits. After all, we live inside this collective energy field, and since our own emotional bodies are made of this type of energy, it stands to reason that we can be affected by the energy. The energy accumulated in the collective field literally pulls on our individual fields. What can this explain that Materialism cannot explain?

The energetic cause of mental illness and addiction

Science has actually made some discoveries that point to the existence of a collective mind or energy field that connects all of us. As one example, there is a certain type of computer called a random number generator. They obviously generate numbers that are meant to be entirely random. Yet scientists have observed that at certain times, when the attention of many people is focused on the same topic, this interferes with the machines and makes their numbers less random. Examples of when this happened was the O.J. Simpson court case and 9/11. Materialism has no explanation, but I think the reason is that there is an energy field that connects us all.

This is underscored by another discovery of quantum physics, which shows that two subatomic particles can be separated by a vast distance, yet a change in the spin of one particle will generate an instant change in the other particle. According to Materialism, the particles are entirely separated and independent, so for a change in one particle to affect the other, a signal must be sent from one to the other. Yet this signal must be sent at or below the speed of light, meaning it cannot generate an instantaneous change. Since an instantaneous change has been observed many times, a different explanation is needed. To me, it is that the two particles are not separated but only appear to be so. They are separated in physical space but still connected by the energy field that underlies the physical world.

Imagine that a spaceship visits the earth and looks down from a great height. They observe that along the coast of Greenland is a number of white things that are moving southwards at the same time. Despite their advanced technology, their scanners cannot detect anything below the surface of the water, but they can detect a very strong wind above the surface. They observe that the icebergs are moving against the wind but they cannot understand why. We of course know that the reason is that the icebergs are moved by a strong current under the water, but if you cannot see that, there is no explanation. Some quantum physicists have now embraced the principle of non-locality, meaning they have left behind the Newtonian idea of separate matter particles, realizing instead that everything is connected at a deeper level of energy.

To me, it is obvious that since every matter phenomenon is the effect of an invisible energy field, nothing is separate because everything is connected through the energy field. Therefore, it follows that all people are connected by a shared energy field, a collective mind or consciousness. No man or woman is an island.

What has that got to do with mental illness and addiction? As a child I was afraid of drunk people because it was obvious to me that they were not acting like they normally did. It was like the person was no longer there and you could not reason with them. I have been an author since 2002 and have conducted a large number of spiritual workshops around the world. I once conducted a workshop in Los Angeles and a man came who himself claimed he was possessed by an evil spirit.

At certain times, his body would tighten up and he would start screaming and yelling something that made no sense. When you looked into his eyes, you could see that is was not a normal human being looking back at you. I think you can find people like that in many mental institutions (in New York City you can find them on the streets). As a child I was very scared of the phenomenon of a lynch mob. I have never actually seen one in this lifetime, but just reading about it made my hair stand up. The reason being that I realized it is possible that a group of people can have their individual minds taken over by a group mind, and now they can do things (such as kill people) that they would never do as individuals. The individual mind is literally replaced by a group mind.

To me, this gives at least one additional explanation for mental illness. Some people can open their individual energy fields (their emotional, mental or identity bodies) to an accumulation of energy in the collective energy field. Yet this collection of energy is not really what people traditionally see as an evil spirit because they give this spirit almost human-like powers of reason. Instead, I see this as an accumulation of energy that does not have a sophisticated awareness. Yet it may have some awareness that allows it to take over people's minds and cause them to do things they would not normally do (I will later talk more about why this happens).

I think that if we could free ourselves from the overlay of Materialism, this explanation would make sense to people who deal with mentally ill people or addicts. As a child, I was afraid of becoming an addict. This was in a sense illogical because I don't have an addictive personality and I have no desire to escape my normal state of mind. I have always wanted to change my state of mind, but not through some chemical but by using the powers of the mind alone. I want to change my mind permanently, not temporarily. Yet because I was sensitive to this non-physical energy, I sensed that addicts do not make a fully aware decision to become addicts. They slide into it because their energy fields are open to the influence of these fear-based energies in the collective field. Their minds gradually become taken over by some being or entity that makes their energy field such an unpleasant place to be that they seek relief by numbing themselves or producing another state of mind. The consequence being that if we do not remove the energy in the subconscious minds, people will be pulled towards addiction for the rest of their lives. And why should people have to suffer like that if there is a viable solution?

I am naturally not bringing this up in order to scare people. I have no desire to cause anyone else to experience the fear that I experienced. However, fear springs from ignorance and in order to overcome fear, we first have to be willing to look at the phenomenon. Once we understand that we have an energy body that can be influenced by certain exterior energies, we also realize that we can protect our energy fields from this influence.

During my childhood and youth my biggest problem was that it was very difficult for me to fall asleep. I would lie awake for 3-4 hours every night because I had so many thoughts coming into my head that I could not relax. Finally, I would be so exhausted that I fell asleep, but I would not get enough sleep so I would be sleepy next day at school or work. Then, in my mid-twenties I finally learned about my energy field and techniques for sealing it from external influences. I realized that I could invoke a shield of high-frequency energy around my field that could seal it from fear-based energies.

Within a few weeks of using such techniques, I could fall asleep within 15 minutes, and it has lasted to this day. I have also met several people who had more severe problems, including hearing voices, and who got over it after a short time of using techniques for protecting their energy field. More on such techniques later.

Okay, so if there really are such collective energy beings, why would they want to take over people's minds? To explain this, we need to talk about money.

15 | THE REAL CURRENCY ON EARTH

As a child, I was told that money is the root of all evil or that everything that happens between people can be explained by their desire for money. I once watched the movie Cabaret in which there is a song with the words: "Mo-ney makes the world go around." I disagree, unless we expand our understanding of what currency is.

Again, my mind has always been able to make intuitive leaps, and when I understood that everything is made from energy, it also became clear that the basic currency of the world is not money but energy. I am not talking about physical energy, such as sunlight or electricity, but about the emotional, mental and identity level energy, or psychic energy.

What really makes the world go around is energy. What makes human beings go around is not just physical energy but also psychic energy. With that I mean energy in our emotional, mental and identity "bodies." Where does this energy come from?

Back in the day when steam engines were the most advanced technology, some scientists formulated what is called the first law of thermodynamics, which says that energy can neither be created, nor destroyed. This was based on the knowledge and the measuring technology they had at the time, which was much more primitive than what we have today. Yet many materialists have expanded this law to be valid for everything in the material universe. They say there is only a finite amount of energy in the universe and that it cannot be expanded.

There is also a second law of thermodynamics, and it basically says that any closed system will move towards maximum entropy, which means a lowest possible energy state in which no work can be performed. Or to say it more bluntly: Any closed system will break down and self-destruct. If you do not maintain a steam engine, it will eventually rust away and if you neglect a civilization, it will decay.

To me, it seems that a strict materialist interpretation leads to a contradiction between the first and the second law. Materialists say there is nothing outside the material universe, and this means the universe is a closed system. They say the universe is driven by a finite amount of energy, and according to the second law, a closed system with a finite amount of energy should be moving towards more and more entropy, meaning that all organized structures should be gradually breaking down. The Big Bang is often compared to an explosion in which all energy was hurled outwards in a seemingly chaotic way. When was the last time you saw a house being blown up where, after some time, the debris spontaneously assembled itself into a house again? Yet, materialists believe, as a basic article of their faith, that after the Big Bang (a situation with maximum disorder) the debris spontaneously assembled itself into the incredibly complex structures we see in the universe. And these structures are becoming increasingly more complex and vast. This requires a degree of blind faith that I am simply not able to muster. It also requires an explanation of why the formation of the universe could violate the second law of thermodynamics, according to which this simply cannot happen in a closed system.

As mentioned, cosmologists are telling us the universe is still expanding after 13 billion years, and the expansion is speeding up. At the same time we see that there is an evolutionary process on earth that is bringing forth more and more complex life forms. We see that human society is evolving towards greater and greater complexity and sophistication. By simply observing the universe, we see that it is clearly moving towards less entropy and more organization and this requires more than a finite amount of energy. I see three options:

- The evolution of the universe from the chaos of the Big Bang violates the second law

- The second law is wrong

- The universe is not a closed system

When we add a certain amount of coal to a steam engine, we get a certain amount of energy out of it to perform work. If we observe that the engine is producing more energy than can be accounted for by the coal we add, we must reason that the engine receives energy from another source. So if we observe that the material universe is performing more work than can be accounted for by a finite amount of energy, we must reason that the material universe is receiving energy from a source outside itself, meaning the universe is not a closed system. In this way, we can keep both the first and the second law intact. These laws simply do not apply to the material universe as a whole. In fact, given the new discoveries that everything is connected, we might ask if there is any closed system anywhere? As I have already mentioned, it seems obvious to me that there are realms or octaves of energy beyond the physical or material. There is a stream of energy that flows from the identity realm into the mental, then into the emotional and then into the physical realm. It is this stream of energy that started what materialists call the Big Bang, but which was really a period of sustained expansion. All of the energy available to the universe was not compressed into a singularity and released all at once. There is a continuous release of energy that keeps the expansion of the universe and the evolution of life on earth going. If we set aside any desire to interpret science within the materialist belief system, this interpretation of observed facts is as scientific and consistent as the current paradigm.

So if there *is* a stream of energy entering the material universe, where does it enter? I think that with today's more accurate measuring technology (or with technology that could be developed) it would be possible to measure this. For example, I think it would be possible to measure that the physical processes that take place in the sun cannot account for all of the energy released by the sun. In other words, the sun is one place where energy enters the material universe from a higher realm. The same might be true for many other phenomena seen in the cosmos, including white holes. On the other end of the scale, the subatomic world may be a portal for the entrance of energy. I already mentioned that it has been observed how particles can seemingly appear from nowhere. Well, what if they are simply lowered in vibration and thus cross the threshold between the material octave and higher octaves?

Where does psychic energy come from?

Now comes the one idea that truly revolutionized my outlook on life. What if the human mind is an entry point for energy from higher octaves? I think it would be possible to measure that the energy we take in through food and other sources is not enough to account for our psychic activity (scientists have measured that when a person dies, there is a small reduction in weight). In other words, the physical body is not a closed system and cannot drive our emotions and thoughts. The physical body is constantly receiving energy from our emotional, mental and identity bodies. The question now becomes where this energy comes from?

In my worldview, there is a stream of energy that enters my physical body. It comes from the emotional body, which is the one that is right above the physical in vibration. The emotional body receives it from the mental body, which in turn receives energy from the identity body. So from where does the identity body receive energy? It comes from a part of our beings that is beyond the material realm, even if we define the material as having the four levels from physical to identity. As mentioned, the world is an energy continuum, and we can go towards higher vibrations. As we do so, we eventually cross a threshold and move beyond the vibrations found in the identity realm. We move into a higher realm.

Almost all mystical and spiritual teachings contain the idea that there is a spiritual realm beyond the material. Many teachings also say that we have a higher part of our minds, a higher self, that exists in the spiritual world. It is this higher self that is the source of our intuition, and it can give us a deeper sense of identity than anything in the material world. Yet it is also the source of life-giving psychic energy that drives our three higher bodies. This idea seemed obvious to me from the moment I came across it, and as with so many other ideas, it was because it harmonized with my experience. When I was a young child, I had a constant experience that there was some non-material being that was always there with me. This was not the "magic helper" that psychologists like to use to explain such "childhood superstitions" because it never did anything for me, and I never asked it to do anything. I experienced that there was a being with me, and all it did was give me a frame of reference that there is something beyond the world in which I am living, and there is more to me than this physical body. Because of this direct experience, I could never believe that I am a material being who is limited by the physical body, nor could I believe that I am a sinner. I always knew that I am a mind and that as a mind I have no limitations other than the ones I accept for myself. Thus, even though I experienced the world as a very limited place, I never felt completely trapped here, and this made my childhood bearable. It is probably what enabled me to survive psychologically in an anti-spiritual society.

Today, I have an even more clear experience of my higher self, and I feel a constant stream of energy from my higher being into my four lower bodies. This is not something I *believe,* it is something I *experience* as a daily reality and of course many spiritual people have a similar experience. Now, why is all this important?

Taking command over our lives

Well, anything we do in life is done with energy. So let us look at a particular person and measure that person's ability to do what he or she wants to do in life. We can define which goals a person has and then we can look at how far the person is from fulfilling those goals. We can readily observe that some people are highly active and able to accomplish many things whereas others are far more passive and get little done in their lives. What accounts for the difference? Well, since everything is energy, at least part of the explanation is that those who accomplish more must have more energy available to drive their efforts.

Again, we take a specific person and define her goals in life. We could then set up a scale for how much energy it would take to accomplish these goals. We could then measure how much energy the person currently has available to her. If there is a discrepancy between the energy it would take for the person to reach her goals and the energy she has available, it is obvious why she cannot reach her goals. So what is the obvious solution? It is that the person needs to get more psychic energy. And where would that come from—probably not from eating more granola bars.

Another perspective is my goal of taking command over my own psyche. I have said that we all might have pools of fear-based energy stored in our emotional bodies. We might also have pools of mental energy in our mental bodies and higher energy in our identity bodies. These pools of energy can pull on our conscious attention and, for example, make us depressed, make us focus on the negative side of life or give us a sense that we can't accomplish anything. "I just don't have the energy." If we are to break free of these limitations, we need to remove that low-frequency energy, and how can we do it? By directing energy waves of a higher vibration into the fear-based energy. We can transform the lower energy by raising its vibration. Yet where is this high-frequency energy going to come from? What if it is readily available to all of us from our higher selves or from the spiritual realm? We can now define a new model for what it means to be a human being. A human being is an energy system. We live in a world that is not made from solid matter but vibrating energy. The physical body is actually an energy field and it can stay alive only by receiving energy from outside itself. Some of this energy comes from the food we eat and other material sources. Some of it comes in the form of psychic energy that flows through our total energy system, from the identity level, to the mental, to the emotional and then into the physical. The energy comes from our higher selves or the spiritual realm, and there is more energy than we could possibly need to accomplish anything we want to accomplish.

The physical energy we get from material sources is enough to keep our physical bodies alive, but it is not enough for us to accomplish much else. In order to function at a higher level, we must have a stream of creative energy from our higher selves. In the ideal scenario, we would have so much energy flowing from our higher selves that we could accomplish any goal we set for ourselves. Since we can observe that this is not the case for most of us, the explanation is that something has blocked or limited the amount of energy flowing from our higher selves. The key to improving both our external circumstances and the condition of our psyches is to increase the amount of energy that can flow from the spiritual realm into our four lower bodies.

To me, this was a truly revolutionary idea because it gave me a practical way to accomplish something I had always known was possible. I knew intuitively that my psyche is my domain, or at least I have the potential to make it my domain. I knew that no external source can influence my psyche unless I allow it to do so, and if I knew how, I could free my mind from all external influences. I always knew that I am not powerless, but learning about the flow of energy was the first time I could explain why I am not powerless and how I can take command over my psyche. I was so excited when I realized the potential for this, and I can truly say that my life has never been the same. But while this may sound good, it probably also sounds quite abstract, so let me be more practical.

What blocks the flow of psychic energy

Let us say that in several past lives I took a stand against various authorities and was imprisoned or executed as a "reward" for my efforts. Although I do not have specific memories, I have a strong sense that I have experienced this in past lives, as do many other spiritual people I know. The trauma of being tortured by the Inquisition, burned at the stake as a witch or shot at dawn as a revolutionary generated a pool of fear-based energy in my emotional body. This energy blocks the flow of energy from my higher self so I have less energy available to my conscious mind and physical body. Yet by learning the proper techniques, I can invoke high-frequency energy from the spiritual realm and direct it into the fear-based energy. Over time, I can transform the fear-based energy and eventually get rid of it so there is no blockage in my emotional body. This will give me more energy, but it still may not be the maximum flow.

As a result of being executed many times, I formed in my mental mind the belief that it simply wasn't worth it to take a stand for anything. "What's the point of taking a stand, when they kill me anyway?" Such a belief obviously limits what I think I can and cannot do in this world, and this will also block the flow of energy from my higher self. My mental beliefs will obviously have created a pool of low-frequency energy in my mental body.

Now, as long as I have an intense pool of fear-based energy in my emotional body, my conscious mind may not be able to penetrate and see the belief in my mental body. Every time I touch the energy, I feel such emotional pain that I pull back and refuse to look further. Yet when the emotional energy is reduced, I can begin to look for the deeper beliefs. By using various forms of therapy or self-observation, I can eventually uncover the belief. I might then use my rational mind to reason that in this lifetime I have been born in a modern democracy where I will not be executed for disagreeing with the authorities. Thus, it is actually safe for me to speak out about my spiritual beliefs. I might be ridiculed but at least I will not be executed. Thus, I can come to a point where I can make a decision that replaces the original decision. I might have decided never to speak out again, and I can now replace that with a decision that does not limit my self-expression. Of course, there may also be some energy stored at the mental level that makes it harder for me to uncover my decisions. But this energy can also be transformed and I can gradually clear my mental body.

As I begin to clear my mental body, I can eventually begin to look at my identity body where by deepest beliefs about what kind of being I am are stored. I might then uncover a set of beliefs that limit my self-expression by making me believe that I either cannot or that I am not allowed to express myself freely on this planet. This can be beliefs such as that I am a sinner and can only wait for Jesus to save me, or that I am an evolved monkey with no higher purpose for my existence. It can also be a huge range of more subtle beliefs, and I have uncovered many of them during my work on my psyche.

The picture that now emerges is that we human beings have a much larger potential than most of us were brought up to believe. In order to fulfill that potential, we have to open up the flow of energy from our higher selves. The basic way of doing this is to purify our emotional, mental and identity bodies from the energies and limiting beliefs that clog up those bodies so the energy can again flow freely.

The potential here is tremendous. By clearing out the debris in our three higher bodies, we can overcome many mental illnesses and develop an empowering approach to life. The process can have such a dramatic impact on our lives that it is difficult for people who have not tried it to envision and believe how much their lives can change. I have experienced how this can make a tremendous difference and I know thousands of spiritual people who have also achieved decisive results from consciously applying this process. Yet it isn't the complete picture and there is more to talk about.

Your higher self doesn't think like your lower self

The picture I have painted so far is a bit rosy. It sounds like we have a higher self that is willing to release unlimited amounts of energy and it is only a matter of unblocking the four lower bodies so the energy can flow. In a sense, this is true, but we also need to consider the intent we have for trying to get more energy from our higher selves. Or we can say that in order to unblock our emotional, mental and identity bodies, we have to overcome the tendencies that make us self-centered and selfish.

To put it bluntly, Adolf Hitler had (at least for a while) a lot of energy to accomplish his goals. Does that mean Hitler received unlimited energy from his higher self? Would a self that resides in a higher realm give a person unlimited energy if that person would use it to control or destroy other people? Do our higher selves think the way we do, or are they really higher, meaning they have entirely unselfish intentions?

The conclusion I eventually came to is that we can roughly divide human beings into two categories: those who are firmly trapped in the basic illusion of earth and those who have started freeing their minds from this illusion. What is the basic illusion that rules the collective mind of this planet? It is that we are separate beings, isolated from each other and from the world we live in. Every man and woman is an island. This gives rise to the belief: I can harm you without affecting myself. I can act as if I really am separated from you and therefore what happens to you will not affect me.

When I look at the history of humanity, I see two forces working to influence people's minds. One is the force of selfishness that is based on the illusion of separation. The other is the "force" of selflessness based on the intuitive realization that we are not separate beings. We are all connected so what happens to you will indeed affect me.

We can also say that there are two tendencies working in the human psyche. One is selfishness, based on the illusion that we are separate beings. The other is unselfishness, based on the recognition that we are all connected. Helping us move out of separation and selfishness into connectedness and enlightened self-interest is the basic process that is driving life on earth. The essence of all religious and spiritual teachings is to help us complete this process, although such teachings (especially when they are turned into closed-ended authoritative belief systems) can also be used to further separation. For 2,500 years, Buddhism has taught the concept of interdependent originations, meaning all life is connected. Jesus told us to do unto others as we want them to do unto us, and most religions say the same.

My conclusion is that all of the conflict and struggle we see in the world is a result of people who are still trapped in the illusion of separation. They see themselves as separate beings, and they are trying to accomplish certain goals that are important to separate beings. Of course, if many people see themselves as separate beings, their goals can easily be in conflict with each other. This creates an inevitable struggle where some people will seek to get what they want by forcing or harming other people.

In contrast to this, there are many people who, over many lifetimes, have had enough of this struggle. Basically, the vision behind democracy is to create a society with less struggle and conflict between people. This can be accomplished only if people have started escaping the illusion of separation and intuitively know that we are all connected and thus what affects other people will also affect myself. Meaning, it is in my own enlightened self-interest to create a society in which all people have equal rights.

Life can therefore be seen as a process where people, over many lifetimes, move from selfishness towards connectedness. This is a process we can call self-actualization or the spiritual path. Many people in the modern democracies have reached a certain stage in this process. They have essentially followed the spiritual path without being consciously aware of it or calling it a spiritual process.

Okay, so back to my starting point of how we receive energy from our higher selves. What is it that makes it possible for us to go into the illusion that we are separate beings? It is that we lose the conscious contact with our higher selves.

I have said that the physical universe is made of energies that vibrate within a certain spectrum. It is the vibratory level of these energies, the density of these energies, that makes it possible for us to think we are separate beings. If we shut down our intuition and look at life only through the senses, we are experiencing ourselves as separate beings. We can therefore use the intellect (which can argue for or against any viewpoint) to come up with supposedly rational reasons for why it is okay for us to do selfish things and why we can get away with it.

Our higher selves exist is a realm of much higher vibrations, meaning they do not see themselves as separate beings. Our higher selves are connected and they experience that our lower beings (our four lower bodies) are not separate beings. We have free will, so we have the right to have the experience of what it is like to act as separate beings. Yet doing so comes with a price because the more selfish we become, the less energy is released to us from our higher selves. Meaning we have less energy available to us for accomplishing the goals of the separate self.

So how do we explain that some very selfish people have been able to accomplish some very destructive acts that clearly required a lot of energy? From where did Hitler get all that energy?

The war over energy

Some people say that all wars are fought over energy, such as oil. I agree that all wars are fought over energy, but we must include psychic energy.

Again, an obvious example is Hitler. In the beginning of the war, it seemed like the German army was invincible. Whatever the Führer directed them to do, they could accomplish. Yet at some point the tide started turning, and the army started losing. How do we explain this?

During the 1930s Hitler conducted a process that had as its main purpose to steal energy from the German people. You can find movies on Youtube about these mass rallies where Hitler gave a speech in front of 100,000 people. He gradually worked people into a fever pitch where their eyes were glazed over and they mindlessly screamed "Heil Hitler" or "Sig Heil." What were they doing? They were giving their psychic energy to Hitler, and it was pooled into a reservoir of energy in the collective emotional, mental and identity bodies of the German nation. When the war started, the German army was riding this wave of psychic energy, and it washed over Europe as an unstoppable tidal wave. Because it was a finite energy, it eventually ran out and now the German army started losing. The dynamic was that the amount of energy that had been accumulated made Hitler feel drunk, and he thought he was invincible, causing him to think he could conquer the entire world at once.

We human beings need psychic energy in order to accomplish anything in this world, even to survive. We can get it in one of two ways. The natural way is to get it from our higher selves, but this requires us to move out of separation and selfishness. If we are not willing to stop acting as separate beings, there is only one way to get energy, namely to steal it from other people. This can be done in two ways: through raw force or through deception. You either force people to give up their energy or you deceive them into giving it voluntarily, perhaps by making them think (as did Hitler) that they are serving a greater cause.

Once I found some teachings that explain this competition for energy, a lot of things started making sense to me, especially because I had been sensitive to psychic energy since my childhood. For example, when I watched one child tease, or rather mob, another, I could feel how the child being hurt was forced to release energy. However, I couldn't understand why until I understood that the perpetrator did this in order to steal energy from the other child.

Why do people argue? I once knew a person who would on a regular basis start an argument. There was often no real reason behind the argument. Once the argument had gone on for a while, it would suddenly be over for no apparent reason. I later realized this was because the person who started the argument had now received enough energy from the other person. She was satisfied, so the argument was over—until next time the person had a deficit of energy.

I fortunately never watched someone being tortured so I could never understand why some people would do this to others. It is a proven fact that any information you get from a torture victim is unreliable because people will confess to anything in order to get the torture to stop. So why do people torture others? Because the torturer is stealing psychic energy from the victim.

To me, this also explains rape, pedophilia and war. Raping another human being forces that person to release energy. Pedophiles must have such a deficit of psychic energy that they need to steal it from children who still have not squandered it through various activities. When someone is violently killed in war, they are also forced to release energy and someone can steal it.

Of course, war is on such a scale that it is difficult to explain it just by saying that some people steal energy from others. Obviously, soldiers don't consciously start wars in order to steal energy. And often the soldiers on both sides are killed and wounded, thereby being forced to release energy. If both sides lose energy, who stands to gain?

I was always aware of war and had a sense that there had to be some hidden reason behind it. The normal causes for war that I was told about in school didn't seem sufficient to explain madness on this scale. It took me many years to piece together an explanation, and it is probably the most controversial thing I have yet talked about in this book.

16 | APPROACHING AN EXPLANATION OF EVIL

When I was 13, I rode my bicycle to school on a beautiful spring day. It was early May and the trees in Denmark had just leafed out, their bright green leaves set against a deep blue sky. It seemed that in every tree a bird was singing, and I thoroughly enjoyed the spectacle as I made my way to school, feeling all was well with the world. The first couple of lessons were normal, but then we were asked to go to the auditorium, which usually meant we had to watch some educational movie.

So I go to the auditorium and sit down, expecting a film about the dangers of smoking or the Amazon rain forest. But instead I get a black-and-white movie that starts by showing an iron gate with the words: "Arbeit macht frei" (work makes you free). Behind that gate was the most sophisticated torture apparatus yet constructed by man, namely the Auschwitz concentration camp. For the next hour, I was transfixed by images of people coming out of railroad cars, being herded into gas chambers, dead bodies being thrown into mass graves, piles of luggage, clothes and human hair. Not to mention crematorium ovens being swung open and revealing a half-burned skeleton with its mouth wide open, as if screaming: "How could this happen?" At least that was the question on my white lips as the horrors finally faded from the screen.

And what did I get? We were told to leave the auditorium without any explanation, and we never had a follow-up to process the movie. We were simply shown this horror and left to ourselves to react. I can still remember walking out into the bright sunshine and seriously wondering how the birds could still be singing after what I had experienced. In fact, I couldn't understand why all activities on the planet had not come to a halt until we had figured out how something like this could happen and how we can prevent it from happening again. Because I don't see how we can prevent it by not talking about it.

So I will talk about evil, even though it is clearly one of the taboos of our oh-so-open democracies. It is the very thing that no one wants to talk about, including many spiritual people who subscribe to the motto that: "It's all good." Their theory is that if we put our attention on evil, we give it power. So they must believe that if we ignore evil, it will go away. I just don't see much historical evidence for that theory.

How we create with our minds

Naturally, growing up in Denmark during the 1960s, Nazism and the Holocaust was the big evil. For me, the question was always how Hitler could have seemingly hypnotized so many among the German people to follow him blindly. I saw movies of the mass rallies and the people in the audience looked like they were in a trance, fanatically screaming: "Heil Hitler" at the top of their lungs. What exactly happened there? Was there something that took over people's individual minds? It took me many years to find a plausible explanation, and it has several levels.

How do we human beings create anything? Well, we can only create something when we have a raw material. As I have described, the real raw material is energy, including (but not limited to) what we normally call matter. We can see that we human beings have created some very impressive things in the physical, visible spectrum, such as large cities or entire civilizations. Yet is our creation only in the physical realm?

I have talked about the four levels of the mind, the identity, mental, emotional and physical. So how do we build a house? Not everyone is capable of building a house. In order to do so, a person needs a shift in his or her identity mind whereby we come to accept: "I can build a house" (whether we do it personally or have someone do it). Then comes a process at the mental level where we make the exact plans for how the house should be built. Yet this isn't enough because we could sit on the plans for years without doing anything. So there has to be a shift at the emotional level where we have the drive to actually start the process, and only then will there be action at the physical level.

My point is that for anything we do at the physical level, there is a corresponding process at the three higher levels. At these levels, we create an energetic structure or matrix and it is this structure that is gradually lowered to the physical level of vibration. How do we create this energetic matrix? We do so with our minds, and the reason we can do this is that our minds are capable of doing something with the energy that exists at the identity, mental and emotional levels. There is nothing mysterious about this. The energy at these levels is as real as physical energy, but it is not visible to the physical senses because they are calibrated to detect only energy in the physical spectrum. Yet our minds can sense the higher energies. Anyone can learn to do this, and spiritual people are spiritual because we have already learned to do this (most likely in a past life).

What is a culture?

One of the things that visibly sets humans apart from animals is that we can create something that is not physical. Why do we have art, music, sports, philosophy or science? Why do we see many different cultures and civilizations throughout history? Because we humans are capable of creating these energetic matrices that are beyond the physical realm. What is culture? It is an energetic matrix that exists at the emotional, mental and identity levels.

How do we create a culture? It is created because a group of people use their individual minds to create a collective structure at the emotional, mental and identity level. This matrix exists in the collective mind, meaning that a group of people (even humankind as a whole) share a collective identity mind, mental mind and emotional mind. The individual minds of those who are part of the group are connected to the collective mind. The individual minds can influence the collective mind, but they can also be influenced by the collective mind, it's a two-way street.

We were all brought up to identify ourselves as belonging to a certain group (family, sex, race, nationality and possibly many other factors). We were brought up to think a certain way and we even took over certain emotions that are common in our groups. All people can sense this, so it is just a matter of realizing that this is not physical but something that exists at the emotional, mental and identity levels of the collective mind. Nothing mysterious, just a matter of becoming aware of what we all sense.

So how did Hitler hypnotize the German people? He started by defining a new identity for them as belonging to the master race, the Aryan super race. He defined a new structure at the mental level, talking about how this master race was destined to rule the world and remove all evil. Then, he gave the anger that was already in the collective emotional mind a direction so the people could direct it against the scapegoat, namely the Jews. In other words, when you see a mass rally where people seemed hypnotized, it was because the individual minds of those people had been overpowered by the collective mind. And the collective mind could then extract energy from the individuals, which became stored in the collective mind.

The energy gradually accumulated in the collective mind until it became so strong that it could overpower most people's individual minds. Once people were overpowered by the collective, they were no longer acting as individuals. They had set aside their individual will and submitted to the collective will. The more energy was in the collective mind, the easier it could overpower individuals and steal more energy. A self-reinforcing circle was created. This is how the German nation was manipulated into following Hitler towards the inevitable disaster. This is how a group of people become a lynch mob that is ready to kill a scapegoat. This is how the Russian people submitted to the terror of Stalin and did not object to the Soviet Union. This is how young girls are seen screaming uncontrollably at a rock concert.

To me, realizing how this works explained so many of the historical events I had read about. There are so many examples of situations where people walked right into a disaster that they could not see, but once the spell was broken, it was obvious.

I could look back at things like the crusades, the Inquisition and the witch hunts and I always wondered how people could not see what seemed so obvious now many years later. How could people possibly believe the earth was flat? Well, there was an energetic matrix in the collective identity, mental and emotional minds and it overpowered people's individual minds until it seemed obvious to them that the earth had to be flat.

The stunning conclusion was that we human beings are able to create a structure in our collective mind that can become so strong that it can influence, even overpower, the mind of an individual. This was at first very scary to me because my greatest fear had always been that something would take over my mind and make me do things I didn't want to do. Yet it was also a liberating conclusion. I realized that the collective mind was there whether I acknowledged it or not. So it would influence me also when I did not see it, meaning that by admitting that it was there, I could now do something about it. And the very fact that I was open to the existence of such a collective mind meant that my mind was not completely taken over by it—or I would have denied its existence.

The unseen power behind addictions

Drugs was not a widespread phenomenon during my childhood and youth, but alcohol was. I had at least two family members who became alcoholics, even though no one really talked about it. What I noticed was that addicts of any kind were not able to reason about their addiction as normal people could do. They could always find ways to deny that they were addicts and explain why their addiction wasn't harmful to themselves or the people around them. This I found difficult to explain, but by building on what I have said above, I found an explanation. As I mentioned, quantum physics has proven that when a physicist is conducting an observation of subatomic particles, the mind of the scientist influences the outcome of the experiment. The scientist is not neutrally observing a phenomenon but is co-creating the phenomenon. As mentioned, this leaves us with two options. One is that our minds can influence matter, normally called telekinesis. The other is that there is a form of consciousness present at the quantum level, and our minds can interact with that consciousness to influence the outcome of the experiment.

Another way to say this is that matter is not matter. It is made from energy, but energy has two aspects. One is movement, and one is direction. Our minds have the capacity to interact with the basic level of the matter world, and it is because the subatomic level is where energy from the three higher realms enters the physical spectrum. Since our minds have an emotional, mental and identity level, they can interact with the energy that makes up the physical universe. This is really not a mystery when we dare to look beyond the Christian and the materialist paradigm.

So our minds can form a matrix and superimpose it upon the basic energy. Yet once that form has been imposed upon the energy, it can continue to exist even when we take our minds off it. When we create a culture, we do so through our minds, but once created, it seems to have a life of its own and can exist even when we are not consciously aware of it.

To me, the simple explanation is that when enough human beings use their minds to create something collectively, what they create takes on a rudimentary form of consciousness. As an example, consider for how long people have been drinking alcohol. Anything we do at the physical level has a component at the emotional, mental and identity levels. So as we partake of that physical activity, we pour our psychic energy into the matrix that defines the activity. This means we endow that matrix with a certain form of consciousness. We are literally creating a living entity that has some form of consciousness. This means we have now created an alcohol entity that is aware that it exists and that it can continue to exist only when people feed it their energy by drinking alcohol.

So as a Frankenstein's monster, the alcohol entity will actively seek to get people to drink or to get people who already drink to drink more. Say we have a child who has certain psychological issues that make it hard for him to deal with life. He has never learned how to deal with these issues, but they cause him constant suffering. He now becomes old enough to drink, and he discovers that being drunk offers him relief from his daily suffering. This person is already vulnerable to having his mind influenced by the alcohol entity, and it can easily start influencing his emotional mind and get him to want the relief offered by drinking. In the longer run, it may influence his mental mind and project into it the age-old excuses people have come up with for drinking. It may even influence his identity mind and make him think it is normal or okay for a person like him to drink or that he is an alcoholic for life.

The scary scenario of collective entities

The stunning conclusion I reached was that we human beings have created numerous such entities that aggressively seek to take over people's minds. These entities are not actually evil. They can be compared to a computer that mindlessly does what it has been programmed to do. The alcohol entity does not have enough consciousness to evaluate whether drinking has negative consequences. It is created by people who want to drink, and it mindlessly seeks to get people to drink and to drink more. So the entity is not evil, even though what it is getting people to do might be evil or have negative consequences.

I understand that this can be a frightening thought, but only in the sense that it was frightening to me to learn about bacteria—these invisible entities that could kill me if I didn't wash my hands. Once you realize that a danger exists, you also see what you can do to escape it, and there truly is a defense against these collective entities. However, I will describe that later because I am not quite finished with the topic of evil.

Once I started realizing that we create these collective entities, it was shocking to contemplate how many of these we might have created. Even more shocking was to consider how many people might live their entire lives having their minds overpowered by these collective entities, never thinking an individual thought or making a free decision. This gave me a very strong desire to free myself from this influence, and it has been one of the driving forces behind my spiritual efforts.

Now, it may be easy to see that something like an alcohol, drug or tobacco entity is a problem. But it may be more difficult or unpleasant to admit that there might be a number of these collective entities that seem benign, even necessary. Given that I am a spiritual person, I have thought a lot about what makes people believe in a particular religion or spiritual teaching. In today's world we have a lot of people who grew up in a Christian culture but who did not become faithful Christians. These people can look at certain Christian beliefs and find it difficult to understand how faithful Christians can believe in them. Yet what if people believe because they grew up in a certain culture and from a young age, their minds were taken over by the collective entity created by that culture? This entity blocks people from questioning the basic tenants of their religion and they end up believing without really having chosen to believe and without knowing why they believe as they do. They just "have faith." It is a blind faith because instead of choosing their beliefs, their minds have been taken over by the collective entity created by their religion.

Obviously this works in connection with what I have talked about before, namely that we have a subconscious database with a Do not question folder. Some of the contents of that folder were put their by the culture in which we grew up, and the fear of questioning these ideas is reinforced by the collective entity of that culture. It is not just our personal fear we are up against but the collective fear of our culture.

Consider how the Catholic church has had 17 centuries to build a collective entity that by now must be very strong. Consider how Lutheran Christianity has built onto the Catholic faith without questioning certain elements of it. So even Lutheran churches have a strong collective entity, which I truly have encountered among fundamentalist Christians in the United States. I could literally see how they were mortally afraid of considering any ideas that were not biblical or scriptural.

As I said, I lived in Estonia for 5 years, and it became clear to me that communism created a very strong collective entity. Most people did not question the system and did not dare to talk about it with anyone. I realize full well that the system (especially under Stalin) was incredibly physically violent, but it was always clear to me that there was an undeniable psychological component. Stalin could not have killed everyone, but he didn't have to. He only needed to make people believe that he was *willing* to kill everyone, and then people submitted to the collective entity that had been created by the Bolshevik revolution.

So how do we explain that the Soviet Union collapsed, that Hitler lost the war or that so many people are no longer blindly believing in Christianity? Some collective entities are primarily emotional. Some induce the fear of questioning authority, but as we can see from the emergence of democracy, humankind is moving away from fear and that is why some of these entities lose their ability to overpower individual minds. Other entities are primarily mental, meaning they are based on certain beliefs. Yet humankind is also in the process of questioning many old beliefs and this makes it easier for people to pull themselves away from, for example, the collective entity of Christianity. Some entities are at the identity level and they are the hardest to overcome because most people are reluctant to question the sense of identity into which they were born. Yet we are indeed moving towards a more sophisticated sense of identity than our forefathers had.

So how do we explain that in the modern world many people have pulled themselves away from the collective entities that dominated people's minds 500 years ago? To me, one of the explanations is reincarnation. After living several lifetimes in fear of trolls and witches without actually seeing one, you eventually come into a lifetime without having this fear in your emotional body. After having lived several lifetimes believing in the Christian promise of going to heaven after this lifetime, yet every time coming back to earth, you eventually see beyond this belief. And after living many lifetimes being brought up to think you are a human being, with all of the limitations that entails, you eventually start realizing that you are more than a human being, you are a spiritual being who is only temporarily embodying in a human body. You are in this lifetime born into a certain culture, but you no longer identify yourself based on that culture. You know there is a higher identity to discover, and you keep searching until you find a teaching that explains who you really are, where you came from and why you are here. Again, there is a collective movement away from limiting beliefs, and spiritual people are at the forefront of it.

Truly evil people

I just want to round off the topic of evil. What I have said above really cannot explain the existence of people who are as extreme as Hitler, Stalin or Mao. One could say that humankind has over millennia created a very strong collective entity that wants people to go to war. This entity receives energy when people are killed in a war, so the more killing, the more energy the entity gets and the stronger it becomes. One could say that Hitler's mind was taken over by the war entity and the entity was using him to create war.

Yet I still never felt this was the whole explanation, and it took me a long time to find a deeper understanding. Part of this understanding is that there are some people who are clearly not as other human beings because they have no sense of empathy, no sense of humanity. There is a growing awareness of narcissists and psychopaths and how they have influenced society. Truly, I think that in the future, someone will take what is known about these psychological abnormalities and study how many leaders were influenced by them and how this has so often altered the cause of history.

Of course, this leaves the question of where such evil beings came from. This understanding is beyond what I want to talk about here. I have already given it in a condensed form in my novel: *My Lives with Lucifer, Satan, Hitler and Jesus*, so for those who are interested, I will refer to that book. But the short answer is that these people have had a very long time to go into selfishness, and they have taken selfishness to an ultimate extreme.

17 | HOW WE CREATE OUR CIRCUMSTANCES

I am going to leave the topic of evil for a while because in order to explain what we can do about evil, we need to understand how we have created the circumstances we face on this planet. In the following I will talk about some things I have already described, but I will give a deeper perspective, so bear with me.

Let me begin by getting the skeleton out of the closet, or rather, getting me into the closet with the skeleton. I mentioned that at an early age, I developed this intense fear of ghosts and skeletons. What really happened was that one of these collective entities in the emotional realm found a weakness in my emotional body. It exposed me to a wave of fear-based energy that overwhelmed me and opened my emotional body to this fear of skeletons. I am not saying this fear was completely debilitating, but it was always there, and even seeing the picture of a skull in a book or on television could trigger an emotional response. I think many children have a similar experience, perhaps triggered by something else, but we live for most of our childhoods with a strong fear of something. And all the adults can do is to tell us that what we fear is not real. *Not* helpful!

There are two things going on here. One is that I think many children are sensitive to energies from the emotional realm. I don't think all children are as sensitive as I was, but many are able to sense that there are certain energies that are dark. I was very sensitive to such dark energies, and, as described, I could even sense that some places have a lower vibration. This was not something anyone had stimulated and it was not something I believed intellectually. I simply experienced it and I experienced it as very real. Now, take note of a subtlety.

I knew, even before I started in school, that skeletons are a collection of bones and they cannot jump out of the grave as a unit and chase after me. But what made me afraid was not the skeletons in themselves, they were simply the trigger. What made me afraid was that I experienced that there are energy beings in another realm and they have an aggressive intention of influencing me. I experienced this as very real, and telling me that this experience was not real simply wasn't helpful to me. As I said, there really are beings in the emotional realm that have an aggressive intent to influence all of us. The reason being that by making us afraid, they can steal our energy and that is how they survive. I was sensitive enough to notice that when I went into fear, energy was indeed flowing out of my energy field. For that matter, I can still sense this although I have now learned to protect myself so it rarely happens. So one element of this situation is that many children can actually experience these energy beings and their aggressive intent. It is simply insensitive, even cruel, for adults to belittle this very real experience.

The other element is that as small children, we are open to almost anything. A famous Italian educator, Maria Montessori, said that until the age of 6, we have an "absorbent mind" that takes in all kinds of impressions from our surroundings. I know many spiritual people who grew up in disharmonious or abusive environments, and they were indeed open to these aggressive emotional beings and energies. So we have a period in early childhood where we are meant to absorb from our surroundings. Then, from the age of 6, we need to become more discriminating or discerning and stop absorbing everything, making more critical decisions about what we take into our minds.

Now, how are we supposed to determine what to take into our minds and what to exclude? Ideally, by using the two faculties that we human beings have for evaluating outside impressions: our rational minds and our intuition. Yet do we receive any rational explanation about collective entities that can influence us? Nay, we are told to use our rational minds to deny the reality of what we experience. This is not very helpful to a child who is sensitive.

In my case, I can see that what I really needed was someone who could have helped me develop my intuition so I could have learned to close my energy field to the influence of dark energies. This is an ability I have developed as an adult and it has been extremely valuable to me. Since I did not learn this in childhood, my only way of dealing with emotional energies was my rational mind. And since feelings are not rational, this will always be a limited tool, as the rise in mental illness actually proves abundantly.

What happened to me was that between the age of 6 and 12, I developed my rational mind and attempted to use it to deal with my fear of skeletons. Now, I am not saying there is anything wrong with using the mental mind to deal with emotions. I have described that we have four lower bodies and that the emotional body is below the mental body. Thus, in an ideal situation, our mental mind is supposed to have command over our feelings so that we can consciously choose what we feel in certain situations. However, in order for this to work, we need to have a mental understanding of the phenomenon that triggers our feelings.

What happened to me, as probably happened to most people, was that as I grew older, my rational mind became stronger, and it became able to suppress my feelings. This allowed me to push my fear of skeletons into the subconscious mind so I noticed it more rarely. This did make my life easier, but as any psychologist can attest, denying an emotion is not the same as freeing ourselves from that emotion. So how did I free myself from my fear of skeletons?

In a dark room with a skeleton

In seventh grade, we started having biology lessons in a special classroom. It had a smaller room next to it, and that room contained the school's collection of stuffed animals, birds, fish and other specimens. One specimen was a full-size skeleton, assembled with wires and hanging on a rack. It obviously wasn't from a real person, but a plastic model. However, it looked quite "lifelike" and was fully capable of triggering my fear. The room was also windowless and the light switch was on the outside.

During recess, the teacher often left the room open so we could go in and look at the specimens. One day, I determined that this was it. As the bell rang for the next lesson, I hid behind a cabinet. The teacher called the students out, took a quick look, then closed the door and turned off the light from the outside. I was now locked in a completely dark room with a skeleton and thus experiencing the worst fear of my childhood.

Naturally, I didn't die. In the beginning, my heart beat faster, but I slowly felt my way to the other end of the room where the skeleton was standing. As I came close, I mentally said: "Okay, if you have any power, come get me." Naturally, nothing happened. I obviously knew nothing was going to happen, but I had a clear intuitive sense that I needed to do this in order to overcome my fear. As I stood there in the darkness, I felt as if something left my energy field and I felt a deep inner peace. Today, my understanding is that by confronting my fear, the energy beings in the emotional realm lost their power to influence me, and they had to leave my energy field (my emotional body).

This was indeed a breakthrough for me, and I have many times since confronted my emotions and gone into them instead of running away from them by suppressing them. President Roosevelt is famous for saying: "The only thing we have to fear, is fear itself." What he didn't say is that fear is a collective entity that aggressively seeks to influence our emotions. Fear actually gets a hold of us because it makes us feel there is something we don't want to experience, we don't want to look at. In order to avoid experiencing it, we try to suppress the fear. Confronting the fear makes us realize that the actual experience is not as bad as we feared and this punctures the balloon of fear.

However, while my confrontational method did help me, it didn't actually remove the fear-based energy that had accumulated during my childhood. That only happened in my mid-twenties when I learned how to invoke spiritual energy to transform the fear-based emotional energy into a higher vibration.

As a result of my spiritual studies, I also gained a higher understanding that allowed me to truly resolve the doubts in my mental body that made me open to the fear in the first place. And this is precisely what my rational upbringing failed to give me, primarily because the understanding I needed was not found in the mental boxes of Christianity and Materialism. As soon as I found the teachings about collective entities that I have described here, my rational mind had the understanding that enabled it to take command over my emotional body and kick the entities out of there. Deciding with the mental mind that something is not real is not understanding but simply denial. In order to overcome something, we need to acknowledge its existence and then decide to kick it out of our energy fields.

So to sum up, I eventually came to see that we human beings have created numerous of these collective entities at the emotional, mental and identity levels. These entities are there whether or not we know about them, and they can influence our subconscious minds even if we consciously deny their existence.

If we take a look at history, we can see how all human atrocities have happened because people's individual minds were taken over by such collective entities. However, we can also see that many phenomena that we see as benign or constructive are also driven by collective entities. We may think a certain endeavor is constructive, but in reality it is driven by a collective entity whose only purpose is to take over people's minds so it can steal their energy and feed itself.

Compare this to what I said about our minds becoming closed systems that only validate the already accepted beliefs. How did so many among the German people come to believe in Nazism? I have already said that they appeared to be hypnotized by Hitler, and we can now see that their individual minds were taken over by the collective entity created by Nazism. While they were still under the influence of this entity, they could not see the errors and contradictions of Nazi ideology nor could they see the warning signs that clearly showed how Hitler was leading them towards a disaster. Yet once the spell was broken, it became obvious to many people and they wondered how they had failed to see it.

The same thing has happened many times in history. Communism also had the ability to hypnotize people, and I have personally met flaming Marxists in Denmark who were literally hypnotized by the dream of the socialist Utopia. For some of them, they broke free when the Soviet Union collapsed, while others broke free when they realized the reality of how communist society functions. However, this was difficult to do because the Iron Curtain blocked information about the reality of Soviet life.

Obviously, Christianity has also created a collective entity that overpowers many people's minds to this day, which to me is the only possible explanation why Catholics have not rebelled against the way the church had handled the pedophilia scandal. If your own children have been abused by a priest, yet you remain loyal to a church that does nothing to stop the abuse, then your mind must be taken over by a collective entity that hypnotizes you. This explains why Christians can't see the discrepancies between Jesus' original teachings and official doctrines. It also explains why materialists cannot see that the findings of quantum physics have proven the limitations of Materialism. Obviously, I see Materialism as another endeavor that has created a collective entity so powerful that it can overpower the minds of many otherwise intelligent people. When I watch Richard Dawkins argue with a Christian, I simply see two collective entities fighting through two individual people. To me, this knowledge can open up for a deeper discussion of evil.

18 | IS THE EARTH A FEED-BACK MACHINE?

As I said, I had a very real experience that there was something evil that was seeking to influence me. This meant I could never quite stop thinking about what was the cause of evil, and the more I learned about history, the more my need for understanding grew. As I was growing up, there were especially two ideas that caused me a lot of confusion and made it much harder for me to deal with evil than it needed to be.

The first idea came from Christianity and it is the idea that evil is caused by some mysterious being, called the devil or Satan. The problem I had with this idea is that it posed several questions for which Christianity had no answers. In other words, the idea of the devil was an attempt to explain evil, but it raised more questions for me than it answered.

My first question was: "Where did the devil come from?" Christianity says that God created everything so does that mean God created the devil? This seems a logical conclusion based on Christian doctrine, but it contradicted my inner knowing. I knew that the real

God simply could not have created a being that was dedicated to evil. In my mind, there was simply no reason conceivable for why God would do this. But I couldn't resolve the paradox so the idea of a devil left me with a lot of confusion.

The second idea came from Materialism, which has no real explanation for evil. In fact, if you take Materialism to its extreme, the concept of evil has no meaning. Evil is an abstract concept and according to survival of the fittest, there is nothing evil in some beings acting aggressively to further their own survival. Moral and ethical considerations are alien to strict Materialism, as it is only a matter of what gives a species, or even individuals within that species, a survival advantage. Killing the competition is perfectly logical to a materialist outlook.

So how do materialists explain that people do so many inhumane things to each other? Well, the only attempt at an explanation I came across was the idea that evil is simply part of human nature. We all – so they say – have the potential to do evil, it is only a matter of certain circumstances triggering this. The example given is the guards in concentration camps who became sadistic towards the prisoners.

The first problem I have with this is that it goes against my intuitive sense that evil is not a part of human nature. I even have a logical objection because Materialism says we developed from animals, and I don't see any animals that deliberately torture members of their own species. So if evil isn't found in nature, why did it suddenly pop up in us humans?

The other problem I have is that if the materialist explanation for evil was true, then how can we explain that I grew up in a democracy that is dedicated to preventing people from doing evil towards others? If survival of the fittest was true, then long ago the most aggressive beings should have been selected out and have out-competed the more benign people, who according to Materialism are simply too weak to survive.

How do we explain that there is a clear movement in human affairs that goes away from evil and aggression towards mutual respect and cooperation?

A couple of years ago, I was talking to someone, and without having thought about it, I suddenly said: "You know, with all of the work I have done on my psychology, I have never discovered anything evil in my being." As soon as I had said it, I had to pause because I realized it contradicted the common view I grew up with that somewhere deep in my psyche, there lies latent the potential for evil. Yet after more than 30 years of using many methods and therapies, including constantly observing myself since childhood, I simply have not connected to anything evil.

I submit that evil is not part of human nature. It was not put there by God, as the Christians say. Even Mother Theresa once said that we all have a little Hitler inside. Well, I can't speak for her, but I am fairly sure (based on her auto-biography) that I have done a lot more work on my psychology than she did, and I have not met a Hitler inside of me. I have also met numerous other people that I intuitively felt do not have anything evil in their beings. (I have met a few that did, but that's another story).

So how do we explain the undeniable evil we see in human history? Well, I said earlier that both Christianity and Materialism makes it seem like we are powerless to overcome evil. Yet once we understand evil, we see that we can indeed do something about it. Knowledge is power.

The human juxtaposition

I have already given a view of the human situation that goes beyond what I was brought up with, and I will now go further.

I will simply look at our situation as we can observe it based on what I have discussed in previous chapters.

We can observe that we are conscious beings and we are creative beings. We have the ability to create something, both on an individual and a collective level. We can also observe that what we create has consequences, as we live in a world guided by cause and effect. Every cause will have an effect so whatever we do, will have an effect. The question now becomes how conscious, how aware, we are of the effects of our choices?

As an example, when I grew up in the 1960s my father had a boat that was anchored in a little bay where a river ran into the fjord. At that time, my hometown allowed all of its wastewater to run untreated into that river and then into the fjord. This obviously had an effect (the water was brown and no fish could live there), but at the time there was no concern for that effect. During the 1970s there was an increased awareness of pollution and the city took steps to treat its wastewater before letting it into the fjord. Yet we are still creating pollution that can have effects on the environment, as the climate change debate demonstrates.

My conclusion is that the earth can be considered an educational device. We human beings are the dominant life-form on earth and we have been given complete freedom to do whatever we want on this planet. Of course, given that we live on the planet, we will also experience the effects of what we create. We have to live with whatever we create. During my entire lifetime, we have had to live with the fact that we have created pollution that affects our environment and our own bodies and that we have created nuclear bombs that could make the planet uninhabitable in 15 minutes. Quite drastic consequences when you think about it, which of course most people don't. So why don't we think about the consequences of our actions?

The evolution of consciousness

We all know that we don't expect young children to be as aware as adults. We start out in life being fairly centered on ourselves, doing whatever we feel like. As we grow older, we are expected to become more aware of what consequences our actions have for others so we can function in society. Well, what if this applies to humanity as a whole? We can observe in known history that human beings during the Stone Age had a much lower awareness of the consequences of their actions than we do today. In a sense, humanity started out at the level of children, and we have gradually grown to become more like adults. Yet given that there is still so much war, conflict and suffering, we might propose that we have not yet developed the awareness that allows us to function in harmony with each other and our environment. In other words, there is still some learning to do, there is still a level of awareness to which we have not risen. We still have not understood the full effects of what we create.

From this perspective, we could say that the evil and suffering we see in the world is the result of ignorance. This is what the Buddha said 2,500 years ago. I don't necessarily disagree, but I have found that we need to consider that there are two kinds of ignorance. For example, when people did not realize that bacteria exist and can cause disease, I consider this *innocent* ignorance. Yet when the Catholic church attempted to suppress the early scientists and squash awareness that the earth is not the center of the universe, I consider this *aggressive* ignorance. When materialists seek to prevent science from investigating consciousness, that is also aggressive ignorance. So we see in human history that there are two seemingly opposite forces. One force seeks to bring us towards a higher and higher awareness of every aspect of life. The goal is to help us discover how life actually functions so we can make choices that do not harm ourselves. The other force seeks to prevent the growth in awareness by defining certain theories, religions, ideologies or -isms that supposedly define how the universe *should* work according to some man-made view.

We can obviously link this second force to what I have said about our need for security. We live in a world with such insecurity and suffering that in order to function psychologically, we need to have some explanation of how life works. Once we have developed that, it gives us a sense of security. If our theory is threatened, we fear being thrown into panic, and we can therefore take aggressive measures to destroy any threat to our worldview. So aggressive ignorance is very much linked to this psychological dynamic. Yet based on the realization that everything is energy, we can take this to a higher level.

The journey from selfishness to social awareness

Most people tend to be focused at the conscious level. We take a certain action, and we tend to think that the reason we made that choice was what goes on in our conscious minds. We also tend to think that the effect of our action is only what is visible at the macroscopic level that can be detected by our senses.

In reality, psychologists have for over a century proven that everything that happens in our conscious minds is the effects of deeper causes in the subconscious mind. The conscious mind is just the tip of the iceberg of the human psyche. At the same time, quantum physicists have proven that the world is made from energy, and that our minds can interact with the basic energy that makes up the world. The level of matter that we detect with our senses is just the tip of the iceberg of the human environment.

We human beings started our history with a very low awareness of the environment in which we live. We didn't understand how it works and therefore we didn't understand what effects our choices would have. As time has passed, we have increased our awareness of how the world works and this has allowed us to make less self-destructive choices, as witnessed by the appearance of the modern democracies in which might is not right. We see that in the pre-democratic era, people were more focused on themselves and what was good for them as separate individuals. In order to create democracies, we had to develop a more social awareness where we look beyond our *narrow* self-interest to what could be called *enlightened* self-interest.

We can compare this to what physicists have discovered, namely that everything in the universe is connected at a deeper, invisible level. We could therefore say that the learning process we humans have been going through is that we started at a level where we saw ourselves based on our senses, meaning we saw ourselves as separate individuals. As I mentioned, I can observe that if I kill *your* physical body, *my* body still stays alive. A the physical level it seems that I am separated from you and what I do to you does not affect myself unless there is a direct, physical consequence.

This is a very primitive view, and a group of people who think they are separate individuals cannot create a democracy. We could only rise to the democratic era by developing a higher awareness that we are not separate individuals. As I mentioned, every religion in the world contains the idea that we should do unto others what we want them to do to us. If we see ourselves as separate individuals, this idea is simply nonsense, even a sign of weakness. This is exactly how Hitler looked at the idea, based on Nietzsche's philosophy about the übermensch (the super human).

The idea of doing unto others has now been supported by the scientific finding that everything is interconnected. If you and I are connected at an energetic level, it follows that what I do to you has an effect at that deeper level. Since I am part of the energy system of earth, that effect will eventually come back to myself. Now, I can observe that if I kill you and society doesn't discover that it was me, there is seemingly no effect of this right now. But when I incorporate the idea of reincarnation, I can see that it can affect me in a future lifetime.

How we create

So how do we actually create? We create through our minds, as proven by quantum physics. The macroscopic level, the level of matter that we detect with our physical senses, is only the tip of the iceberg of a larger energy system that has four levels. Quantum physics has proven that our minds can interact with this energy system, and we do this through the four levels of our minds.

Our creation starts at the identity level. Here, we have a certain sense of identity that defines how we see ourselves in relation to the world we live in. For example, we might define ourselves as physical beings who can only change our environment through our physical bodies, as we have done for most of our history and as most people still do today. This will then limit the options we can see and the actions we will take. Based on how we see ourselves, we will formulate an image in our identity bodies, and we will project it upon the energy at the identity level. The next step in the creative process is that the image from the identity body descends to the mental level. Here, we have a more concrete view of what we can and cannot do in our environment. For example, if we think we are physical beings, we believe we have to work at the sweat of our brow in order to get what we need to feed our bodies. At the mental level, we make the mental image more concrete and it then descends to the emotional level.

The emotional level cannot change the image that it receives from the two higher levels of the mind, but it can influence our willingness to act on it and the force with which we act on it. For example, many people are capable of formulating an image, often called a dream, for what they want to achieve. This can be very elaborate and detailed at the identity and mental levels, but somehow these people can never put it into action. The reason being that something at the emotional level blocks the image from being projected into the physical level. In my own case, I had a mental image that skeletons were not alive, but for some time my emotions blocked me from letting myself be locked into that room with the skeleton. Once I experienced that there was no real danger, my emotions came back into alignment with my mental body.

The conclusion being that our minds are creative because they can formulate images and bring them down through the levels of the mind and project them upon the basic energy that makes up the universe. This is the energy that quantum physicists discovered back in the 1920s and that they have proven our minds can interact with. But what's the point of this?

The feedback machine

I have said that the earth is an educational institution in which we are meant to grow towards higher levels of awareness. This allows us to use our creative abilities in ways that are not harmful to ourselves, others and the environment. Another way of saying this is that the universe (with its four levels of energy) is a feedback machine. There is something called biofeedback machines, which can be a heart monitor that shows our heartbeat on a computer screen. We can learn to use a mental technique to lower our heart rate, and we can see our progress on the screen. Well, the universe is a feedback machine that shows us how well or not well we are using our creative abilities. How does it do this? By outpicturing as physical circumstances the images we have in our minds. We can measure this in many ways. One obvious way is to look at the amount of suffering that exists on earth. Another measure would be mental illness, or whether people are happy or not happy.

Now, a biofeedback machine is something entirely neutral. It simply shows your heartbeat, and there is no philosophical overlay saying whether it is good or bad. In the same way, the universe is a completely neutral feedback machine. It simply outpictures at the physical level the mental images that we human beings hold in our individual and collective identity, mental and emotional minds (or bodies, as I have called them). The universe doesn't judge what we create, it simply makes it physical. This allows us to see a physical outpicturing of our mental images so we can decide: Is this what we want? Do we want *more of* this, meaning we have not had enough of experiencing this physical condition? Or have we had enough and now we want a different physical condition, we want *more than* this?

What must we do if we want a different physical condition? Well, if we want a different effect, we must change the cause, meaning we must change the mental images that we are projecting unto the basic energy that makes up the universe. If we want a different external condition, we must change our internal condition. Although this is simple logic, it obviously goes against everything we have been brought up to believe.

So why were we not brought up with an understanding of how the universe works?

There are two main reasons for this, one external and one internal. The external reason is that someone does not want us to know. As I said, there are some beings (both in physical embodiment and in the emotional, mental and identity realms) that have no empathy with the rest of us and only want to control and manipulate us. Even mainstream psychology is beginning to recognize the phenomenon of narcissists and psychopaths. My conclusion is that there is a certain type of beings who have an aggressive intent to control the rest of us (and they work through the collective entities that they have manipulated us into creating).

Over a long period of time, they have managed to make us forget the basic functions of the universe. They have made us forget that our external circumstances can only be a reflection of our internal circumstances. Instead, they have made us believe that we are the products or victims of our external circumstances, circumstances over which we have little or no control. Obviously, this makes us vulnerable to being controlled by a small elite of beings with an intent to manipulate.

Yet how have they been able to make us forget this basic fact? It is because there is an internal factor that in a sense makes us prone to forgetting, or even makes us want to forget.

19 | HOW WE PROGRAM THE SUBCONSCIOUS COMPUTER

Although this isn't the full explanation, the easiest way to explain this internal factor is to use the example of one of our ancestors who is sneaking through the jungle with a spear, hunting for food. He suddenly hears a rustling sound in the dense brush and sees a movement out of the corner of his eye. Now, if he calmly stood there, took a closer look and used his rational mind to analyze what made the sound, it is likely that he would have been eaten by a saber-toothed tiger and his genes would not have been carried on. Instead, he needed to instantly, and without any conscious thought, take evasive action. How did he take such instant action? Well, not by making a conscious decision. It happened below the level of conscious thought, namely what we often call instinct.

What is instinct really? I submit that it is something programmed into our subconscious minds, meaning the identity, mental and emotional bodies. We can compare it to a computer program that most of the time lies passively waiting. Yet in some situations it is triggered and now takes over our actions without any conscious thought. As an example, think about how you learned to ride a bicycle. In the beginning, it was very hard to keep your balance, and it required all of your conscious attention to hold the bicycle upright. After a while, you could easily hold your balance without any conscious thought, and your mind was freed up to enjoy the surroundings. If you haven't been on a bicycle for ten years, you won't forget how to hold the balance. The moment you get on a bicycle, the subconscious program is triggered and it takes over the mechanics of riding the bicycle.

Some psychologists talk about the reptile brain, which they describe as a part of our brain that has evolved from the reptile level and therefore still responds with the flight or fight response seen in animals. I don't disagree that we have these responses that are the result of countless generations of animals and humans having to take flight or fight a predator. Yet I submit that these responses are not confined to the brain. They are programmed into our emotional, mental and identity bodies. To me, this is proven by the fact that we can learn to consciously override this fight or flight response so we can cooperate with other people and create a democracy. Our modern democracies prove that we have collectively learned to override our most basic fight or flight response, and I think this would be difficult if it is coded into our brains. It is easier to do if it is coded into our three higher bodies. Why? Because it is easier for our minds to take conscious control over the three higher bodies than the more dense physical body.

My point here is that we humans do indeed have an ability to create something similar to computer programs in our subconscious minds. This is practical in many situations, not only in terms of danger, but also when we perform mechanical, repetitive tasks. I have had several jobs where I performed mechanical tasks, and my body could do it automatically while my brain was free to think about spiritual topics. In a sense, it was harder to have an office job where my mind was constantly occupied with a mental task and could not think about something else. What we now see is that our subconscious minds can be compared to a computer, and we can program it to automatically perform certain tasks, meaning the subconscious mind takes over and the conscious mind is not involved. We now need to add that there is no limit to what can be programmed into the subconscious computer. While creating a program for riding a bicycle is obviously benign, creating a program that determines how you react to other people may not be so constructive. For example, my father had a program that made him distrustful of other people, and it affected his life negatively. We can probably all see examples of people who have such programs that take over their reactions, and once they are in the pattern, it is almost impossible to talk to them or reason with them. I have already talked about reactionary patterns and that the goal of the spiritual path is to overcome our destructive patterns and take command over our minds. However, we can now go further.

Creating without awareness of how we create

Take note of what is really at stake here. I have said that our physical circumstances are a reflection of our internal circumstances, our mental images. We experience as physical circumstances what we project upon the quantum energy with the four levels of our minds. We now see that most of what we project is something we are not consciously aware of. Much of what we project comes through these subconscious programs, because some of these programs are based on the images we have of ourselves, the world and how we can and cannot interact with our surroundings. These images exist at the identity, mental and emotional level and we may not be consciously aware of them.

In an ideal world, we would consciously create our subconscious programs and we would be able to evaluate whether they are helpful or whether they limit us. We would be aware that we have such programs and we would be able to make them conscious and then change them if we wanted to. Instead, what has happened is that we have been manipulated into forgetting this basic mechanism of how we create our physical circumstances through our minds. This has happened because we have created programs in our subconscious minds, but we have forgotten that we created them or why we created them.

This gives us another layer of our understanding of the human juxtaposition. We experience that we live in certain external circumstances. We experience that we did not create them and that we have little influence over them. Instead, we feel our only option is to react to these circumstances. Yet even our reactions are not something we can choose consciously. A specific outer situation may trigger a subconscious program that takes over how we look at ourselves in that situation, how we see our options for responding and what we feel about the situation. We no longer have the freedom to make any conscious decision we want because the subconscious program simply rides the bicycle for us, and all we can do is hang on to the handlebars while we are rolling down the steep hill.

The scary fact is that if we look at human beings, we can see that the vast majority of us are not making conscious decisions in most situations in our lives. Instead, the lives of most people are almost entirely determined by their subconscious programs. Most people are simply responding to their external circumstances through these programs instead of making conscious decisions about how to change their circumstances.

I earlier argued that we do have free will, but I also said that the real question is how free our will really is. We can now see that if our decisions and reactions are determined by our subconscious programs, our will may not be very free. One could question whether many people live an entire lifetime without making a truly free decision, meaning a decision where they are consciously deciding instead of letting the subconscious mind take over.

Obviously, you are not one of these people. How can I say that? Because if you were, you would not have started reading this book and you would not have continued to this point. The fact that you are reading this means that you have realized that you have the potential to free yourself from your subconscious programs. It is therefore a matter of building on this realization and making the process more conscious.

Different types of subconscious programs

In the process of freeing myself from my own subconscious programs, I have discovered quite a variety of such programs. But in order to avoid making it seem too overwhelming, let me focus on a few types:

- Practical programs. Some programs are aimed at enabling us to perform practical tasks automatically, meaning without tying up our conscious minds in the process. Examples are walking, riding a bicycle and similar tasks. Obviously, such programs are largely helpful.

- Action programs. Some programs relate to what actions we take in specific situations. For example, some people automatically respond with physical violence if they feel threatened. Other people respond with submission in similar situations. In my own case, I have never been violent and as a child I tended to respond non-aggressively if another boy bullied me.

• Emotional programs. Some programs determine how we feel in certain situations. For example, some people immediately respond with anger if things don't go the way they want. In my case, one of the most persistent programs I have had is the tendency to feel embarrassed in seemingly insignificant situations, such as if I crack a joke and nobody laughs or if I think I have done something stupid.

• Mental programs. These programs determine how we think about certain issues or ideas or they relate to what we think we can do in life. Some people are very intellectual and tend to think carefully about everything, analyzing all options. Other people are more spontaneous and will do things without thinking about them first. Some people think they can do almost anything in life, whereas others think they are not very capable and they wait for others to tell them what to do.

• Identity programs. These relate to how we see ourselves and how we see our relationship to God, other people and the world we live in. I have met Christians who identify themselves as sinners and are always looking for a reason to feel guilty or ashamed. I have met atheists who feel they can do anything they want and don't need to feel guilty about any of it. These programs are the deepest and most difficult to resolve.

Where subconscious programs come from

So where do our subconscious programs come from? Well, this is where the picture is not as easy to simplify, but let me give some of the most common ways in which we acquire these programs:

- Almost any repetitive task can create a program. Riding a bicycle is a practical example, but if we are often in a specific situation, such as being verbally abused, this will also create a program.

- Some programs we create ourselves in childhood, and we obviously are not consciously aware of doing this. Being a small child in this world can be a daunting experience, and we create a variety of programs in order to just deal with life on this planet. The more difficult or abusive our childhood is, the more programs we create.

- We continue to create programs all of our lives. Naturally, when we start having romantic relationships, this is a potent source of emotional and mental programs. Our studies and work situations are another source of programs.

- Any kind of difficult or traumatic situation is the source of creating programs.

- Some programs we have created ourselves, but they were not created in this lifetime. They were created in past lives, in many cases in response to very traumatic situations. Just look at history and see how you could very likely have been exposed to war and other atrocities that could have forced you to create programs. For many of us, our response to traumatic situations in this lifetime does not create a new program. It simply activates a program created by traumas in a past lifetime.

• Some programs we take over from our family and immediate environment. I mentioned that young children have absorbent minds, and we can easily take over certain programs from our parents. How many of us have been affected by a teacher in school, either positively or negatively? Did we take over that teacher's program about learning or our own abilities? If an adult has a program that gives a negative self-image, how easy is it for a child to take on that program?

• Some programs we take over from society. Every culture, nation, race, nationality and ethnic group has created its own programs. When we are born into that environment, we take over some or all of these programs without being aware of it. I have lived in four different countries, and it became very obvious to me that each nation has its own subconscious programs that affect most of its citizens. For example, the United States prides itself on being the first modern democracy, but most Americans have a subconscious program that makes them far more suspicious of their own government than what you see in Denmark. In Sweden they have programs that make most people believe you resolve conflict by not talking about it and waiting for it to go away by itself. This makes it difficult for Swedes to get along with Danes, who have another program making us think we have to bring things out into the open.

• Some programs are common for humanity as a whole. Over the course of history, all humans beings who have ever lived have contributed to creating programs in the emotional mental and identity realms. Just consider how much conflict there has been and how this has created some very strong programs that cause people to respond with violence. I have experienced in Israel how the people in the Middle East are programmed to respond with anger and hatred, and we obviously still see this in many places around the world. Yet we also see that in the democratic nations we have started to free ourselves from these programs and find a non-violent way to interact.

• All programs are created in response to specific situations. In some cases these situations simply happen as we interact with other people. But in some cases we are manipulated into creating certain programs. I have hinted that there is a certain force that seeks to manipulate and control the general population, and they have, throughout history, manipulated us into creating certain programs that make us easier to control. As just one example, consider the feudal societies of medieval Europe. One nobleman owned a huge piece of land. He obviously couldn't farm this land by his own labor, but he didn't have to because there were 500 peasants who lived on the land and did all the work for him. How could one nobleman keep 500 people living as his slaves? Well, only because the peasants had been raised to take in a set of subconscious programs that made them accept their lot and think there was no alternative to that way of life. Just look at history and see how many similar situations we find. Why have we so often submitted to a small elite? Because we had taken over a set of subconscious programs that made us think there was no alternative.

Avoidance programs

Some programs are purely practical, but many programs are avoidance programs. In the past we were exposed to a situation that we experienced as very unpleasant or traumatic, and we decided we never wanted to experience that again. So we created certain programs in order to avoid similar situations:

- Such programs can be at the level of actions and are aimed at avoiding actions that have previously led to negative consequences. I have learned that in a past life I was killed for speaking out against authority. I created a program that was aimed at preventing me from speaking out against authority so I would not be executed again.

- Some programs are at the emotional level and are aimed at avoiding certain feelings. For example, I was deeply embarrassed in a very public way in a past life, and this came as a complete surprise to me. This created a program meant to avoid the possibility that I could ever be that embarrassed again. This caused me to withdraw myself and always look at my actions from the outside. If I monitored myself constantly and anticipated other people's reactions, then I would not be surprised and then I would not feel as embarrassed as the first time.

• Some programs are at the mental level and they are aimed at avoiding a situation where we are proven to be wrong or stupid for holding certain viewpoints. For example, I have met Christians who have elaborate programs aimed at discrediting any argument that could disprove Christian doctrines or worldview. I have met Muslims who have similar programs about Islam and materialists who have similar programs about Materialism. However, there is an infinite variety of such programs that are aimed at preventing us from being proven wrong as individuals. Many of these programs are aimed at justifying certain actions, giving us an excuse for continuing to do what we intuitively sense might not be constructive. Just look at what people will say on order to convince themselves that smoking will not kill them even though it did kill their parents.

• Other programs are at the identity level and are aimed an avoiding the feeling that we are wrong by being who we are. Many of these programs take the form of making a certain group of people feel superior so they could not be wrong. As an obvious example, the German people had a certain sense of superiority before the first world war. It was shaken by their defeat in the war, but Hitler managed to rekindle it by his idea of the Aryan super race. One could therefore argue that a subconscious program led to the second world war.

Decision-making programs

Another type of avoidance program is meant to justify that we avoid making decisions. These programs are very understandable when we consider how much suffering and conflict there is on this planet. We have all of us, in this or past lives, experienced that we made a decision that had disastrous consequences. So is it any wonder we seek to avoid such consequences by not making decisions?

I earlier said that there is a mechanism that wants us to forget that we have created subconscious programs. Our unwillingness to make decisions makes us want to forget that we have created programs that justify why we are not making decisions. I have met Christians who always pray for divine guidance and who believe they are told what is God's will for their personal decisions. I have met many spiritual people who go to astrologers, numerologists, psychics or use other methods to find some higher meaning to their lives so they don't have to make a decision. Other people think their lives are guided by destiny or fate, meaning some higher power is showing them what to do.

All of this is aimed at justifying that we don't need to run the risk of making our own decisions and experiencing the consequences. Yet what have I said is the basic principle of our creative efforts? It is to make a decision based on our present level of consciousness and then see the consequences, using them to raise our consciousness. We all know intuitively that it is our responsibility to make decisions and that is why we need to justify not making them. This justification shows us that there is something that we need to look at and overcome.

Of course, this is what the spiritual path to self-mastery is all about. When we clear out our subconscious programs, we will again feel free to make decisions and learn from them.

We will also free ourselves from being controlled by the programs, by other people or even by the power elite that wants to control the population. There is no more powerful way for an elite to control the population than to get all people to create subconscious programs that cause them not to want to make decisions. These programs make us vulnerable to submitting to an elite that claims it can make all of the decisions for us.

Labeling or judgment programs

There are many subconscious programs that are aimed at making a judgment by creating a label for a certain issue. I have talked about how we have a subconscious database with a folder that contains ideas we consider absolute true and that we do not question. Every civilization, culture, nation, race, ethnic group and religion has created a number of collective programs that define judgments about what is true or untrue, good or evil. The effect of this is that those who are members of the group come to (often without seeing this) take on these programs and therefore close their minds to any and all ideas that are labeled false by the program. I have met many fundamentalist Christians in the United States whose entire view of life is driven by such programs. They hear a certain idea, and it is instantly labeled as "occult" and therefore judged as being of the devil. I have met Arabs who had instant judgments about Jews and Jews who had their own programs about Arabs. I have met materialists who had programs judging any non-materialist idea as subjective superstition and at the same time judging any materialist idea as absolute truth (without seeing that their judgment was also subjective).

As a child it was a shock to me to realize that some societies have taboos, meaning there are certain topics that people are not allowed to talk about. One such taboo was sex, causing many people (even in today's world) not to understand what causes pregnancy. There are of course numerous others.

I was also shocked to realize just how many judgments we have about other people, other nations and other cultures, often without having actually experienced them for ourselves. Just look at the society in which you grew up and see how many prejudices you were exposed to and supposed to take on in order to fit in. Obviously, those of us who are spiritual people simply could not accept all of these prejudices, especially the ones about ideas beyond the mainstream mental boxes. We kept asking questions that were judged as dangerous by our society and that is how we ended up finding new ideas that gave us a spiritual understanding.

How subconscious programs run the world

How come such collective subconscious programs can build in intensity over time, and how come they are able to take over the minds of individuals to the point where people are not making conscious decisions? Well, we can reach back to my previous talk about collective entities. We can say that when a subconscious program has been sufficiently reinforced, we are actually creating an entity with a rudimentary form of consciousness that wants to survive. Yet we can now go deeper into this.

I have said that quantum physicists have proven that at the most fundamental level of matter, our consciousness can interact with the basic matter/energy out of which the material world is made. Matter is actually energy waves, but waves require some form of medium in which they can vibrate. A wave in water moves because it makes the water molecules vibrate. So what is the basic medium in which energy can vibrate? It is consciousness.

I have said there is an emotional level beyond the material. There is a mental level above that and an identity level further up (in vibration). When we go beyond the identity level, we reach a higher level, and we can call it the spiritual realm.

As soon as I heard about the concept that there is a spiritual world beyond the material, it was immediately obvious to me because it simply verbalized my inner experience. Yet it took me many years to rise above some of the subconscious programs about the spiritual realm that have been created by several of the world's religions. The three great monotheistic religions, Judaism, Christianity and Islam, promote the image of a remote (and angry) God in the sky. God is up there in heaven, we are down here on earth and there is a fundamental, qualitative separation between heaven an earth.

What I eventually came to see (and which quantum physics has also shown) is that there are no real divisions in the world. Everything is interconnected because everything is made from the same stuff. The spiritual realm is made from consciousness and it is inhabited by conscious beings. The world we live in is made from the same stuff and it is also inhabited by conscious beings (us). The difference is that the basic "stuff" in the spiritual realm vibrates at a higher level than the material realm. What we call matter and energy is the same stuff as in the spiritual realm, but it has been lowered to a different level of vibration. Therefore, the matter world seems more dense to our physical senses and also to our minds.

The main difference between the conscious beings in the spiritual realm and ourselves is that because of the density of matter, we have forgotten what spiritual beings know. Spiritual beings know that the world is made of consciousness and that they create their external circumstances with their own minds.

They create the same way we do, by formulating images or matrices in their minds and superimposing or projecting them onto the basic "stuff" out of which the spiritual realm is made (without thinking they are separate beings). We have forgotten how we create, and that is why we are not aware of how our minds interact with the basic energy/consciousness out of which the world is made.

We can also say that spiritual beings know that they create everything with their minds. What they see around them is a direct outpicturing of the matrices in their minds. We have forgotten this, which means we are not creating directly. We are creating indirectly because we are not superimposing matrices with our conscious minds. We have stored our creative matrices in our subconscious minds, and we are superimposing them through the programs, entities or selves in the emotional, mental and identity minds. That is why our conscious minds are so often surprised by what we see in our physical circumstances, making us feel we are victims of circumstances beyond our control. That is why we have created these thought systems that portray our situation as created by a remote God in heaven or by impersonal laws of nature—both of which are beyond our control.

How subconscious programs control us

I have so far talked about subconscious programs in order to compare it to something with which we are all familiar. Yet this is where the computer analogy breaks down. Unless we consider the popular theme in science fiction movies where a computer eventually becomes so powerful that it acquires a certain consciousness and now seeks to control the people who created it. This is exactly what happens when we create subconscious programs. In order to create such a program, we must formulate an image in our minds and we must project it upon the basic stuff out of which the world is made. We use our consciousness to form the image, we use our consciousness to project it and the stuff onto which we project it is also made from consciousness. This means that when we project the image with a certain repetition and intensity, what I have so far called a program actually becomes a conscious entity. This does not mean we are creating something that is self-aware as we are. We are creating something that has a lower level of consciousness than we ourselves have.

Although it isn't entirely accurate, we can compare the entity we create to an animal. A tiger is not self-aware and it cannot choose to consciously alter its behavior. Yet it has a form of consciousness that makes it aware that it needs to eat in order to survive, and it will therefore attack anything that it considers food. Whether the tiger comes across a dear or a human being, the tiger has no moral considerations that it is wrong to eat human beings because we have a higher con-sciousness than itself and therefore deserve the chance to live. To the tiger, we are simply food and in many cases easier to catch than a dear.

Once we have created a subconscious entity, it also does not have any moral considerations. It has enough awareness to know that it needs food in order to survive. What is the food of such a subconscious entity? It is the psychic energy that we used to create it. Thus, the entity will seek to get us to continue to give it food so that it can survive and even grow. To the entities we create, we are the source of food.

How can such entities influence us and get us to give them energy? Well, we created them so they exist in our identity, mental or emotional bodies. At the physical level, we know that once a certain mass has accumulated, it exerts a gravitational pull on anything near it that also has mass. There is a similar phenomenon at the emotional, mental and identity levels. Any energy that accumulates to a certain intensity will exert a pull on its surroundings, any energy field will pull on any other energy field.

Say I create an entity in my emotional mind (for example). This entity was created because I felt angry so it was created out of a specific emotional matrix and energy. Whenever I feel angry, I use my mind to qualify the basic stuff out of which the world is made with the vibration of anger. I actually take the energy I receive from my higher self and qualify it with a fear-based vibration of anger. This is what created the entity, and it is what feeds the entity. Thus, the entity has some awareness that in order for it to survive, I need to be angry.

Once such an entity has reached a certain level of intensity, it can exert a pull on my emotional body. It can agitate my emotions, and this means I will now have a tendency to react with anger to more situations than before I created the entity. The entity pulls me into reacting with anger so it can be fed and even grow. I have met people whose default reaction to almost any situation in life is anger. There is often no outer reason for their anger. They react with anger to situations in which most people would never become angry. So there is no rational explanation for their anger. But the deeper explanation is that they have created a very powerful anger entity in their emotional bodies and it pulls them into acting with anger even when there is no discernible reason for it. In a sense, their entire lives have now been swallowed up by feeding this anger entity, and they are looking for enemies everywhere. They are often defending themselves without having been attacked and they often attack others in order to get them to react with anger.

How collective entities influence history

Now, let's take this to the collective level. The universe is an interconnected whole, so my emotional body is not separate but connected to the collective emotional body. What determines the nature of this connection is the entities or selves I have created in my three higher bodies. For example, if I have created an angry self in my emotional body, it will connect me to the collective anger entity. This collective entity can then use my individual self to make me angry so that the collective entity can steal my psychic energy.

When we look back at history, is it so hard to see that we human beings have created these semi-conscious entities in our collective mind or energy field? How is it possible that people in the Middle East have been fighting amongst themselves for thousands of years? One group is seeking revenge for something the other group did to them. Yet the other group did it in order to get revenge for what the first group had done to them. No one can remember when this cycle of seeking revenge for revenge started, and it doesn't matter. There is no rational reason for the aggression. It is simply that there is a gigantic collective entity over the Middle East that pulls on people's emotional bodies so they go into aggression and thereby feed the entity. There are even entities in the mental realm that make Arabs feel it is justified that they are angry with the Jews and that make Jews feel justified in defending themselves against the Arabs. They all think they are doing this for some greater purpose, but the only purpose is to feed the collective entities. How will we ever make peace there as long as these collective entities sabotage any move towards peace?

I lived in the United States when 9/11 happened. I watched how the Bush administration unleashed a propaganda machine (remember the Weapons of Mass Destruction that couldn't be found?) in order to pull America into the war in Iraq. This was a nation that had gone through the trauma of the Vietnam war and was reluctant to go to war. Yet the American people have created a very powerful collective entity that pulls them into being patriots (something virtually unknown in a small country like Denmark). So when the President declared war, no one dared to object for fear of being labeled unpatriotic. Because I was not an American, I was not caught up in this and I could clearly see that this would end in disaster, as I think has been proven by events. Obviously, many Americans could see it as well, but no one, from the Democrats, to the press, to the people dared to object.

Then, look at the second world war. For generations, three nations, Germany, France and England, had been building national entities that made each nation feel they were the superior nation in Europe (and the world for that matter). Obviously, this took an extreme turn in Germany with the Aryan race, but can we really say that the war was created only by Germany? Was it not simply these three national entities that created such a tension that they had to fight it out in order to establish who was superior? Did anyone really end up feeling they had won the war? Well, certainly the collective entities won by being able to absorb all of the fear-based energy released by the suffering of so many millions of people. Of course, we humans have also created a very powerful war entity and one could argue it was this entity that benefited the most. What a feast it had from stealing so much energy from so many people.

What have we now established about evil? Well, at least part of the explanation for what we call evil is that we have created these collective entities that can overpower individuals and pull them into certain forms of behavior. The deeper purpose behind this is to simply feed the entities so they can survive and even grow. Do the entities have any purpose for doing this? Not beyond their own survival and growth.

What would happen if the war entity would manage to create a war of such proportions that it killed all people on earth? Well, at first the war entity would feel incredibly powerful from all the energy. Of course, that energy would eventually dissipate and if there were no people to feed it, the war entity would eventually die. But the war entity is not self-aware and it cannot reason this way. It will mindlessly continue to seek to get people to go to war even if it leads to its own destruction. The question simply is how long we human beings are willing to go along with this mindless game?

I know very well that this idea of collective entities is hard to accept for most people because it threatens their sense of security. But just ask yourself if you can possibly see another explanation for the situations I have described and many other situations. I have always been fascinated by situations in which a large group of people believed in something that was later proven to be false, but there was no way they could see it because they were seemingly hypnotized.

Consider how people believed the earth was flat and that it was the center of the universe. Consider how people did not object to the Inquisition and the witch hunts because they were hypnotized by their fear of the Catholic church. Consider how the Germans could see no way to object to the madness of Hitler, and how the Russians could not object to Stalin. Consider how in so many countries Catholic priests were systematically abusing children, and it was often public knowledge that this was happening but no one could break the spell and get society to act upon it. Can you give me another more plausible explanation for the observable fact that in so many situations people have literally been hypnotized and no one could break through and change the equation.

20 | WHAT CAN WE DO ABOUT EVIL?

One consequence of our explanation problems is that there are certain questions that are rarely asked. One of them is: "What can we do about evil?" Considering the immense suffering that evil has caused throughout history, how come we are not making it a priority to use all of our sophisticated scientific resources to answer this question? Why don't we have a special study of evil at the world's universities? Given that the Latin word for evil is "malum," we might call it: Malumology.

Based on what we have discussed up until now, it becomes relatively easy to see what we can do about evil. Let us start with the personal level. Here is how I see my personal situation. I live on a planet that exerts a gravitational force on my physical body. This is quite benign and practical as floating off into space has never been a dream of mine. Yet I also live in a world that has an emotional, mental and identity realm. In each of these realms are a number of collective energy beings or entities that exert a pull on my emotional, mental and identity bodies. These entities are constantly seeking to pull me into fear-based forms of behavior. The reason being that these entities need energy from people in order to survive. They cannot get this energy from the spiritual realm. So they need to manipulate me into taking the energy that I receive from my higher self and lowering it to a fear-based vibration that they can absorb.

I live on earth, meaning I live inside the collective energy field. As my physical body is affected by the pull of gravity, my emotional, mental and identity bodies are affected by the pull of the collective energy bodies. Most people are so affected by this pull that they live most of their lives being so overwhelmed by the collective that they cannot make truly individual decisions. Yet we all have the potential to free ourselves from this influence and seal our energy bodies from the collective energy bodies.

I still remember the incredible excitement I felt when I first realized that this is a real possibility for me. During my childhood I had sensed that there were energetic beings seeking to influence me, but because I didn't know what it was, I felt powerless and stuck. Once I realized that there is something I can do to free myself from the pull of the energetic beings that I had sensed all of my life, I became very excited and very determined to pull myself up.

How can we overcome this collective pull? This involves two elements. The first one is a purely energetic element. We simply need to realize that lower energy is less powerful than energy of a higher vibration. For example, high-frequency energy can form a shield (as we see with spaceships in science fiction movies) that lower energies cannot penetrate. So we can learn to seal our personal energy fields from any fear-based energies. We can learn to invoke high-frequency energy from the spiritual realm and seal our auras from the collective energies. We can also recognize that the fear-based energy we have accumulated in our auras will be the "mass" that the collective energy will pull on. By invoking love-based energy from the spiritual realm, we can transform the fear-based energies in our auras so there is nothing for the collective to pull on. This is relatively mechanical and something that is quite easy to do (if we are willing to go beyond the mental boxes of Christianity and Materialism).

When I learned how to do this, it had some dramatic effects on my personal life. I have already described that after a few weeks of invoking spiritual energy, I was able to fall asleep very quickly. After a few months, I noticed that there was a painful situation from my teenage years (involving a girl I had a crush on) that would often haunt me. Whenever the situation came to mind, I would feel this emotional pain, almost like a stab in the heart. After invoking spiritual energies for about three months, I suddenly realized I could now think about the situation without feeling the pain. The reason being that I had transformed the energy in the emotional body that caused the pain.

While invoking spiritual energy can be effective in itself, it is not enough to free us completely from the collective pull. We also need to recognize that what makes us vulnerable to this pull is the subconscious programs we have in the emotional, mental and identity bodies. The fear-based energy is created through these programs so only when we resolve the programs, will we be permanently free. This is a more difficult process, but once we do resolve the energies, it becomes easier to uncover the programs and consciously dismiss them. The trick being that while we can *create* a program without being aware of what we are doing, we cannot *uncreate* a program without seeing it and making a conscious decision to dismiss it.

What do we need to do to uncover and dismiss these subconscious programs? We need to make them conscious and how do we do that? Well, as we can observe from the emergence of democracies, our planet is in an upward spiral where we are raising the collective consciousness. In order to create democracies, we had to raise the collective awareness so a critical mass of people became aware of the subconscious programs that made them accept the feudal system. Once a critical mass of people freed themselves from these entities, we could make the leap as a society to institute democracy.

So we can say that there is a general raising of awareness whereby we become aware of these programs through our physical experiences. However, what drives this process is that some people become aware of their individual programs and overcome them. This happens because these people observe themselves – over many lifetimes – and think about their situation so they become able to detect a certain program and ask themselves: "Why do I react this way, what is behind it?"

We can say that so far, humanity has progressed because some people have used self-observation to dismiss some of their individual programs. This process has been going on for centuries because after experiencing suffering for many lifetimes, we eventually start considering what role we ourselves have in creating our suffering. We become open to looking at the beam in our own eyes instead of focusing on the splinters in the eyes of other people. Many of the people who have driven this movement are what I today call spiritual people. There are millions and millions of such people, and they may not all be consciously aware of what they have been doing. The raising of consciousness that we have seen over the past centuries has been largely unconscious, meaning people have not been consciously aware of the process. In many cases they have not done this to raise their consciousness but to escape specific forms of suffering. They have, over many lifetimes, come to the point where they have decided that they have had enough of suffering and they have started looking for a way out.

A result of our anti-spiritual societies is that we do not understand how we are controlled by our subconscious programs. What has motivated people is that they have experienced such personal suffering that it forced them to look for an explanation that was beyond their existing worldview. I have said that our worldview gives us a sense of security so in order to question it, something has to make us willing to go beyond our sense of security. All too often this is such immense suffering that we cannot live with it and thus we force ourselves to look for an alternative explanation in the hope that it can alleviate our suffering.

To me, this is so unnecessary because by being conscious of the spiritual path, we can question our worldview and expose our programs without having it be driven by this intense suffering. I have met so many spiritual people who were driven by severe psychological problems to look at spiritual teachings. But why should it be that way? Why shouldn't we be able to grow up in a society that gives us teachings and tools for overcoming the very thing that makes our lives miserable? Is that really too much to ask for in a society that claims to be sophisticated and free?

There is a tremendous potential for more and more people becoming conscious of the process. Once we realize what we want and the mechanics involved, we can make much faster progress on the individual level, something I have proven myself and that I see thousands of other people proving also. As soon as more people start doing this consciously, we will have a much bigger impact on the collective and shift our societies away from conflict, war, poverty and suffering.

I still remember having an intuitive experience where I saw this potential, and it literally sent shivers down my spine and tears down my cheeks. It was such a powerful experience of the immense potential for improving conditions on this planet, conditions that had been so disturbing to me as I grew up. Instead of feeling powerless in the face of these conditions, I now saw that by making the process conscious, we can achieve tremendous progress.

Are we all alone in the universe?

No, I am not here going to talk about alien spaceships coming to save us from ourselves. I said that the rise in the collective consciousness has been driven by a few individuals who have been willing to overcome the limitations in their own psyches. These people can be found in every historical epoch, in every culture and every religion. However, they have not been like the average follower of, for example, Christianity. They have looked beyond the official doctrines and accepted a more open-ended worldview. One word to use for such people is to say they are "mystics."

There are some people who talk about Christian mystics or Muslim mystics, but personally I think "mystic" is a universal term. I see myself as a mystic, and that means I do not define myself based on any particular religious tradition. However, I don't have a problem with some people being mystics and pre-ferring to express themselves by using the words and imagery from a certain tradition, such as Christianity. I have written books about my mystical view of Christianity because I grew up in that tradition. Yet I have also written books that go com-pletely beyond any tradition.

Okay, so what is the core of being a mystic? It is that our approach to spirituality is not based on believing a certain tra-dition or set of doctrines. It is to some degree driven by the desire for a deeper understanding of the fundamental questions of life, but it is not limited to seeking understanding. A mystic is truly a person who has realized that while *understanding* spiritual topics may be helpful, it can also be a hindrance to growth. This is, for example, outpictured by the scribes and Pharisees who attacked Jesus (who was a true mystic) and the Hindu brahmins who attacked the Buddha (another true mystic). So the core of being a mystic is that you look beyond understanding and seek a direct, inner, intuitive experience of the spiritual side of life.

You are not simply seeking to understand the spiritual realm. You are not content to believe in a doctrine that describes this realm. You are not content to leave the questions of whether there is a spiritual realm beyond the material world open, or open to interpretation and proof. You want to experience the spiritual realm in such a way that the experience becomes as real (or even more real) than your experience of the material world. This is what has traditionally been called mystical experiences, but we could also call them intuitive experiences. What's the significance of this?

Well, I have said that I have personally had mystical experiences since I was a child. I have met many spiritual people who have also had such experiences. Yet I have also met spiritual people who have not had the direct experience but who have still been open to looking for answers to the deeper questions and looking for those answers outside traditional worldviews. That is why I have so far given a lot of ideas that seek to stimulate understanding. This is done to help open-minded people gain a deeper understanding of the situation we face and what it takes to raise our consciousness.

I am now going to change my approach slightly because I am going to talk about a topic for which I cannot give any concrete proof or even a final argument. I have said before that due to our perception filters and subconscious programs, there is no final argument that can be given. So I am not going to present an argument but simply describe what mystics have experienced throughout the ages and what it means for me. I am not seeking to convince you of anything. I am only asking you to pay attention to your intuitive reaction (which is centered in the heart, not the head) as you read the following.

There are many types of mystical experiences, but they have one thing in common. I have said that due to our subconscious programs, we have come to see ourselves as separate beings. We see ourselves as separated from each other, the planet we live upon and our source. I have also said that our minds have become closed, self-validating systems. The core of a mystical experience is that we glimpse a state of awareness that is beyond the sense of separation and the closed mind. We somehow glimpse that there is a state of oneness above and beyond the consciousness of separation. We glimpse there is a more expanded view than the unquestionable beliefs in the subconscious file folder.

This has caused mystics throughout the ages to experience directly that we human beings here on this little planet (that is like a speck of dust in the expanse of the physical universe) are not the only self-aware, intelligent beings in the larger creation. In my view, the majority of mystics agree that there is a form of beings who exist in a higher realm (a higher vibration) than the material universe. Some of these beings have the function to help us expand our awareness and raise our level of consciousness. Mystics can describe them in different ways and use different names, but the basic idea is that we do have the option of working with beings who have more experience and a higher level of consciousness than ourselves.

I personally prefer to call these beings "ascended masters." This name signifies that many of them have been in embodiment on earth, so they have experienced what we are experiencing. Over many lifetimes, they discovered and followed the spiritual path that we are following. Eventually, they took this path to its logical conclusion, meaning they had purified their four lower bodies to such an extent that there was nothing pulling them back into embodiment on earth. Thus, they could make a quantum leap and go through a process called the ascension. When you ascend (as we all have the potential to do), you do not come back into embodiment on earth but achieve a permanent existence in the spiritual realm. You become an ascended master, and you do this by mastering your own mind until it is free of all pulls from earth. More about ascended masters later.

How free will can limit free will

What's the significance of this? Well, consider what I have said about free will. We human beings here on earth have the power to create a set of physical circumstances that cause immense suffering (as we can observe that we have done). This is really an outcome of the observable fact that we have free will. Our will is so free that we can create any kind of mess we want to create (even what we don't consciously want to create). Yet what have I said about how we create? We create through our consciousness. We formulate mental images in the three higher levels of our minds and then we project them upon the basic stuff that makes up the matter universe.

The consequence is that our will is so free that we can limit our free will. We can collectively create circumstances that are so far beyond what we can create individually that we begin to believe we have not created this ourselves. Thus, we come to believe that the suffering we see in the world was not created by ourselves. In a sense it wasn't. The suffering in your personal life was not exclusively created by you, it is to some degree a product of the conditions we have created collectively over a long period of time. Your part of it was not created by you in this lifetime but over many, many lifetimes. The result of all this is that when you look at your situation in this lifetime, it seems like you are the powerless victim of circumstances beyond your control.

But why does it seem that way? Because over many lifetimes you have created a set of subconscious programs in your emotional, mental and identity bodies that make it seem real that you live in a world that limits you and that you can do nothing about it. In other words, if you look at most human beings, they have created subconscious selves that form a self-reinforcing illusion. Their view of the world has become so persuasive that they think it is real. They think they are limited beings and therefore they do not try to look beyond their subconscious programs and raise their consciousness. They continue to project the same mental images upon the quantum energy and thus they literally become self-fulfilling prophecies.

This leads to two questions. If we accept that we human beings here on earth can create certain physical circumstances, we obviously have not created every aspect of our physical circumstances. We didn't create the earth, the sun, the Milky Way or the billions of distant galaxies. So where did this all come from? Well, the mystic's answer is that the universe was created by beings in the spiritual realm. These beings also created planet earth and they created us in our original forms. We were then allowed to take embodiment on earth and because of free will, the ascended masters who created us are not allowed to interfere with what we do once we are here. That is why our source beings have allowed us to create the mess we currently see.

The second question is: If we accept that there are beings who created the entire universe, they must be relatively smart. So couldn't they foresee that if they let us loose on this planet with free will, we might make a mess of things? And if they did foresee this, do they have a way out? Is there a Plan B—or is there a part of Plan A that we are not aware of?

How we forgot where we came from

Now, I may have said some things that sound like I am not too enthusiastic about the Bible, especially the Old Testament. But I do find that there is one useful idea in there, and it is the story of Adam and Eve in Paradise. I have already said I never believed there was a time when there were only two people. Yet what if we look at Genesis, not as a literal account but as a symbolic account of what has happened to all of us.

The story portrays Adam and Eve as being in two fundamentally different states. At first, they were in a situation where they had the constant contact with and guidance from a being with a higher level of consciousness than themselves. I don't see this as the ultimate God of the universe, but as one of the source beings who created planet earth. We might say that we all started out in a state where we had guidance from one or more spiritual teachers.

We then see that Adam and Eve went into a different state where they had lost contact with this spiritual teacher. How did this happen? Well, what is the "fruit of the knowledge of good and evil?" Could it be a symbol for the state of consciousness we are now in, the consciousness that we are separate beings? Look at what the so-called serpent said to Eve: By eating the fruit, you become as a God, knowing good and evil. Is that not a symbolic description of the state of consciousness I have described? Have we not created perception filters and subconscious programs that make us believe we are like Gods because we have the power to define what is real and unreal, true and untrue, good and evil? Is not the very source of conflict that many different groups of people have defined separate and conflicting versions of what is good and evil? Is not our willingness to kill in order to establish our version of truth as the superior one a proof that we have lost the awareness that we all came from the same source and that we are all connected?

It is simply a matter of realizing that there is an unavoidable risk by giving us free will, namely that we can create an illusion that seems so real to us that we are convinced it is not an illusion but a real world. And once we are in that state of separation, we have lost contact with our spiritual teachers and we have even forgotten that they exist (perhaps having replaced them with an angry God in the sky).

As a child, I could never understand why a good God had planted that tree and allowed the serpent to be in Paradise. I now understand that the "tree of the knowledge of good and evil" is a symbol for the fact that if we have free will, we must have the option to create our own world and forget about our origin. The serpent can be seen as a symbol for beings who have taken this process to the extreme and become completely self-centered and narcissistic, seeking to deceive and control the rest of us. Most people are innocently ignorant and behave like Gods without thinking we are Gods. Those in the serpentine consciousness believe they *are* Gods and that they can define how the universe *should* work.

Everything I have said previously, my long explanation about perception filters and subconscious programs, actually leads up to explaining why we find ourselves in our current predicament. Obviously (I hope), it also explains how we can get out of our current situation and what we can do about evil.

The human predicament one more time

What many mystics have come to realize as a result of mystical experiences is that humankind at large has been "cast out of Paradise" because we have fallen or sunk into a lower state of consciousness than where we started. Before this fall, we had contact with our spiritual teachers and we had an awareness that we all came from the same source and thus we are all connected. We knew that because we are part of a whole, what we do to others, we are also doing to ourselves. It is enlightened self-interest to work on raising the whole. In reality, we were not cast out by our spiritual teachers. We used our free will to lower our consciousness to where we can no longer perceive our spiritual teachers, our true natures or our common origin.

After we descended into separation, we have now become blinded by an illusion that has made us forget who we are, where we came from and that we are all connected. Some of this illusion we have created through our own choices, but some of it we have taken on because we have been misled and manipulated by beings who have taken the self-centered state of consciousness to the extreme. These serpents have created numerous illusions (religions, political theories, philosophies and what not) that all claim to define how the universe really works. They also define it as an epic cause to get all people to follow one worldview and eradicate all conflicting views. And this is all done partly to give these narcissistic beings a sense of power but also to get people to misqualify energy that can be stolen by the narcissistic beings and by the entities in the emotional, mental and identity realms.

Once we are trapped in this situation, our collectively created illusion becomes self-reinforcing and causes most people to live lifetime after lifetime in this state of blindness from which there seems to be no way out. Yet there *is* a way out, and it is what mystics have discovered throughout the ages. The way out is defined by a spiritual law that defines the parameters for free will.

This law says that once a planet has been turned over to a group of beings, they have the free will to create their own situation. If they choose to go into separation, the ascended masters must stand by and allow people to do this. They are not allowed to interfere—until we ask for help. Why have we seen a raising in the collective consciousness? Because over time, some people have been asking for help, and the law says that when the student is ready, the teacher must appear. In other words, when a human being on earth asks for a way out of its current state of consciousness, our spiritual teachers must present us with something that can help us walk the path beyond separation.

But wait a minute, now. Throughout the ages, numerous people have been in great suffering and they have prayed to a variety of Gods without receiving any help to relieve their suffering. The explanation is simple, although it will seem harsh to most people. Free will gives us the right to create any circumstances we want. We create through our consciousness. Once we have created a set of circumstances through our consciousness, it does no good to pray to some supernatural being to relieve us of our self-created consequences. Our spiritual teachers are not allowed to respond to such requests. They are allowed to respond only when we start taking responsibility for ourselves and instead of asking for a way out of the unpleasant consequences, we ask for a way out of our present state of consciousness.

As I have said, planet earth is an educational institution. We learn in two ways. One is the School of Hard Knocks in which we learn by seeing matter outpicture the images we hold in our minds, individually and collectively. The other way is the spiritual path, the School of Inner Direction, in which we receive help from our spiritual teachers to raise our consciousness and escape our perception filters and subconscious programs. These teachers are allowed to help us in two ways. One is to give us teachings that help us increase our understanding. The other is that we can invoke their spiritual energy to transform the energies that have accumulated in our emotional, mental and identity bodies. Once we have used these methods to raise our consciousness, we can also receive direct inner directions from our teachers.

In a sense, we could say that we human beings are caught between the narcissistic beings, the serpents, who want to keep us trapped in the illusion of separation and our spiritual teachers who want to set us free. Why have we never heard of such spiritual teachers or ascended masters and why do both Christianity and Materialism (and many other thought systems) deny or ridicule the idea that they exist? Because the serpents will do anything to keep us trapped in illusion, and they have done everything they could to make us deny the very teachers who could help us get out.

What we can really do about evil

Here is a short summary of what we can do about evil:

- Raise our consciousness on an individual level and thereby pull up on the whole. This can be done by using many forms of ideas, such as traditional psychology, ideas about personal growth but also spiritual teachings, many of which are inspired by or directly released by our spiritual teachers.

• Invoke spiritual energy from the ascended masters so we can transform the fear-based energies in our personal energy fields. There are many techniques for doing this, including some released directly by the masters.

Once we have pulled ourselves somewhat free from the pull of the collective consciousness, we have options for working directly on the collective:

• We can help raise awareness of the dynamic that is happening on the planet where a small elite of narcissistic beings are seeking to deceive and manipulate the rest of us. This can be done through psychology or a study of history. Our spiritual teachers have also given many teachings to help us understand our situation.

• We can invoke the energy from our spiritual teachers that will directly transform the energy in the collective emotional, mental and identity bodies and thereby reduce the pull that the energetic beings have on people. This will make it easier for other people to free themselves from the collective illusion.

• On a personal level, we do not have the power (the energy) to remove the energetic beings in the collective energy field. The ascended masters do have the power to do this, but they don't have the authority to do so, as we who are in embodiment have the ultimate authority for what happens on earth. Yet by using specific techniques, we can give our spiritual teachers the authority to remove these energetic beings so the masters can use their power to help us raise the planet to a higher level.

• We can become conscious of what is happening on earth, and we can decide that a certain manifestation is no longer acceptable to us. It may seem insignificant that a few people do this, but because we are all connected, we can pull up on everyone else. Along with taking the steps described above, we can bring about a situation where a critical mass of people decide that a certain manifestation of evil is no longer acceptable to them. Again, how did we manifest democracies? Because a critical mass of people decided that the feudal society, where most people were slaves of a small power elite, was no longer acceptable to them.

I have experienced in my own life that this has tremendous power on the personal level. I have seen how a group of people have called forth spiritual energy that has had an effect at the collective level. Can I prove this beyond any doubt? No, and that is why I am saying it is a matter of feeling whether this appeals to you in your heart.

I have come to understand that most of the people who are spiritual have come into embodiment with a plan for what we wanted to do in this lifetime. Many of us have as part of this plan what we want to accomplish in terms of raising our consciousness but also what we want to accomplish in terms of raising the collective and freeing the planet from certain manifestations of evil. We each have our individual life plans, so it is a matter of you using your intuition to sense whether what I am presenting here could be part of your own life plan? Does it seem self-evident? Does it excite you? Does it make your heart burn within you?

21 | ARE WE ALL TRAPPED IN AN ILLUSION?

When I was young and had found my first spiritual teaching, I went through a transformation or a conversion that happens to a lot of spiritual people. I realized that as I was growing up, I had been trapped in an illusion, namely that there is no spiritual side to life and no way for me to know anything about it. I felt, as many spiritual people have felt, that I had now awakened from this illusion because I had found a teaching that to me proved that it is possible to know something about the spiritual side of life. I also felt that all of the atrocities and conflicts I had been so concerned about came from the fact that we, meaning humanity as a whole, didn't know about the spiritual side of life. I therefore, reasoned that if only all people could be awakened to a spiritual teaching, things would radically change. Of course, I also reasoned that if only people could be awakened to the spiritual teaching I had found, then this would change the world. Unfortunately, many other spiritual people had found other spiritual teachings and they thought it was *their* spiritual teaching that would save the world.

It took we about four decades to develop a higher understanding of what is really going on here on this planet. In a sense, my first realization was correct: It is indeed because we human beings are trapped in a state of illusion, a lower state of consciousness, that we have created so much misery and suffering. I just hadn't even started seeing what this state of consciousness was about. I thought it meant that people just had never heard of the spiritual side of life, and if only they were told, they would naturally accept it. Yeah, right!

The dualistic extremes

Another misunderstanding of mine was that I thought awakening from the state of illusion was a matter of gaining knowledge, of coming to a higher intellectual, rational understanding of how life really works. It took me over two decades to realize that no amount of intellectual understanding will free us from illusion. It requires a fundamental shift in consciousness, a shift in perspective. I know now that I cannot bring about this shift by giving an understanding, but I will still attempt to explain the basic dynamic that causes us to be in illusion. It has been my experience that it is helpful to start out with an intellectual understanding, which can then become the basis for an intuitive leap, and it is such a leap (or rather several) that can free us from illusion.

Let's begin with the observable fact that people have a hard time agreeing on a lot of things. As I said before, I was always very concerned about the fact that two people can be presented with the same information but they reach opposite conclusions. I felt it was very important for me to understand why this is so and I kept studying a variety of teachings in order to grasp what is behind this.

We can observe that there is a tendency for debates to become polarized. In other words, the debate becomes centered around two positions that are often defined in diametrical opposition to each other. This causes the formation of groupings of people who see themselves as being in opposition to each other, and this so often leads to violent conflict. Now, when I was young, I fully realized that once we resort to violence, we have crossed a boundary. At the time, I saw violence as being clearly unacceptable according to my inner sense of how human beings should behave. Yet despite knowing intuitively that violence is not acceptable, I was still convinced that there has to be something that is true and something that is false, something that is right and something that is wrong, something that is good and something that is evil. I suffered from a cognitive dissonance because I could not see that it is precisely the division into true and false, right and wrong, good and evil that causes most conflicts.

The consequence of this blindness was that I saw only one solution. In order for us to remove conflict, all other people had to be convinced that what I saw as true was really true, what I saw as right was really right and what I saw as good was really good. I could not see that my mindset was the same as all other people had taken throughout history. They were all convinced that *their* truth was the ultimate truth and therefore removing conflict required all other people to come to accept this one and only truth. In other words, I could not see that I was using the same mindset that had created conflict to try to remove conflict. And I could not see this despite the fact that I had read Einstein's famous saying that we cannot remove a problem with the same state of consciousness that created it. Today, I see that when we allow a debate to become polarized, we enter into a specific form of thinking that I like to call "black-and-white thinking." The reason being that we think an issue can be defined and debated based on only two nuances, namely one black, one white, one right, one wrong. This is a binary approach, like a computer that operates with signals that can be either on or off and nothing else (which is one reason computers can't think like humans, and some humans think like computers). Once we have done this, we lose all of the nuances that exist between black and white. It is like going back to the time when all televisions were black and white. We think life is so simple that it can be reduced to two options and we have to choose one over the other. This is incredibly simplistic because we can observe from history that everything that involves human beings is very complicated.

So why is this black-and-white thinking so appealing to some people? Because of their need for security. As I said, the world presents us with an overwhelming insecurity, and it is easy to reason that this is because everything is so complicated. If only we could reduce everything to a very simplistic view with only two options, one right and one wrong, then our problems would seem simpler to solve and we would feel more secure. How simple if all of our problems were caused by a clearly identifiable group of people so all we had to do was build some camps with gas chambers and eliminate those people. Or, as some people in the United States still think, if only we could ship all the black people back to Africa, then we white people wouldn't have any problems getting along with each other.

The value judgment

Where does black-and-white thinking start? Well, it actually starts with our physical senses and the brain processes tied to the senses. Let's go back to my example of our forefather who is sneaking through the jungle. He hears a sound and sees a movement, and in a split second he has to determine whether this means danger and what causes it. So our senses are designed to detect differences, such as the difference between a circle and a square. The brain processes that use the senses are designed to categorize differences and sort them into various categories in our subconscious databases.

When we look at only the senses and the brain processes, they are quite neutral, we might even say objective. Our eyes can detect the difference between a circle and a square, and the brain processes do not label a circle as good and a square as evil. However, this becomes more complicated when we deal with an animal we call a lion and which we, naturally, have labeled as dangerous. Or we might have experienced that some people can be dangerous and want to do us harm.

How easy it is for the subconscious part of our mind to attach a value judgment to the differentiation made by the senses and the brain. If we have a pool of fear-based energy in our emotional bodies, it is easy for us to label a lion as a bad animal. It is easy for our mental minds to reason that it would be better if lions were eradicated so we no longer need to live in fear of them. Likewise, if another group of people have caused us to build fear or anger in our emotional bodies, it is easy for us to label them as bad or evil people. In our mental minds, we may construct a theory that labels them as fundamentally bad and even justifies why they should be eradicated. In our identity bodies we might start seeing ourselves as being the enemies of these people and being in a fundamental, irreconcilable conflict with them.

The epic thinking

Once we have built a value judgment about another group of people, it is easy to take the next step. It is to construct a theory or worldview that contains an epic sense of importance. This has the following elements:

- The theory is not a theory but comes from an unquestionable authority. This might be the supreme God of the universe, historical necessity, a philosophy, scientific findings or a particular guru or prophet.

- The theory defines a goal that must be reached and steps to get there, including obstacles that must be overcome.

- There is always an epic importance to reaching this goal. There is a carrot if the goal is reached, an ideal state that will be manifest (Paradise on earth or a communist society). There is a stick if the goal is not reached, a calamity that will happen (all people going to hell, the eradication of the human race). Thus, it is of the utmost importance to reach the goal and prevent the negative outcome.

- This leads to an attitude that the ends can justify the means. Because the goal is so important and the opposite is so terrible, it is acceptable to force or kill other people. In fact, it might even be for their own good to kill them so their souls will not burn forever in a fiery hell. Or it may be best for the whole to kill one group so the entire human race is not polluted with their impure genes.

Here are some examples: The ancient Jews thought it was epically important for them to move into the land promised to them by their superior God, and thus it was acceptable to kill all men, women and children who already lived there. The Romans thought it was epically important to conquer the world and bring their superior civilization everywhere. The medieval Catholics thought it was epically important to maintain their stronghold over Europe and kill all Protestants. The Soviets thought it was epically important to spread communism around the world. George Bush thought it was epically important to bring freedom and democracy to the Axis of Evil. Obviously, the list is almost never-ending.

The overlooked irony of human history

We now come to the overlooked irony of our history. Let's go back to what I said about the story of the Garden of Eden. We have the concept that there is a "fruit of the knowledge of good and evil." This implies that before they ate the fruit, Adam and Eve had no knowledge of good and evil. And this implies that they were in a state of mind where they did not think in a polarized, black-and-white way where every issue had to be reduced to only two polarities and they had to choose one over the other. In other words, they could still see the nuances, the colors beyond black and white. They also saw themselves as one with each other and one with their source, meaning their spiritual teacher.

The fruit of the knowledge of good and evil is a symbol for the dualistic state of consciousness. We could say that when we are not in this state of mind, we do not think in terms of polarities because we have a wider frame of reference. This is because we have an intuitive connection to something (our higher selves or a spiritual teacher) that shows us the underlying oneness of all life. Therefore, we experience directly that what is good for us as individuals is what is good for the whole. There is no conflict between us because I would never do to you what I don't want you to do to me and vice versa.

Once we go into duality, we now start thinking dualistically, meaning everything must be reduced to black and white, true and false, good and evil. Yet how do we define what is right and wrong? We define this in relation to ourselves because now we see ourselves as separate individuals, not part of a larger whole. This gives rise to a form of selfishness that we did not have before. We see ourselves as separated from each other, so now it seems to me that I can do something to you that will not affect myself. We think we can do something good for ourselves by harming someone else, or do something good for the whole by harming one group.

So here comes the great irony. Before we fell into duality, we had a frame of reference that was beyond our own minds. We had direct contact with our spiritual teachers, and they did not show us what was right and wrong. They showed us what was based on oneness and what would help all of us grow (the individual and the whole growing together).

After we fell into duality, we no longer had this frame of reference based on oneness. We are now trapped in a certain perception filter that is based on separation. Yet we do not see this. In fact, we now define self-centered causes based on a frame of reference that is not beyond our own minds but that is defined entirely within our now separate minds. Yet again, we do not see that our frame of reference is self-centered and relative. We think it is absolute and objective because it is defined as an epic cause coming from the highest authority. In other words, we think what we are doing is justified by a higher authority (a frame of reference beyond ourselves), yet our actions are entirely self-centered and relative to our own narrow self-interest as separate beings. We could also say that before we fell into duality, we were in a state of mind that we experienced as Paradise because our own state of mind did not cause us to suffer. After we fell into duality, we experienced constant suffering, but we retained some sense or memory that there had to be something beyond suffering.

So in a sense all of the striving we have seen human beings engage in throughout history is an attempt to bring ourselves back to Paradise. The problem is that we are seeking to create Paradise on earth by using the very mindset that caused us to fall out of Paradise. We are trying to get back into a state of oneness by using the consciousness of separation. So many of the theories, ideologies and religions we have seen have been created from the consciousness of duality, and that is why they have defined the epic cause that requires the use of force against other people. How can this ever take us back to oneness? Nothing we do from separation will take us back to Paradise. Any attempt at forcing others can only reinforce separation and cause us to fall deeper into duality. The only way out is to transcend the consciousness of separation and duality.

Duality causes us to run away from oneness, and how can you ever arrive at a goal by running away from it?

Where do these epic theories and causes come from? In my view, they are deliberately defined by that small elite of narcissistic beings who are seeking to manipulate and control the rest of us. They are doing this in order to gain power and to steal energy. Considering how much conflict such epic causes have generated, it is clear to me that some very powerful collective entities have been created in the emotional, mental and identity bodies of the planet. This explains why people are so reluctant to question the epic causes. Their minds become influenced by these entities and people are easily overwhelmed by fear of questioning authority, as we saw with Catholics in the Middle Ages and Soviet citizens in the last century. Yet as the advent of democracy proves, we have indeed started to free ourselves from this downward pull and question the epic mindset that divides us so the serpents may conquer.

As I said, it took me several decades to realize this, but when I finally saw this in an intuitive flash, my entire perspective on life changed. I suddenly saw what is the real cause of conflict and how naive it had been that I was trying to remove conflict by getting everyone to agree with a perspective that I now saw as entirely relative and self-centered. I saw that human history has been a process where people have argued about ideas, but all of the ideas have been out of touch with the underlying reality that all life is one. They have all been relative ideas defined by camouflaged self-interest, relative to a single person or a group of people. In a way, this insight was incredibly liberating, but for several years it was also disheartening because how on earth could we possibly change the situation?

What can we do about the epic mindset?

When I first started grasping the dynamic of the dualistic consciousness, it was somewhat frustrating to me because I couldn't see what could be done about it. At the time, I still had a strong feeling that human suffering was wrong and should be avoided. I then started seeing that human suffering is a consequence of the duality consciousness that causes us to see ourselves as separate beings. I also saw that the more people become enveloped in the relativistic logic of duality, the more their minds are closed to the insights that could set them free. Duality taken to its extreme leads to fanaticism that completely closes people's minds. So I couldn't see what could be done.

For a time, I thought that maybe it would be possible to start a campaign to educate people about duality and its consequences, but I soon realized that this is a delicate task. After humanity became blinded by duality, we have created a number of collective entities that pull on people's minds in an attempt to keep them trapped. Thus, if I fought or opposed other people, I would only feed my energies to these entities and therefore reinforce the grip that duality has on this planet. So whether I joined the fanatics or opposed them, I would be part of the problem, not part of the solution.

If we are concerned about current conditions and would like to help improve them, what can we possibly do? Well, the first thing I realized was that I could raise my own consciousness and free myself from even the most subtle illusions of duality. I could also invoke spiritual light from our teachers in order to transform the fear-based energies that keep people trapped. I could call for the purification of my own consciousness, the consciousness of other people, even the collective consciousness. I could also call for our spiritual teachers to step in. I could authorize them to use their power to set people free from the mass entities and the lies of the serpents. I could also do whatever I could to make other people aware of duality and how it limits us.

All of these things were valid enough to do, and for over a decade, I spent countless hours making calls to our spiritual teachers. Yet I eventually realized that I had done this with the state of consciousness I had at the time, and I still had some fear and some elements of duality. Thus, I started seeing the need to step up to a higher approach. This took me many years to piece together, but I will present it here in an abbreviated form.

22 | THE REALITY SIMULATOR CALLED EARTH

I have said that earth is an educational institution. I would like to take this one step further by comparing earth to a reality simulator, like a flight simulator or a pair of virtual reality goggles. So this planet is designed as a device for simulating an environment that, when we are inside of it (seeing it through the goggles of our physical senses and outer minds) seems like a real world.

The purpose of the simulator is to put us in an environment that stimulates our long-term growth by giving us certain experiences. When we look at human beings, we can see that it is possible to have many different experiences in the reality simulator of earth. People find themselves in many different environments and they have many different experiences of life that all seem real to them.

If we step way back, we see that there are two basic types of experiences we can have. One is an *immersion* experience where we believe what our physical senses tell us, namely that we live in a real world made of solid matter. We also believe that this world sets some limitations for what we can do, we may even believe we are products of this world and that we are defined by the world. This is perfectly fine for us, as long as we are in the immersion phase. We are meant to immerse ourselves in life on earth and believe it is a real world because this gives us a certain type of experiences.

The second type of experiences we can have on earth is an *awakening* experience. When we have reincarnated many times on earth, we may eventually come to a point where we have had enough of the immersion experience and we start to wonder whether there is more to life than what we have experienced so far. This is when we gradually (over many lifetimes) start questioning our senses and outer mind, eventually beginning to doubt whether we live in a real world that defines us.

We can then start what I have called the spiritual path, which is basically an awakening process. We awaken to the reality that we are spiritual beings who are not defined or produced by the reality simulator. We originated in the spiritual realm and have simply entered the reality simulator in order to have the experiences it can give us. We also begin to see that we don't live in an objective world, but a world that responds to our state of consciousness. The simulator mirrors back to us, as seemingly physical conditions, what is in our consciousness. Thus, the only way to change our *external* circumstances is to change our *internal* circumstances. Eventually, we can complete the awakening process by going through the ascension process whereby we become ascended masters, having a permanent existence in the spiritual realm.

Selfishness is part of the design

As long as we are in the immersion phase, we will, due to the way the simulator simulates "matter," see ourselves as beings who are separated from our environment, other people and anything outside the simulator. We can then use the duality consciousness to reinforce this sense of separateness, causing us to become increasingly selfish and narcissistic. And while this has created immense amounts of suffering, it is simply one of the types of experiences we can have in the reality simulator of earth. The simulator is calibrated to give us these types of experiences if that is what we want. However, the consequence is that when we create an illusion in the emotional, mental and identity bodies, it becomes self-reinforcing. It blocks our contact with the teachers that are outside the simulator so we lose any frame of reference that there is something outside the simulator.

We do not start out our journey in the simulator at the lowest possible level. We start at a fairly neutral level where we see ourselves as separate beings, but we are not selfish. We can then go up from there and expand our sense of connection to other people, whereby we eventually regain our connection to our spiritual teachers. We can also go down from the starting point and go deeper into separateness and selfishness.

If we go up from the starting point, we receive help from our spiritual teachers to grow. If we go down, we cannot and will not listen to our spiritual teachers. We therefore enter the School of Hard Knocks, which means our environment (including other people) becomes our teacher. This means we will often have to have these types of experiences for a very long time, until we have had enough of them and start wondering if there is a better way. While we are going down, we deny that our own state of consciousness has created our external situation. When we come to a turning point and start going up, it is because we begin to take some responsibility for having created our own suffering. We become somewhat willing to change ourselves in order to improve our situation.

While we are going down, we need to build and uphold the illusion that we live in a real, unchangeable environment. This justifies why we act as selfish beings. In order to achieve this, we use the duality consciousness to create a worldview that is entirely self-centered and relative to our state of consciousness. This process is for most people helped along by the influence of a small group of beings who have taken the process to the extreme. These serpents or extreme narcissists have created the epic thought systems that pull people further into selfishness and justify what they are doing.

Again, there is nothing inherently wrong with this, as this is still the type of experiences the reality simulator is designed to facilitate. We can say that the reality simulator is like a sand box. We can build any kind of sand castle we want because it cannot hurt the sand. Neither can it hurt the permanent part of our beings, the one that descended from the spiritual realm.

Making peace with being on earth

These ideas helped me greatly. I had always been concerned with alleviating suffering. I now realized that suffering is a result of people's state of consciousness. I did not put other people in *their* state of consciousness, I only put myself in *my* state of consciousness. Thus, I am not responsible for other people's suffering and it is not my role on earth to remove other people's suffering. If they are not willing to change *their* state of consciousness, who am I to tell them that they should live their lives according to *my* state of consciousness? Why should I seek to get people to change the experience they want to have based on the experience I want them to have? Of course, this also means I don't need to let other people's suffering affect me negatively so I don't feel I can enjoy life on earth or be myself here. I can live and let suffer, something I found it difficult to do when I was younger. I realized through some difficult lessons (involving three ex-wives and many other people) that I cannot change another human being. If they are not willing to change their consciousness, nothing I say can change their minds. I then realized that I don't have to change *any* other human being, let alone *all* other human beings. Since childhood, I had always had the sense that there was a purpose for why I am on this planet, there was a mission I had to accomplish, some contribution I had to make. Yet I now started seeing that this didn't mean I was here to change all other people and remove all suffering. I realized that I am at a certain stage of the awakening process. I can help and inspire those who are at a lower stage of the process than myself. But I cannot help those who have not yet started the awakening process, and neither is it my mission to do so.

This helped me overcome the pressure and frustration that sprang from the feeling that I was here to do something positive but not being able to see how I could do so. I felt that if there was a person I could not help, it was because I was not capable enough to help that person, and I should attempt to change myself so I could help anyone. I now realized that I can help a certain amount of people who resonate with my level of consciousness and are open to me. So I can feel at peace with focusing on the people I *can* help and taking my attention away from the people I *cannot* help. I leave them to follow their own path, either finding someone else to help them or remaining in the School of Hard Knocks. This was an incredible relief for me, as it has been for other spiritual people I know.

How do we escape duality?

How do we even begin to escape duality? I found it very helpful to realize that I have been on this planet for a long time. Therefore, I might have some internal programs (spirits or selves, we could also call them) that I have reinforced over a long period of time. I cannot expect that they can be whisked away in a moment by some magical formula, spiritual teaching or technique. I need to approach the spiritual path as a life-long, gradual process.

In the beginning, this was very difficult for me because I am a result-oriented person. I came to see that the goal of the spiritual path is to reach a higher state of consciousness, and I wanted to reach it as quickly as possible. Thus, I became very eager to practice the techniques for invoking spiritual energy and often spent hours every day doing so. This was not an invalid approach for me. As I have explained, we live in a world with a very dense collective consciousness that is constantly pulling on our emotional, mental and identity bodies. It will take a determined and constant effort to clear our higher bodies from fear-based energy so the collective has less of a pull on us. I have seen spiritual people who gave up before they had freed themselves from this pull, and they were pulled right back into it. So we need to put in a very determined, unwavering effort to get beyond the downward pull of the collective mind. Yet once we have done so, we also need to realize that what took us to that stage will not take us further. It is like the Space shuttle that has stages. The first stage is a huge booster rocket that will take it to a certain altitude. Once there, the booster rocket has done its job, and it needs to be released. Attempting to keep it attached will only hinder the upward climb.

The next stage is to begin to contemplate perception and how everything is affected by the contents of our emotional, mental and identity bodies. This is where a spiritual teaching that talks about duality can be invaluable. Let's look at a simple example. Let us imagine that you and I are sitting across from each other and having a conversation. You are seeing *my* body from the outside, but you are not seeing *your own* body from the outside. I am seeing *your* body from the outside, but I am not seeing *myself* from the outside. We are each seeing a different image because we see the same situation from different vantage points, different perspectives.

Let's now reach back to everything I have said about perception and the reality simulator. There are people who say that the material world is not real and that the entire world is created by our consciousness. I do not see that as correct. We live in a world that was created by our spiritual teachers, the ascended masters. They created the world from their own consciousness. They defined the four octaves, namely the identity, mental, emotional and physical, meaning they generated energy that vibrated within four consecutive ranges or octaves. This energy is the basic building material of our world. They then superimposed certain thought matrices upon the base energy and this caused the energy to take on certain forms.

So there was an objective world before we were sent into it, but we are not seeing that world. We can come to see it, but only when we purify our four lower bodies from all energies and thought matrices that spring from duality and separation.

Then, we can see the world as it is. What do we see until then? Well, we can observe that there are many different people on this planet and that they have many different ways of looking at life. Yet most of them are convinced that *their* view is the only truth and that what *they* see is a real world. In other words, people have many different experiences but they all believe that their experience is real. How is this possible when they all live in the same world?

It is possible because we live in a reality simulator. The simulator itself is made from energy. As our four bodies interact with the energy waves sent at us by the simulator, we are not seeing the energy waves. The reason is that in our four bodies we have certain energies and thought matrices. As the energy waves from the simulator enter our four bodies, our internal energies create an interference pattern with the waves from the simulator. What we perceive is this interference pattern and not the pure waves from the simulator. The interference pattern is therefore highly influenced by the contents of our four bodies, but as long as we are unaware of this, we will be convinced that what we are perceiving is a real world. We think the interference pattern is the original world defined by the simulator.

Many years ago, I visited a science museum in Seattle in the United States. They had one of the first versions of virtual reality goggles. A child was wearing a pair of goggles and was walking around in an open space. A large computer monitor showed to the audience what the child was seeing from inside the goggles. We could see the underground tunnels through which he was moving and thus understand why he was turning when he did. Now imagine that you took two children and gave them each goggles. Yet the goggles displayed different images. As they talked about what they saw, they might very well end up in a big argument because they were each convinced that what they were seeing was real.

This is essentially what has happened on earth. We have seven billion people who are each interacting with the same energy patterns produced by our common simulator. Yet we each have an individual set of reality goggles that gives us a different perception. Some us belong to groups that have many common traits to their goggles so they see a somewhat similar vision. Yet others groups see an entirely different vision. Because we are all convinced that the interference patterns we see are the real world, how could we possibly avoid conflict and suffering?

So what do we do as spiritual people? Well, it essentially depends on whether you have had enough of the kind of experiences you have so far had in the reality simulator. If there is something you really want to experience on earth, you should do what it takes to have that experience. There are certain experiences I have wanted in this life, and I have pursued them until I have had enough of them.

If you have an inner resolution that you have had enough of the kind of experiences that the reality simulator of earth is currently offering, then you have two options. You can learn how to consciously change the experiences you are having inside the simulator (either in this lifetime or in a future lifetime). And you can learn how to permanently exit the simulator by making your ascension and becoming an ascended master.

Either way, the process is much the same. You need to recognize that the experience you have had so far in this lifetime is to a very large extent a product of the energies and thought matrices (the programs, entities and selves) you have in your emotional, mental and identity bodies. Some of these you have created yourself in this and many past lifetimes. Others you have taken over from your family, nation, race, ethnic group or from humanity as a whole.

There is only one way to change the experiences you are having inside the reality simulator, and it is to change the contents of your three higher bodies. There is only one way to exit the simulator, and it is to purify your three higher bodies of *all* matrices created through the duality consciousness so you can shed the illusion that this is a real world. You cannot exit the simulator as long as you think it is a real world. You can only exit the simulator by transcending the illusion of reality and coming to see it as just a simulator. And you can only do that by coming to see and question all of the elements in your three higher bodies that were created inside the simulator based on the illusion of separation that springs from duality.

How do you know whether you are ready to start this process? Zen Buddhists have a concept: "I clutch my ideas." In other words, you are seeking to hold on to your current ideas instead of being willing to question them. The most important quality that will bring you forward on the spiritual path is the willingness to question your ideas, including the ones that your subconscious mind (your programs and selves) tell you that you should not question.

This does not mean you have to do this all at once because we all need a certain sense of continuity. I have met a few people who had such violent experiences (such as a kundalini awakening) that they lost their sense of continuity, their "grip on reality." None of us can go through an instant awakening. We need time to adjust our sense of reality so we can still function in our daily lives. I have not (in this lifetime) been attracted to extremism because I have always sensed that in our time, the goal is to integrate spirituality with everyday life. So I have always wanted to be able to function in a somewhat normal life (many would argue with my definition of normal) while pursuing spiritual growth.

The thing is, many of us have already been pursuing spiritual growth in several past lifetimes, meaning we have the potential to make much faster progress in this lifetime. What I have so far presented in this book is definitely not something that all spiritual people are ready for, and I am in no way thinking that everybody should accept what I say here. Yet I know that many people are ready for what I present.

How do you know if you are one of them? Well, if you had not been willing to question the things I have brought up so far, you probably would not have read to this point. You would have come to an idea that you were not willing to question and something in your subconscious mind would have come up with an excuse for rejecting the book or at least that particular idea. If you were not ready to question your subconscious programming, that excuse would have seemed real to you and you would have stopped reading. So let's move on and question some of the thought matrices that many of us were brought up with in our sophisticated modern democracies.

23 | WHY CAN'T WE TALK ABOUT RELIGION?

In school, I learned that some societies had taboos, meaning that there were certain things people were not allowed to talk about, even certain words (such as the name of God or the devil) that people were not allowed to say. This was presented as a form of superstition, like thinking it was bad luck if a black cat crossed the street in front of you. The teacher made it sound like we no longer have taboos in our modern democracies because we have freedom of speech and are allowed to talk about everything. Well, in my experience, having the *political* freedom to talk about everything is not the same as having the *psychological* freedom to talk about everything. I think our modern democracies have a lot of taboos, and two of the most powerful ones are God and Jesus. However, there really isn't much point in talking about God and Jesus until we have talked about religion. After all, it is religion (including the religion of Materialism) that makes it so difficult to talk about God and Jesus.

As I said, I did not grow up in a religious environment and I did not have religion pushed upon me, at least not in a direct, personal way. Yet, religion still pervades our societies and the collective consciousness, even in a secular democracy like Denmark, so who can grow up without being influenced by religion in some way?

Despite my non-religious upbringing, I always had one particular issue with religion. Even as a young child, I had my mystical experiences, and they showed me that God, or the spiritual realm, is completely beyond all human opinions, beliefs, theories, doctrines and rules. As I grew older, it became clear to me that religious organizations were not beyond human idiosyncrasies and that they were often directly responsible for some very inhumane acts.

I was probably around 10 years old when I heard about the crusades, the witch hunts and the Inquisition, and it was clear to me that such acts were not sanctioned or encouraged by the transcendent God I experienced. It was a clear expression of human power plays. Now, one could say: "Well, but is that specific to religions? Don't we have many other man-made organizations that have power plays and that have precipitated inhumane acts?" Of course we have, but my problem with religion is that it does not present itself as just another human organization. Many religions present themselves as being created or sponsored by God, and they even claim they represent God to human beings, often that they are the only organization that represents God.

These claims are completely out of touch with my experience of God as a formless being who is beyond all human idiosyncrasies. This God does not favor one group of people over another and this God cannot be confined to a particular set of doctrines. Consequently, the transcendent God cannot be represented by only one organization and would never sanction that one religion killed all non-believers on his behalf. In other words, it was always clear to me that when one religion feels justified in killing other people, this was a completely man-made phenomenon and was never, *ever* sanctioned or initiated by God. God has no desire or need to have one group of people kill any other group of people. Such behavior is completely out of touch with the reality of God and it only demonstrates that the people doing it have never had a direct experience of the formless God. Instead, they worship a man-made idol, a false god, a collective spirit—which does need people to kill each other in order to steal their energy.

The central challenge of organizations

How do we explain that some religions have been able to persuade their followers to go to war against the followers of another religion and commit wholesale slaughter of men, women and children—as the Christian crusaders undeniably did towards Muslims and as Muslims did towards Christians?

Let's begin with a story I once heard. Saint Peter and the devil are walking down the street one day. They see a man on the other side of the street bend down and pick up something from the sidewalk. Saint Peter says to the devil: "Did you see that man, he just found the truth, now you have a problem, don't you?" The devil replies: "Oh, I'm not worried, I'll just ask him to organize it."

Obviously, it's a silly story because there is not just one truth that we can find, but to me it always made a point about what happens when we organize something. Even as a young child, I was aware that the most important thing for me was my individual existence, or my existence as a distinct individual. I saw that it was a great gift that I lived in a society based on the idea that I have rights as an individual. One of my democratic rights is the right to be different, the right to not follow the crowd and do, say or think as everyone else in my society. This was caused by the fact that in previous lifetimes, I had come to a certain understanding of the spiritual path so I knew that I needed to raise myself beyond the collective consciousness.

I was not very old when I started seeing that there is always a conflict between any organization and the individual. Now, don't get me wrong here. I was never a rebel or anti-social in any way. I didn't have a problem submitting to the rules of my parents or the rules in school or in society in general. I never rebelled against authority in an outer way, but I was always aware that I needed to make use of my freedom to think for myself and not follow group think. Therefore, I could always see that any organization does define a certain group think, and it forces it upon its members, often even seeking to force it upon non-members and society as a whole.

From the time I heard about the Inquisition, I knew intuitively that this was wrong (the only word I could use at the time). I knew that the transcendent God would not want a particular religion forced upon every human being on earth. As I grew up in the 1960s and 70s, a minority of Danes believed in socialism or communism. It became clear to me that these people wanted to force socialism upon Danish society with both parliamentary and non-parliamentary means. I intuitively sensed this was wrong and that there was something wrong with communism (even though I couldn't formulate what at that age).

To me, there is nothing inherently wrong with human beings organizing themselves into groups. Obviously, we can achieve more by working together than by working as separate individuals. Furthermore, seeking to cooperate can be a very efficient method for growing spiritually. Ideally, working together with others can be a means for us to escape the dualistic sense of separation and move towards oneness.

The problem is that the duality consciousness so often distorts the purpose of an organization, especially if it becomes large and starts having influence upon society. The organization then becomes taken over by people who are into power plays, and the organization now becomes a tool for furthering the power plays of some very self-centered and narcissistic people, what I have earlier called those in the serpentine consciousness.

To me, an organization is ideally meant to serve people. Once it is taken over by power plays, the organization now becomes a tool whereby a small elite can suppress and control a large number of people. I see this so obviously happening with the Catholic church and the Communist party after the Bolshevik revolution.

So the central challenge of any organization is to continue to serve the people and avoid being taken over by a small elite seeking to use the organization in its power plays. Does it serve a large number of people or does it serve a small elite who are using the organization to control a large number of people? *That* is the question.

Organizations and individuality

As a child, I also saw that organizations can have a hypnotic effect on their members, and it was very scary to me. This was very obvious to me concerning the medieval Inquisitors. Here is a person who spends the day torturing other people, and then at night he goes into the church, looks up at the crucified Jesus and he is sure that Jesus looks back with approval of what he has done in his name. Or you take the Nazi concentration camp guards who poured the Cyclone B pellets into the ventilation shafts of the gas chambers, feeling they were doing a good and necessary thing. So another challenge of organizations is to avoid creating a mindset that overpowers the individuality of its members. How can this be done unless we know about energy and that we can create these collective entities that can overpower individual minds?

It is clear to me that any organization will create a certain thought matrix. This is inevitable because an organization must be defined, and it is a thought matrix that defines it. Once an organization reaches a certain size, it will inevitably create a collective entity. This happens whenever a group of people focus their minds on something. Now, this isn't necessarily a negative. I don't believe that an organization will necessarily suppress the individuality of its members. Yet if an organization draws a clear boundary between its own members and non-members, this is a danger sign. If the organization is based on black-and-white thinking and defines an epic goal that must be reached and a scapegoat that must be forced or eradicated, then this is an even bigger danger sign. Such an organization will inevitably create a powerful collective entity, and it will inevitably overpower the individual minds of its members.

As just one example, consider the Catholic church, which claims to be the only organization on earth that can guarantee your entry into heaven. All obedient members are guaranteed to go to heaven, whereas all non-members are guaranteed to spend an eternity in hell. Can there be a more sharp boundary between members and non-members? The epic goal is that only by making all people members of the Catholic church, can God's goal of saving humankind be reached. During the crusades, it was said that killing Muslims was actually merciful because if they continued to live as Muslims, they were guaranteed to burn forever in hell. To me, it is obvious that during the past 1700 years, the Catholics who went to church every Sunday have been feeding their energy to the collective entity created by the Catholic church, and by now it has become quite strong. I experienced this directly when I visited the Vatican a few years ago. I remember entering Saint Peter's square and being struck by the architecture. Given that I have a degree as an architect, I know something about the purpose of architecture, and the Vatican is obviously designed to portray the Catholic church as powerful, even invincible. The effect is to crush the individuality of all who enter.

I also remember watching a documentary about the sexual abuse by Catholic priests and its first exposure in Boston in the United States. The program followed one man who had been abused by a priest and as a result had severe mental health issues. There was an interview with the man's parents, but despite the fact that their son had been abused, they did not dare to say anything about the Catholic church. Even when the diocese sold the church that the parents had been attending all of their lives in order to pay for the legal costs, these people remained members. Why? Because they were convinced that only by remaining members of the Catholic church would they go to heaven.

I have met many fundamentalist Christians in the United States who are mortally afraid to question any so-called literal interpretation of the Bible. As if any "interpretation" could ever be literal. If it is literal, it is not an interpretation, is it? Anyway, it is impossible to have a normal conversation with such people about anything related to religion, God or Jesus. Their minds are simply completely controlled by a collective entity that makes them mortally afraid to think for themselves.

The real problem with these collective entities is that once they reach a certain size, they want to survive and they want to grow. This means the survival and growth of the organization becomes a goal in itself. It becomes an end that can suddenly justify means that go against the organization's original purpose. I mean, what did Jesus come to accomplish? Well, if he really was sent by God, as Christianity claims, he came with a purpose that is beyond human power plays. We might even say he came to set us free from human power plays, from the human condition.

So if the Catholic church really represents Jesus, it should primarily be concerned with setting people free from human power plays. What sense does it make that the church has been an instrument for getting people to submit to human power plays? For almost a thousand years, the population of Europe lived in feudal societies where the majority of the population were the literal slaves of a small power elite. This society could not have emerged or survived for so long had it not been for the Catholic church that supported the power structure. My point being that instead of setting people free, the Catholic church became a powerful tool for enslaving people. I can only explain that by saying that the Catholic church created a collective entity, and when it became powerful enough, it took over the minds of the leaders of the church so that they turned the church into an end in itself.

The goal now changed fundamentally. The original goal that was beyond earth had now been replaced by a goal defined by the most narcissistic beings on earth. The goal was no longer to set people free but to perpetuate and expand the church as an organization. Or rather, it was to ensure the survival and growth of the collective entity that now controlled the church, preventing anyone from questioning the power structure. It simply clouded their minds with such fear that no one dared to cry out: "But the Pope has nothing on."

I am not against religion

Despite this, I am not actually against religion. I *was* against religion when I was younger, but I have now made peace with it. What helped me do this was the idea that earth is a reality simulator and that people are allowed to have any experience they want for as long as they want it. If the majority of people on earth want to have the experience of belonging to a religion that claims to be the only one and that claims it can guarantee their entry into heaven, who am I to say that they should not be allowed to have that experience? I was always against people being forced *into* a certain religion, so how could I allow myself to think people should be forced *out of* a certain religion?

Today, I see that the Catholic church could only have grown and could only have survived if it fulfilled the needs that certain people have. Obviously, those who are members of the church today have certain needs, and the church is still fulfilling them. One such need could be that many people are not ready to accept the ideas I have presented in this book. They are not ready to contemplate that it is our own state of consciousness that determines whether we will go to heaven or remain in our self-created hell on earth. They have a need to believe that being a member of an outer organization and following a set of outer rules is enough to secure their entry into heaven. And perhaps they need to live several lifetimes with this belief before they are ready to question it. Who am I to judge them or interfere with their growth process? Yet why should I let my own growth process be affected by *their* choices—or rather non-choices?

What I have come to is that I will not in any way allow any religion on earth to distort my personal, inner relationship to the God who is above and beyond anything on earth. I claim my right to think independently of any religion. I claim my right to strive for a direct, inner, mystical experience of the spiritual realm so I can free my mind from any thought matrix that springs from duality and separation. I claim my personal independence from any man-made, dualistic idea about God.

The original purpose of religion

I am obviously very critical of religion, but this doesn't mean I think that religion is necessarily problematic. I have already said that I think there is a group of spiritual beings who are assigned to help us overcome the illusion of separation and duality. Throughout history, these teachers have attempted to help us by giving us various spiritual teachings. For example, I see Jesus as a spiritual teacher who was working with the ascended masters to bring forth a teaching that was originally non-dualistic. Jesus demonstrated a path whereby we can raise our consciousness beyond duality.

I see religion in its original form as being a way for our spiritual teachers to help us raise our consciousness. The problem comes in because so few people have understood this, mainly because most people have been blinded by duality. That is why the serpentine beings have been able to distort most religions so that instead of serving to set us free from duality, religion has become a tool for keeping us trapped in duality, even for misqualifying energy that can be stolen by the serpentine beings and the collective entities.

So if religion is true to the purpose of freeing us from duality, I have no problem with religion. And since there are different groups of people, I have no problem with there being several religions. I think there can be several religions that are all valid, if they empower their members to raise their consciousness beyond duality. I also think that any religion that keeps people trapped in duality could be called a false religion, especially if it also keeps people in a struggle against those who belong to other religions.

I have come to see that there are certain beings who will use any human activity in their attempts to control us and steal our energy. I have met many Christians in the United States who believe there is a devil who is working against God's purposes. Yet they still believe the Bible is the pure word of God and that their church's literal interpretation is literally true. These people truly believe that their form of Christianity is pure and will protect them against the devil. To me, this is a rather naive belief, and none are more trapped by the devil than those who believe an earthly institution can protect them from the devil. The only escape from the devil is to raise our consciousness beyond duality so the prince of this world comes, and has nothing in us.

24 | WHY CAN'T WE TALK ABOUT JESUS?

The concept that Jesus represents is simply so loaded with all kinds of feelings and tension that it is virtually impossible to have a free, neutral and constructive conversation about Jesus. This is not only true about those who are openly Christians but also about many spiritual people.

Many spiritual people have in past lifetimes had enough of the hypocrisy and dogmatism of Christianity, and they have given up on this religion and often on all formal religion. I fully understand this sentiment, because until the age of 30 I largely ignored Jesus. I eventually came to see that this was not very constructive for me because there is a vast difference between Jesus as a spiritual teacher, an ascended master, and the religion that has hijacked him and everything he stands for. Since Jesus is an inescapable part of the spiritual or religious life on earth, as a spiritual seeker I need to make my peace with Jesus. So let's talk about Jesus.

After having lived in the United States and being exposed to fundamentalist Christianity, I can say that I am extremely grateful that my parents didn't push Christianity upon me. The worst case scenario I can imagine (in the modern world) would be to have had a father who was a fundamentalist Christian preacher who expected his son to follow in his footsteps and every Sunday scream "DJEEEEE-SUS" from the pulpit. It would not have been pretty.

Instead, I grew up in Denmark where Christianity isn't really pushed on anybody, and my parents certainly didn't push me at home. To the contrary, I would have liked it if I could have had a conversation with my parents (or anybody with a pulse) about certain topics, but that wasn't possible.

Even though Christianity wasn't pushed on me, it is nevertheless still there as a force in the collective consciousness. For almost two millennia Christians have created numerous powerful energetic beings in the collective consciousness, and they will seek to influence anybody, but especially people who are open to the spiritual side of life. These beings want us to come into the fold so they can milk us for our spiritual energy by getting us to misqualify it with the fear that permeates the official Christian churches.

So let me talk about some of the problems I have with the official Jesus.

Should I be afraid of Jesus?

If you accept the official image of Jesus, whether it comes from a Catholic or a fundamentalist church, you should either be afraid of Jesus or at least be afraid to talk about him and question official doctrines. I absolutely never could see anything scary about Jesus himself, although I obviously felt the projection of fear coming from the Christian religion. Yet when I read about Jesus' life and what he said (as fragmented of an account as we have in the official scriptures), I don't see him encouraging people to fear him—or God for that matter. I see him as a mystical teacher who encouraged people to go within (the kingdom of God is within you) and have mystical experiences. And if you have fear, it will block you from having a mystical experience.

I clearly see that the official Christian churches encouraged people to have fear, but I just cannot see it coming from Jesus. Neither did he encourage people to believe in the angry and judgmental God portrayed in the Old Testament. In fact, if you look at the image of God found in the Old Testament, it is incompatible with the image of God given by Jesus. Jesus' "Father" is not the angry God in the sky but a loving God who wants us to inherit his kingdom: "Fear not, little flock, for it is the Father's good pleasure to give you the kingdom."

Why is there so much fear in the Christian religion? Because people at the time responded to it, so it was an efficient way to control them. But the underlying reason is that Christianity has created a collective entity that wants to be fed. And since the entity was created out of fear, it can only absorb fear energy. Again, we have a worldwide organization whose main purpose has become to feed this entity that is not truly alive but not dead either.

The only son of God?

I might have been seven or eight years old when I heard the concept that Jesus is the only son of God. My instant reaction was: "But then where did *I* come from?" I didn't mean only myself, but if Jesus was a son of God, then it was obvious to me that all other human beings also had to be sons and daughters of God. It made no sense to me that God would have created only one son. It made no sense to me that God would create all of us as sinners, and then he would create one perfect son and send him down here so we could really see how imperfect we are compared to Jesus. This idea simply contradicted my inner experience and I never accepted it for a second. So what was Jesus? To me, Jesus started out as a human being. He had many embodiments on earth, and during those many lifetimes, he gradually raised his consciousness as we all have the potential to do. This caused him to raise his consciousness to a level where he was selected for a special mission, namely to bring forth a new spiritual teaching.

As many other spiritual people, I accept that there are certain ages or cycles in the evolution of history. They are commonly named by referring to the precession of the Equinoxes, a movement of the stars that has nothing to do with spiritual beliefs. It is an astronomical phenomenon that is independent of human beliefs. So the 2,000 years before the birth of Jesus was the Age of Aries. Jesus was born at the start of the next age, namely the Age of Pisces. This was part of a process initiated by our spiritual teachers, who wanted to bring forth a new spiritual teaching to replace the teachings that dominated many people on earth. As an example of this, the Old Testament contains the idea of "an eye for an eye" and Jesus told us to "turn the other cheek." It is clear to me that the Old Testament ethos was dualistic, whereas Jesus' ethos is non-dualistic.

So Jesus is a human being who had reached a higher level of consciousness than most people at his time. Yet the consciousness he had reached was not beyond what all of us have the potential to reach. Jesus was therefore primarily meant to serve as an example of the fact that we can all follow a systematic path to a higher state of consciousness. Now, at the time, the general public was not ready to follow this path in its purest form. That is why Jesus, as even evidenced in the scriptures, taught the multitudes through his parables and then expounded all things to his disciples. Jesus gave a general teaching for the broad population and to his disciples he gave a more advanced teaching about the spiritual path.

The plan was that both the general and the higher teaching would be kept alive by the Christian movement, so that in the following centuries more and more people would become ready to follow the inner path. This did not come to pass. In the first couple of centuries after Jesus' death, there were Christian sects who taught the inner path. But this was decisively suppressed when the Catholic church came to dominate Christianity. Thus, for 17 centuries, the inner path taught by Jesus has been largely lost. Yet it is my understanding that in today's age many more people are ready for this path. We are ready to see Jesus as an example to follow rather than as an exception. We are ready to give up the idea that Jesus was the *only* son of God and claim our true identity as sons and daughters of God.

Is Jesus the Saviour?

I have already said that earth is an educational institution or a reality simulator that is designed to give us an environment where we can experiment with free will. The purpose is that we raise our consciousness until we can follow in Jesus' footsteps and ascend from the cycle of birth and rebirth. So how on earth could God's purpose for earth be fulfilled if all we had to do was wait for Jesus to come back and save us?

As I described earlier, even as a child I had a sense that I am responsible for my own situation. I am an individual with free will, and I am responsible for the choices I make. I can make any choice I want, but I can also undo any choice I have made in the past. Yet it is up to me to undo my past choices and to do so consciously. I have to be willing to see the beam in my own eye, namely my unresolved subconscious programs, spirits or selves.

It would not in any way facilitate my growth towards a higher state of consciousness if Jesus came and saved me by doing all the work for me. Jesus came to show me that I too can escape the dualistic consciousness, so he can serve as an example. The dream of a savior is based on the lie that we can enter heaven without changing our state of consciousness. I never could believe that, as I always knew there are no selfish beings in the spiritual realm.

Why did Christianity elevate Jesus to be the Savior? Partly because of the Jewish misconception of a Messiah who would come and save them, and partly because of a human power play. As I said, the Catholic church was created by the Roman emperor Constantine, who saw it as a political instrument for controlling the people and keeping the Roman Empire united under his rule. There was a point where it hit me that the only real problem with the Catholic church is that it is generally presented as a religion. The reality is that it's a *political* instrument.

As I mentioned, the Jewish religion had made the Jews believe that their entry into heaven depended upon the outer religion and its priesthood. Jesus actually came to set us free from this dependency upon a religion on earth. Yet Constantine didn't want that, so he (and the willing clergy) turned Christianity into the same kind of religion that had Jesus killed. They changed the story of Jesus so he was portrayed as being so perfect from the beginning that he could not serve as an example. Instead of the independent inner path to a higher state of consciousness that Jesus taught, they changed the teaching so it seemed like Jesus was the Saviour and that we could not get to heaven without him. And since the Catholic church was the only true church that represented Jesus, that meant we could only get to heaven through the sacraments administered by the Catholic clergy. Christians were then in the same situation that the Jews were in when Jesus came to set them free. Truly, this is one of the saddest ironies of history.

Now, it is my understanding that there is a group of spiritual teachers, the ascended masters, who are assigned to oversee the growth of humankind. And these beings have various spiritual offices. Thus, Jesus has since his ascension been holding an office that is called the Planetary Saviour, meaning we all have to go through his office in order to ascend. So in this sense I can accept him as my savior, but not because he will do the work for me but because he will show me how to do the work for myself.

Has Jesus paid the price for our sins?

So what about the claim that it was Jesus' death on the cross – and the spilling of his blood – that paid for our sins? Again, since earth is an educational institution, how would it help my growth if Jesus paid for my sins and whisked them away? Besides, to me the spilling of blood is clearly dualistic. It implies that the sin of killing people can be paid for by another killing, that the sin of spilling blood can be paid for by spilling more blood. This never computed for me.

I do think that after Jesus ascended, he was allowed to take upon himself some of the sin, karma or misqualified energy we have in our four lower bodies. However, the purpose was not to free us from this permanently. The purpose was to free us from the heavy burden of this energy so we could more quickly raise our consciousness to the point where we could take back this energy from Jesus and transform it ourselves. Jesus did not free us permanently, but gave us a chance to grow more quickly.

I also don't see sin in the linear way it is normally portrayed. God has given us free will, so we really do not need to be forgiven by God or Jesus for what we have done with that free will. God is not the angry judge who is willfully keeping us out of heaven until our sins are paid for. Instead, sin is made up of two elements. One is the beliefs or subconscious programs we have created over many lifetimes on earth. Another is the fear-based energy that has accumulated in our four bodies over many lifetimes.

It is this burden that has a gravitational force that pulls us back to earth and prevents of from permanently ascending. So as soon we remove this burden (by transforming the energy and resolving our dualistic beliefs) there is nothing for gravity to pull on and we will naturally ascend. No one needs to pay for our sins, we simply need to clean up after ourselves.

It is not the choice of God or Jesus who will be saved or who will not be saved. It is the choices of each human being that determine whether that person will be pulled back towards earth or can rise to the spiritual realm.

The difference between Christ and Christianity

As I was growing up, I had a clear animosity towards Jesus. I intuitively knew how Jesus had been used to manipulate human beings and how his name had been used to justify so many inhumane acts. I clearly resented this, but the reason was that I was not able to see that there is a difference between Christianity and Christ. I could not see how the organization that claims to have a monopoly on Christ had distorted the message that Christ came to bring. I could not see that there is a vast and fundamental difference between the *official* Jesus and the *real* Jesus.

As I started realizing that there *is* a huge difference, I started gradually reevaluating my view of Jesus. I eventually came to see that Jesus is the most misunderstood and misrepresented spiritual teacher on earth. The Buddha was also a spiritual teacher, but his teachings have not been distorted or misrepresented to the same degree. I came to realize that Jesus came to set us free, but he has been misused to enslave us even more than we were before he came. However, this is obviously not *his* doing but the doing of a small elite of beings in the serpentine mindset. They took the non-dualistic example of Jesus and dis-interpreted it through the dualistic consciousness, thereby creating an organization that from its inception was dualistic in nature. And the Catholic church is still a dualistic organization 17 centuries later.

I came to see that all of my objections and resentment of Jesus were actually directed against the image of him presented by the official churches. I therefore gradually came to make my personal peace with Jesus as a spiritual teacher.

Has Jesus left us behind?

One thing I could not understand as a child was why Jesus had seemingly left us and has had nothing to say to us for 2,000 years. I had an intuitive sense that Jesus was a significant spiritual figure. I also sensed he was significant for me personally, and that is why I resented the official Jesus. Because I sensed I had a personal connection with Jesus, I could not simply leave behind the official Jesus. Yet neither could I have a personal relationship to that Jesus, so I felt stuck between a rock (and it wasn't the rock of Christ) and a hard spot. I couldn't ignore

Jesus but I couldn't relate to him either. I now see that Jesus never meant to leave us behind. It is the official religion that has cut or blocked out direct contact with Jesus. Why did they do this? Because they wanted to make us dependent upon the earthly institution, and if we had direct guidance from Jesus, we would not be obedient to the Catholic clergy.

Today, I see Jesus as one of the spiritual teachers assigned to assist humankind in our growth towards a higher state of consciousness. I see Jesus as one ascended master among many ascended masters. I also understand that in order to ascend, we have to fully and finally leave behind everything on earth. This means we have to leave behind the consciousness we have developed over our many lifetimes on earth. Therefore, I realize that Jesus as an ascended master is above and beyond any man-made image of him, even if it is based on what he did and said 2,000 years ago.

I have gone through a long process of freeing myself from my own and the official images of Jesus, and this has made it possible for me to develop a personal relationship with the Ascended Master Jesus. I have come to understand that I am one among 10,000 people who took a vow to support Jesus' mission 2,000 years ago. We took the vow to continue to embody during the Age of Pisces in order to help preserve and promote the true path taught by Jesus. Thus, we vowed to help Jesus fulfill his mission. We each have our individual role to play in this work, and for me it has meant to create a website and publish several books about the mystical teachings of Jesus. The important point is that we all have the potential to become the modern-day disciples of Jesus and work on developing a personal relationship with the Ascended Master Jesus. How I came to accept this is a long story that I will tell in one of the coming books in this series. In this book I want to focus on the relationship of spiritual people to our anti-spiritual societies, so let's look at how these societies deal with the topic of God.

25 | WHY CAN'T WE TALK ABOUT GOD?

Why can't we have a normal, peaceful conversation about God? Well, in a sense it is because God is the ultimate topic to talk about and because so many religions have claimed to have a monopoly on the truth about God. Since these many religions differ widely on how they define the ultimate truth about God, they obviously can't all be right. Yet since they all insist that they are right, there goes any chance of constructive dialogue.

Let me start with a simple question. We see that there are many religions, including the religion of Materialism, who claim they have the final, the absolute and the one and only truth about God and can define whether God exists and what form God has or has not. They have very different, often mutually exclusive, definitions of God, so they obviously can't all be right. But there is another possibility: What if none of them are right?

I have said that planet earth is a reality simulator that is designed to give us an immersion experience and an awakening experience. In order to have an immersion experience, we define a worldview that gives us a sense of reality, but we define this from the duality consciousness. This state of consciousness makes us see ourselves as separate beings, meaning we are separated from God. How likely is it that we can come up with a definition of God based on the consciousness of separation and that this definition is accurate? How likely is it that we can use the intellect, the rational mind to define God or define whether or not God exists? If God is the originator of everything, then God must be beyond duality. So what sense does it make that we try to define God while we are still in duality? Wouldn't it be more constructive to raise ourselves beyond duality and then see if that gave us a different perspective on God?

I am aware that these questions will seem reasonable only to people who have started to awaken from duality. People who are still in the immersive experience will be convinced that their dualistic definition of God is accurate because it isn't their definition. It comes from an infallible source. And in my experience there is nothing one can say to such people, which is why it was such a relief for me to realize that I don't have to say anything to these people. The School of Hard Knocks will in time teach them, and I can focus on working with people who have started to go into the awakening experience.

Arguments for or against God's existence

A number of years ago, I felt exited when I started reading Richard Dawkins' book, *The God Delusion*. I expected that a university professor would list all of the arguments for or against God's existence. I was rather disappointed since I found neither the traditional arguments nor any original thinking about the topic. But I did find these arguments in a book by Gary Cox, called *The God Confusion*. He describes the traditional ideas about God and the arguments for and against God's existence and he discusses the connection between evil and God. It was interesting to me that since the 1300s Catholic theologians had found it necessary to come up with arguments that supposedly proved God's existence. I had to wonder why, since at the time the Catholic church had the power to burn at the stake anyone who questioned God's existence? Nevertheless, Gary Cox describes the arguments from ancient to modern times and also talks about how to counteract the arguments for God's existence. Reading the book crystallized for me what I had sensed intuitively, namely that we can never resolve the question of God's existence through rational, intellectual arguments. I have already gone into great length about perception and how the intellect can argue for and against any topic without coming up with a final argument. What makes an argument seem final to a given person is the person's subconscious perception filter. This is why an argument that seems valid to one person can seem completely invalid to another. What can we do as spiritual people when it comes to the question of God's existence? Well, we can first of all realize that we are not in a high enough state of consciousness to experience a final truth. We can acknowledge that we have started the awakening phase, but we are not necessarily at the higher stages of it. Thus, our present level of consciousness may indeed block us from resolving the question of God's existence. Thus, it is more constructive to put the question on the shelf and focus our energy and attention on raising our consciousness. I personally did this for more than a decade before I started looking at the question again. Before I describe what I eventually realized, let me first deal with the fear of God. After all, so many people fear to even consider the question of God's existence that it is impossible to have a conversation with them about God.

Dealing with the fear of God

As I said, since my early childhood, I had the experience that there was a spiritual being with me. This experience was in sharp contract to the image of a remote, angry and judgmental God presented to me by the Christian religion. Even into my adult years, this caused a lot of confusion, and the confusion opened me up to some of the fear of God that the Christian religion has foisted upon our societies.

I can think back and remember how I did feel a certain fear about questioning God or God's existence. I was afraid to question the official Christian image of God, even though it was in stark contrast to my experience of a loving, supporting Presence. I was afraid that the angry God would punish me for questioning him, and I felt that this God was always watching my every thought and feeling. It took me several decades to come to the point where I was willing to consider some of the questions I will present in the following. Where did this fear come from?

Today, it is obvious to me that the fear I felt was projected into my emotional body by the huge collective beast that the Christian religion has created since the year 325 when the Catholic church was formed. In Denmark this fear has some hold on people and it makes them very reluctant to even talk about God. In the United States, people often use the word "God," but most Christians I have met are mortally afraid of questioning church doctrines and the image of God portrayed by the church. They are afraid to question the image of an angry God because they think that if they do, that angry God will punish them by sending them to hell. Today I see this as the archetypal example of how taboos become a closed circle, a catch-22, from which there is no escape. The image of the angry God prevents people from questioning the image of an angry God, but what if the angry God isn't the real God? How will people ever find out if they don't question the image?

It took me a long time to get over this fear to the point where I could actually start questioning the Christian image of God. What helped me was partly my experience of being in the closet with the skeleton. I started seeing that if the angry God had the power to destroy me, he would probably already have done so. It was also very important that I realized the importance of invoking spiritual light from the ascended masters. I was not particularly doing this to overcome my fear of God, but by clearing out the fear-based energies in my emotional body, I eventually also cleared out the fear of God and I was able to start questioning the things I had previously been afraid to look at.

I have experienced that people who are in the immersion phase will be so burdened by their fear of God that they will not be able to consider anything I say here. But I also realize that such people are not likely to read this book. So let us look at the image of God based on the Old Testament where God is clearly defined as angry, judgmental and as residing in a remote heaven.

What helped me start questioning the Old Testament image of God was that I started seeing that Jesus gave a very different image of God. The Old Testament God is very conditional and seems determined to keep us outside his kingdom unless we fulfill all of his requirements. Jesus' God is a loving father figure who takes good pleasure in giving us his kingdom. I realized that if I want to be a modern-day disciple of Jesus, I should pay more attention to *his* image of God than the Old

Testament one. Obviously, Jesus had been willing to question the old image of God, so how could I claim to follow him if I was not willing to question that image? I also gradually gained a deeper understanding of free will, and this made me realize that God is not seeking to keep me outside his kingdom. God has given me free will so it is only my own choices that keep me outside by keeping me in the consciousness of separation. Once I free myself from the illusions (the subconscious programs or internal spirits) based on duality, I am free to enter God's kingdom. In fact, I will *be* in God's kingdom instead of thinking I am outside. So if the key to entering God's kingdom is to overcome illusions, I obviously also have to overcome all illusions about God. And how can I do that if I don't dare to look at the illusions I have about God?

I then started realizing that if we look beyond the image of infallibility projected by Christianity, the Old Testament originated in a specific historical situation. At that time, there were numerous tribes in the Middle East, and each of them had their own God. Then, one of these tribes started developing the idea that there was only one true God and that the gods of the other tribes were merely idols. Why did this tribe come to accept this idea? Because it gave them something, it fulfilled a need they had. And that need was obviously the need to feel that they were *special,* that they were *superior* to the other tribes (probably other tribes had the same need, but maybe it was stronger in the Jews?) As soon as they had accepted the idea that they had the superior God, this instantly made them special and they then accepted the idea that they were the chosen people of this superior God. In my observation, this dynamic followed the Jews throughout the Old Testament period and, after visiting Israel, I realized it is still haunting them today. It's not easy to believe you are God's chosen people.

Did we create God in our image?

Now, when I was younger, I was still so affected by the Christian projections that I thought: "Well, intuitively it feels right to me that there is only one God, so since the Jews believed this, perhaps they did have some contact with this one God? Perhaps the Old Testament God really is the one God?" I was gradually able to question this because I realized that it didn't really make sense that the superior God of the universe would be partial to any group on earth, let alone a small tribe in the Middle East who was so obviously willing to kill other tribes, even each other.

I still remember as a child having been with my parents to visit my uncle. It was a clear night, and as we were walking home, I for the first time truly noticed the Milky Way. My parents told me it was created by millions upon millions of stars like our own sun. As I looked up into this amazing spectacle, I had an experience of the incredible vastness of the universe.

This experience gave me a sense of just how incredible of a universe I live in, and I realized that a being who could create such a vast world had to have a form of consciousness that was completely and utterly above the consciousness we human beings have here on earth. I later learned in school that medieval Catholics believed the earth was a flat disc and that the sky was a dome extending over the disc. Right above that dome was heaven where the supreme God of the universe was looking down upon his most important creation, namely us here on earth. In other words, these people believed the earth was the center of the universe and that everything we do is very important to the supreme God of the universe, meaning *they* were the center of the universe. When I contrasted this with my experience of the vastness of the universe, I simply couldn't reconcile the two. It was obvious to me that the creator of the world was so far beyond anything on earth that it made no sense that he would be partial to a particular group of people, whether that was a small tribe in the Middle East or those belonging to the Christian religion.

Another thought was that according to the Bible, God has created everything, including all human beings. So why would this God create some people as being superior to others so they would be his chosen people? Why would God create some people in such an inferior state that they were almost guaranteed to go to hell? This simply didn't compute.

As I have explained earlier, when we go into immersion, we create a worldview that is based on the illusion that we are separate beings. Because of the uncertainty in the world, we have a need for security, and one way to fulfill this is to create a worldview that makes our group seem special. What better way to gain security than to define that you have the only true God and that you are his chosen people? So it became clear to me that our image of God is to some degree created by our own needs for security and that it springs from duality.

Yet I also gradually learned that there is a group of beings (both in embodiment and in the emotional, mental and identity realms) who have taken the duality consciousness to the extreme. They see themselves as being fundamentally superior to us human beings, and some of them even think they know better than God how the universe should function. These beings have an insatiable desire to prove themselves right, and in order to do this, they seek to control all people on earth.

It became clear to me that one of the most efficient means of control was the image of an angry and judgmental God from which we could hide nothing and who was ready to punish us with an eternity of suffering in a fiery hell. Of course, this idea was coupled with the claim that this superior God was not present here on earth and that we could obtain his mercy only through a religious organization defined and run by those in the serpentine consciousness. I realized that from 381 and up until the modern era (and for many people it is still true in the modern era) the Catholic church had almost absolute power over the people of Europe because they believed that blind obedience to the church was the only thing that could secure the mercy of the angry God and prevent them from going to hell. What an incredible hold that the serpentine beings had on people through the external institution of the church.

I eventually realized that there is a sentence in Genesis that says that God created man in his own image and after his own likeness. This made no sense to me because I could not see the creator of the universe having a human form. Yet I could see that we were originally created with a non-dualistic state of consciousness just as the creator must have a non-dualistic state of mind. So I realized that after we descended into duality, we created a God in our own image and after our own likeness, meaning we gave God the selfish qualities that we had acquired in duality. And that is why the Old testament God is a rather unpleasant being. He was created by the most narcissistic beings on earth and that is why he has all the characteristics of a narcissist.

I also realized something very simple. Why do we need an *image* of God? Well, because we have become separated from God. Before we fell into duality, we had a direct experience of a spiritual being, and thus we needed no image, no idol. Yet this understanding was merely intellectual, and what really gave me the courage to question the official image of God was a direct experience.

Resolving the question of God's existence

No question is ever settled through arguments. Any question will be settled through an experience that gives us a sense of reality. The question now becomes whether we have that experience through our perception filters or by going beyond those perception filters?

If we have it through our filters, then those filters are created in the material world. Since God is beyond the material world, no matter what kind of filters we have, they can never give us an accurate experience of God's existence. We might use our filters to create certain images of God, and we may experience a given image as real. Yet, how could any image of God created through the dualistic consciousness ever have any resemblance to the real God? It could only be an image, an idol.

Seeking an experience that is beyond our perception filters is what I call the mystical approach that many mystics have taken throughout the ages. A true mystic realizes the limitations of his or her present level of consciousness and that it distorts perception. Thus, the only way to get a more accurate perception is to reach beyond one's present level of consciousness, one's present perception filters. This can be done by gradually clearing our four lower bodies from fear-based energies and illusions. Yet as proven by countless mystics, it is possible to have an experience of momentarily stepping outside of one's perception filters and experiencing something that is outside of those filters. A mystical experience can take many forms, but once we have had one, we now have a frame of reference from outside our perception filter. A mystical experience is so real that one can never again fully believe that one's normal perception is fully real. Let me describe the mystical experience that forever changed my view of God, my relationship with

God. As I have described, I had many mystical experiences during my childhood and later. I experienced going out of my body and having an expanded sense of awareness. So the following experience was not entirely alien to me although it was still beyond anything I had experienced before.

The experience happened in a particular setting, but it isn't important to the story so I will not describe it. What I need to describe is the worldview I had developed. This view was that there is a spiritual realm beyond the material world (with its four levels). In the spiritual realm there are also gradations, going towards higher levels of vibration. On each level there are conscious beings, what I call ascended masters. There is a hierarchy of ascended masters that reaches from the level right above earth to the highest level, something called the Central Sun, which is presided over by two ascended masters, called Alpha and Omega.

Now, let me describe my experience. I was sitting in a large group and receiving a spiritual teaching about harmony. We were asked to visualize the highest representation of harmony that we could conceive. I had not really considered this before, but the thought came to me: "Oh, that must be Alpha and Omega in the Central Sun." In a split second, I was transported out of my body, and I found myself in a huge hall. It was round and had enormous white pillars around the perimeter. They were made of a white material that radiated light. Above the hall was a domed ceiling, but it was so translucent that it sometimes looked like clouds. On the floor was an amphitheater with semi-circular rows of seats, descending towards a stage. Suddenly, I found myself standing in front of the stage. On the platform were two white thrones, and on each sat a being. These beings did not have a human form. They appeared as clouds of white light, but in the center of them was a set of eyes so I could make eye-contact with them. Between the thrones was a cube of a white, translucent material. I then became aware that there was a flow of energy between the two beings, and it appeared as a horizontal figure-eight. My attention was drawn to the nexus of this figure-eight, which was above the white cube. As I focused on the nexus, it was as if an entirely different world opened up. It was as if I was seeing outside the world in which we live, the world of form. I did not see any-thing (any *thing*), but I had the sense of an infinite space, what many mystical teachings call a void. I then sensed that there was a being in the void, but it had no form that could ever be compared to anything on earth or that could be described in words. It was a conscious Presence, and I felt with a total realism that this was my Source, my Creator. I felt something coming to me from this Being, but it truly cannot be described with words. For years, I called it unconditional love, but even that is not a sufficient description. It had no form, it was inde-scribable, yet indescribably real.

I have no idea how long this experience lasted as time had lost all meaning. I next found myself sitting cross-legged on this white cube between the two beings that I saw as Alpha and Omega. After some time of experiencing their energy, my attention was drawn to the physical universe and I had the sense that I was seeing all of the millions of galaxies from above. My attention was drawn downwards towards a partic-ular galaxy, then a sun, then a planet and then I found myself back in my seat, feeling like my entire energy field and being was shaking. I had to leave the lecture hall and go sit under a tree for a long time before I could even consider facing other people and going back to a normal, human existence. It took me several years to begin to process the experience and adjust my view of God accordingly.

What's the point of describing this experience? Well, first of all, I am not the only one who has had this type of experience.

The ascended masters have a saying: "What one has done, all can do." We all have the potential to have mystical experiences of going beyond the perception filter in our four bodies.

A mystical experience gives us a direct experience that is beyond any intellectual, analytical argumentation. We have an experience that is clearly outside our normal perception filter and that feels real in an entirely different way than our normal perception. When we have had such an experience, we have a frame of reference that allows us to question whether our normal perception shows us reality or a distorted image. So to me, it is clear as crystal that a direct experience is the only way to truly resolve the question of God's existence. But we can go even further.

The real God is beyond form

What mystical experiences have shown to many people is that our normal perception is not ultimately real because it is defined by the forms we find in the material world. It is not that these forms do not have any reality, but they are not the ultimate reality. There is a deeper reality beyond all form, and it is that every form sprang from one, undivided source. Any form is defined, and what defines it is that it is different from any other form and different from nothingness or the formless void. A circle is different from a square and they are both different from formlessness. What my experience of God demonstrates to me is that there is a being who is the source of me and every other self-aware being. I am connected to this being because my self-awareness is an extension of the self-awareness of the creator. And all other self-aware beings are also extensions of the creator. Every mind is an extension of the One Mind. And this mind is everywhere present in its own creation. We are never separated from the mind of God. We may think and experience that we are separated, but this illusion is created entirely within our own minds.

Why have we created this illusion? Because we have come to accept an image of God as a being that has form. We have also come to accept an image of ourselves as beings who are defined by form. So the graven image of God and the graven image of ourselves as defined by form makes us experience ourselves as separated from our source. Yet this image is not created by God but is a creation of our own minds, the matrices we hold in our emotional, mental and identity bodies.

My experience made it clear to me that the angry and judgmental God is a graven image created from the duality consciousness. A mind separated from the formless God created an image of a God who has a particular form. That image has nothing to do with the real God but is entirely a creation of the separate mind. I therefore realized that any image that ascribes a particular form to God is a false image, an illusion, a mirage. The real God is formless or beyond form. Any attempt to confine the formless God to a particular form can only create an illusion that will imprison all those who believe in it. So does this mean I am saying that the angry, judgmental God of the Old testament does not exist? Well, not so fast.

Does the Old Testament God exist?

I found the spiritual path when I was 18 and as of this writing, I have been on that path for 44 years. Yet it took we over 40 years before I was ready to consider the following question: "Is the Old Testament God – Jehovah – the ultimate God or the ultimate idol?" Is Jehovah a real God or is he the most powerful false God created by humankind?

Based on the preceding discussions, I guess my answer is obvious. As I see it, the Jews back in Old Testament times started creating a collective entity based on their image of a highly selective God that favored themselves. This entity gradually grew, but didn't become that strong until the Catholic church was formed and more or less took over the Old Testament God. Since the year 381 millions upon millions of Catholics and other Christians have worshiped and feared this God, and it has consequently grown very strong, fed by all of the energy people have given to it. It is today one of the most powerful collective entities created by humankind.

So, in a sense Jehovah does exist as a conscious being, but it has only a temporary existence. It is fundamentally different from the formless God because the formless God exists on its own. The formless God has no need to be worshiped or feared by human beings because it doesn't need energy from our level. How could the God who created the entire universe need energy from us humans on this little speck of dust of a planet? Yet Jehovah obviously wants people to worship and fear him, which shows me that it is an entity created by human beings.

Does such an entity have certain powers? Well, it has a rudimentary level of consciousness and it has a large reservoir of energy. It can therefore project such energy into the three higher bodies of human beings and, for example, overpower their emotional body with fear or a sense of awe. In my view, many people have had genuine mystical experiences of something beyond the four levels of the material universe. However, a certain percentage of so-called mystical experiences happen when people go beyond their normal level of consciousness (focused on the physical world) and make contact with a collective entity in the emotional, mental and identity realms. Some entities, such as Jehovah, exist on all three levels, so they can project not only emotional energy but also thoughts and even a sense of identity into people's minds. Thus, there are people who have had what they thought was an experience of God, but it was the Jehovah entity they encountered.

Likewise, Christians have created a collective entity that presents itself as Jesus. I have met fundamentalist preachers in the United States who believe they have direct contact with Jesus, and I am not doubting that they have contact with *something*. But since their Jesus validates their black-and-white thinking and their dualistic mindset, I simply cannot see that as the Ascended Master Jesus who is beyond duality. For example, before the invasion of Iraq in 2003 the leader of one of the largest fundamentalist churches in the United States said publicly that God and Jesus had told him this was a just war. In my view, there is no way that the formless God or the Ascended Master Jesus would encourage one group of people to kill another group of people. Thus, this can only be the collective entities that have been created from the dualistic mindset and that are pretending to be the real God or the real Jesus. These entities will simply implode when people stop feeding them energy. When might that happen? Well, I'm not holding my breath. If I were to point out one thing that I think is the most ridiculous thing seen on this planet, it would be the fact that human institutions think they can use the duality consciousness to define God. Once one has experienced the formless God, it becomes obvious just how pointless this is. Of course, Christianity is not the only religion that has defined a false God. Islam clearly has also defined a dualistic God that wants to be worshiped by all people on earth. The Hindu religion has defined their own entities and even Buddhism has defined a false Buddha that apparently needs to be worshiped by people praying to huge golden statues in elaborately decorated temples, whereas the real Buddha sat under a tree. Many human institutions have thought they could define a God *into* existence or could define God *out of* existence. So let's take a quick look at atheism.

It was interesting to me when I read that atheism doesn't literally mean the denial of any form of spirituality or deity. Atheism is strictly speaking anti-theism and theism is a particular image of god, namely the one promoted in the Old Testament. Atheists often argue as if the only possible image of God is the theistic God, but that isn't the case, as a quick study of other religions will show. Of course, atheism has little to say about the God that I experienced, namely a God who has no form. You cannot really argue against a God who has no form. Of course, I cannot argue *for* a formless God either, which is why I am saying that God's existence cannot be determined through arguments but only through experience.

Why hasn't God proven he exists?

People often ask why God – if he does exist – hasn't given us an indisputable proof of his existence. The answer is free will. If God had given a proof that could not be doubted, then there was suddenly a range of experiences that people could not have on earth. They obviously couldn't have the experience of denying God's existence, but neither could they have the experience of defining their own God. And since most religious people on earth are still very attached to defining their own God, this would interfere with their right to have any experience possible in Reality Simulator Earth for as long as they want it. In other words, there must be plausible deniability and plausible plausibility. Another answer is the question: How could God possibly prove its existence in a way that could not be doubted? I have said that everything we perceive is distorted by our perception filter. The human intellect can argue for or against any issue without coming up with a final answer. In the duality consciousness people can create an illusion yet be absolutely convinced it is real. So what proof could be given that could not be doubted or rejected by some people?

In fact one might say that God has already given a pretty solid proof that there must be some form of conscious intent behind the creation of our incredibly complex universe. It has always seemed obvious to many spiritual people that a universe as complex as ours could not have come into being through a random process guided only by chance. Nor could the laws of nature have just appeared spontaneously from the primordial chaos of the Big Bang. We are spiritual because it seems real to us that there is some form of intelligence behind the design of the universe and thus our existence and lives have some form of purpose. It isn't all random nonsense.

Obviously, this isn't obvious to everyone, but it only took me 40 years to realize that this is exactly as it should be. Thus, it is not my responsibility to go out and try to convince everyone to accept a spiritual outlook on life. I can have my own experience in the reality simulator and let everyone else have the experience *they* want.

Atheism and defining God out of existence

There is an incredible spiritual pride in a human being or a religious institution that thinks it can define how God is and what God wants human beings to do. This pride is however rivaled by the intellectual arrogance of a human being who thinks he or she can define God (and any spiritual reality beyond the material universe) out of existence. This is outpictured in the phenomenon that The Wall Street Journal named "Militant

Atheism." I guess it got started in 2006 when Richard Dawkins published *The God Delusion,* which was then followed up by three other authors, namely Sam Harris, Christopher Hitchens and Daniel Dennett. The first three called themselves "the unholy Trinity" and the four of them called themselves "the four horsemen of the apocalypse." I watched some Youtube videos with them, and it seems they really think that because they have written their critical books, it is now only a matter of time before all religion collapses and we have a new atheist Utopia on earth. Obviously, several other authors (such as Nietzsche and Karl Marx) have thought the same thing about their own books in the past, yet religion hasn't gone away.

To me, the reason for this is the collective entities that religious people have created over millennia and that have such a powerful hold over people's minds that no intellectual argument could ever have an impact. Dawkins may think he has invalidated all intellectual arguments that religious people can come up with, but in my experience most people are not religious because of intellectual arguments, they are religious because of raw fear. No intellectual reasoning will even make an impact on this fear. The only factor that will gradually change the equation is a raising of the collective consciousness. Of course, Dawkins is a strict materialist and probably rejects the idea of a collective consciousness that exists independently of the brain.

After studying the phenomenon of this very aggressive form of Materialism, I had an intuitive insight into its cause. It hit me that the timing of militant atheism was somewhat curious. If we look at the modern democracies, most churches are losing members. Naturally, there are some strongholds, such as the Bible Belt in the United States, but overall our societies are becoming less and less influenced by Christianity. So why launch a campaign that is so aggressively directed towards Christianity? I know Richard Dawkins has stated that he reacted to the popularity of intelligent design and the teaching of this as an alternative to evolution in some public schools in the United States. But surely, this is a temporary phenomenon and not about to take over the world.

I then realized that the professed goal of counteracting Christian fundamentalism was just camouflage. I am not saying these four authors are consciously aware of this, but I see their efforts as directed towards scientists. The purpose is to literally scare scientists into remaining in the fold of strict Materialism. For this purpose, there is the creation of a scapegoat (Christianity) and a threat. What is being said between the lines to all scientists is: "Look, you have to stick with strict Materialism because the only alternative is that we go back to the superstition of intelligent design and other forms of Christian nonsense." In other words, Materialism is under threat and scientists have to remain loyal (pretty much the same arguments have been used by Christians to keep their followers loyal). It's Materialism or back to medieval Christianity, a classical example of black-and-white thinking.

Why would anyone want to communicate this message to scientists? I guess because Materialism really is under threat. But is it under threat from Christianity? To me, Materialism is under threat because science itself has made so many discoveries that point to the necessity for scientific inquiry to free itself from the philosophical and political shackles of Materialism.

I have already mentioned many of these discoveries, such as the fact that the universe is made from energy and that consciousness must be present at the quantum level. In fact, even in biology scientists are starting to raise serious questions about Darwin's theory of evolution. Richard Dawkins of course calls himself "Darwin's Rottweiler" and has vowed to defend evolution to his last breath. Yet this is not a strictly *scientific,* but a *political* position because if scientific evidence invalidates a theory, then any true scientist will discard the theory.

I realized that these authors are (probably without seeing this consciously) seeking to defend Materialism by holding back scientific research that points to the need to go beyond Materialism. They are very like the medieval Catholics who frantically attempted to defend the infallibility of Catholic doctrine when it had been proven that the earth is not flat and that it is not the center of the universe. They also did not want scientific research to invalidate their doctrines.

The center of this entire circus is really the issue of consciousness and the potential for developing human consciousness. I have said that there is a group of beings who are completely blinded by the duality consciousness, even to the degree that they think they know better than God how the universe should be working. These beings are attempting to enslave all human beings on earth, and they do this primarily by upholding the illusion that we are separate beings and that we are isolated on this planet.

One of the accusations often raised against spiritual people is that we are brainwashed cult members. What I have read about brainwashing is that the most important condition is that you isolate the subjects so they do not have a frame of reference from outside what the brainwashers are telling them. This is exactly the situation that has been created on earth.

We human beings have been told for millennia that we are isolated on this planet. We do not have access to any frame of reference from beyond what is being told to us by the authorities. These authorities take many forms, and many of them have obviously been religious authorities. I have already mentioned that for over a thousand years, the Catholic church was the instrument for keeping the population of Europe as slaves of a small elite of kings and feudal lords. Yet the Communist

Party was another such authority that also kept the population in the Soviet Union and China isolated from anything that challenged the party line. To me, the materialist establishment is just another such authority that attempts to keep our modern democracies stuck in the materialist paradigm and seeks to discredit any ideas that could provide an alternative to the materialist worldview. Just look at how many scientists find it impossible to conduct research that does not fit within the parameters defined by Materialism. In his book *The Science Delusion,* Rupert Sheldrake describes these restraints on research and he says that when many biologists are asked about Darwin, they say: "Oh, that's just the party line." It's clear to me that there is a rising tension in the scientific field with more and more scientists realizing the need to look beyond Materialism.

The control game of earth

To me, there is a group of beings (some in physical embodiment, some in the emotional, mental and identity realms) that for a long time have attempted to keep the broad population trapped under their power and control. For a long time, they achieved this through various religions, and the claim was always the same. There is a God, but he is remote. He resides so far above our level that ordinary human beings have no chance of communicating with him. Only the specially appointed prophets and clergy of the only true religion can communicate directly with God and bring his commands to the people. Thus, the people are the slaves of these authorities. The communist party claimed that there was a truth, a historical necessity, but ordinary humans could not know it. Only the prophets and clergy of the communist religion (Lenin and party leaders) could divine this historical will and give it to the people. In our modern democracies, Materialism has taken up this role. Again, we ordinary human beings cannot conduct scientific research or interpret the results. Only the prophets and clergy of Materialism can divine scientific truth and bring it to the people.

To me, the collective consciousness has now been raised to a level where we are very close to breaking through to a new era in human history. We are about to throw off the shackles imposed by a small elite who claim that only they have the power to tell us how to live our lives. How can we do this? Only by accepting that the human consciousness has the potential to reach beyond the collective and contact a frame of reference that is above and beyond all human power plays and all theories and doctrines defined through the illusion of duality and separation. After 44 years of studying spiritual teachings and seeking to raise my own consciousness, my experience is that we do have access to a frame of reference that is beyond duality and beyond the serpentine elite who wants to control us. That frame of reference is the ascended masters who have risen above all human power plays and only want to set us free by setting our minds free from duality. It is precisely these ascended masters who over the centuries have brought forth various ideas that have raised the collective consciousness to its present level. All it takes is that a critical mass of people realize the potential we all have for receiving teachings from a non-dualistic source instead of a dualistic power elite who wants to keep us as slaves.

The message I have attempted to get across in this book is that each and every one of us has the potential to raise our consciousness beyond duality so we can know a non-dualistic reality. I have done this myself, many other people have done it throughout history and what *one* has done, *all* can do. The ascended masters are always ready to help us go through this process individually. They will work with us individually, but most of us are not ready to do this. I certainly wasn't ready for a direct working relationship with the ascended masters for the first many years after I found the spiritual path. Thus, I needed to find teachings that had been given by the ascended masters through people who had been trained to receive messages directly from them.

The possibility that we can receive teachings directly from the ascended masters is the greatest potential we have for growing individually and thus also collectively. That is why the forces who want to keep us under their control will do everything possible to discredit this possibility and the people who serve as messengers for the ascended masters. However, this is something I will talk more about in a coming book, because it is beyond the topic of this book.

26 | WHAT KIND OF BEINGS ARE WE (PART 2)

I earlier said that we are psychological beings because our response to external circumstances depends on what is happening in our psyches. We can now go further with our considerations of what kind of beings we are.

Many people would say that what characterizes human beings is that we can think. Some have even called us thinking apes, which I obviously don't subscribe to. Of course we think, but we do much more than that because we have three layers of our psyches, namely the emotional the mental and the identity levels. Together, these three levels produce something that is beyond just thought, it is a total experience. Thus, we can say that we human beings are *experiential* beings. Part of the reason we are here on earth is to have certain experiences.

How do we have these experiences? Partly because we live in an external environment that is exposing us to a framework that we can react to. Partly because we create for ourselves a framework (a family, society or culture) that we can react to. However, what gives us an experience is not the external framework because our experience of being on earth takes place inside our four bodies. Our experience is therefore a combination of the impulses we receive from without and the reaction that these impulses create inside our emotional, mental and identity bodies. As I have said, that reaction, that energetic interference pattern, is in a fundamental way shaped by what is in our minds.

The theater of earth

We can compare this to a theater. We have a stage with sets and props, and this compares to the external environment we encounter on earth. Then, we have a number of roles that can be acted out on the stage. These roles are defined by what kind of play is being put on. Given what I have said about free will and how we can create collective entities, we can say that conditions in human society make up a play that we human beings have defined for ourselves over a long period of time. Within the overall framework there are many smaller plays enacted by local groups. But all together they make up the total number of roles that have so far been defined as possible for a human being to play.

Before we come into a given embodiment, we are choosing which role we want to play on the stage called earth. Some people are content to take on a predefined role and act it out for their entire lifetime. This is perfectly fine because these people obviously have not had enough of this kind of experience. They are not ready to define their own roles. Other people are ready to take on a role but, once they are in embodiment, go beyond the script. The first type of people are still in the immersion phase, and the second have started entering the awakening phase. There are thus two types of roles we can play in the theater of earth. One is that we are completely identified with our role and simply act it out without deviating too much from the script or the constraints imposed by the costume. The other is that we change the role, test its parameters or even transcend it and define a new role for ourselves. Some people are constantly pushing the boundaries for what kind of roles human beings can play. This is what most spiritual people do, and it is one of the reasons we are on this planet.

The immersion type of roles can be played only by people who still believe the theater is a real world. This causes people to identify themselves with the role they are playing. They think they are the type of being defined by the role and they never question this. This is because they never look beyond the impressions they get through their physical senses and they never think beyond the worldview that their role is based on.

All of the roles defined in the theater of earth are based on a particular worldview. None of these worldviews represent an absolute or final truth. They have nothing to say about the real world outside the theater because they are entirely defined by the people who are inside the theater and who have not experienced anything outside. They are defined to give people inside the theater a certain experience. What both religious people and materialists are doing is to take the roles they have defined and project that they have some universal validity because they can say something about what is outside the theater.

Religious people are like people watching Hamlet, and they are analyzing every little detail of the script because they think this can tell them what Shakespeare was like, thereby creating their own image of him. Materialists are like people watching Hamlet, and they are analyzing every little detail of what takes place on the stage, but their only purpose is to deny that Shakespeare ever existed. Of course, both groups do this because this is the kind of experience they need, and as I have said, plausible deniability and plausible plausibility means you can believe any role is real.

When we look at the roles that people are currently playing, some roles represent a very narrow, self-centered sense of awareness whereas other roles represent a broader sense of awareness. We can then set up a scale, and at the lowest level we have roles that allow people to act as if they are completely separate individuals who can do whatever they want without paying any attention to how their actions affect other people. This is the role of being a narcissist or psychopath without any sensitivity or empathy for others. At the other end of the scale, we have roles where people are fully aware that we are all connected and that the only way to raise ourselves is to raise the whole. Obviously, most of us are somewhere in between these two extremes.

This now makes it possible to say that the overall play defined for the theater of earth is one that gives us the choice to go in one of two directions. We can lower ourselves towards still more self-centered roles or we can raise ourselves towards less self-centered roles. In other words, life is offering us a path where we can walk in two directions. What determines whether a given person goes down, up or is standing still at a certain level? Well, we could say that it depends on the person's overall level of consciousness, even self-awareness.

What do I mean by this? Well, if the earth forms a theater in which we, over many lifetimes, have played various roles, we could say that after having played certain roles for a long time, a person might start having had enough of that experience. The person might then start wondering if a different, perhaps even a better, experience is possible. Obviously, we can all see that some people have easier lives with less suffering than others so we are aware that many types of experiences are possible. This can eventually lead a person to start observing how people play their roles and thereby develop some understanding of how the theater actually works. At the lower levels of awareness, people believe they are entirely defined by the role into which they have been born in this lifetime. As we go higher, we begin to realize that we can raise ourselves above the role we were born into. We can do something about our lives and we can even define our own role to a very large extent.

Although this represents a higher level of awareness of how the theater works, it does not necessarily represent progress towards a less self-centered level of consciousness. For example, Hitler was quite aware of how the theater works and that is why he was so good at manipulating other people into becoming supporting characters in his personal play. Yet he was obviously at the lowest level of consciousness possible on earth, meaning the most self-centered. As we go towards the lowest level, we can become quite powerful in defining our own roles. We can even seek to redefine the play itself by creating the epic dramas that say there is a goal that must be reached and a calamity that happens if it is not reached. Thus, this drama specifies that all those who oppose the epic goal must be eliminated. We can say that the theatre of earth has layers:

- First, we have the layer where we are completely identified with our role and think it defines who we are and what we can do.

- The next layer is where we begin to define our own roles in order to get whatever experience we want.

- The next layer is where we begin to realize that some roles are defined through the consciousness of separation and duality, and these kinds of roles always produce suffering because they put us in conflict with other people. Thus, we begin to see that although most roles currently defined on earth are defined based on separation and duality, we can actually transcend this and define a different kind of roles that are based on an awareness of the underlying oneness. This can give us experiences that do not lead to suffering.

• The final layer is when we begin to realize that all roles that could possibly be defined on earth are just roles, and it is possible to transcend these roles and permanently exit the theater. This is when we become open to the process of the ascension, which is our final exit from earth. How do we ascend? By coming to the full awareness of how the reality simulator works, namely that our *external* circumstances are a reflection of our *internal* circumstances. Thus, instead of seeking to control our environment, we aim for mastery over our own minds.

We can therefore say that all of the roles possible on earth, and the theater itself, has as the overall purpose to teach us how to master our own minds. Self-mastery is the very purpose for everything that we see on earth. Obviously, most of us first have to live many lifetimes learning what self-mastery *is not,* but we can all eventually realize what self-mastery *is.*

A brief history of earth

The ascended masters have given quite detailed teachings about how the earth was designed, and they explain how the planet started at a higher stage and how it ended up in its present condition. They also explain the different levels of consciousness we can have on earth. So let me summarize these teachings here.

The earth was designed by seven ascended masters, called the Elohim. It was designed in a pure state, meaning it did not have a collective consciousness. Or rather, it did have the four levels of the physical, emotional, mental and identity but there were no predefined roles or collective entities that could affect human beings. The first human beings who embodied on earth therefore started with a blank slate upon which they could write whatever roles they wanted. Among other things, this meant they did not have to struggle in order to provide what the physical body needs.

What was predefined for earth was a range of 144 levels of consciousness, from the lowest and most self-centered to the highest less self-centered. The first beings who embodied on earth did not start at the lowest level. They started at the 48th level, which is a third of the way up. This is a level where we see ourselves as individual beings and we are quite focused on ourselves and our own growth. But we are not in duality, meaning we are not using the polarized consciousness to create the epic dramas. In order to do this, we have to go below the 48th level, and we do this by using the duality consciousness to create new roles based on the illusion of separation. Below the 48th level, we define roles based on varying degrees of separation, meaning we begin to believe we are not connected and therefore can harm others without affecting ourselves.

When the first human beings took embodiment on earth, no one was below the 48th level. All people who embodied had contact with the ascended masters who were working with people to help them raise their consciousness from the 48th level and up. This is in symbolic form what is depicted in

Genesis and the story of the Garden of Eden. Going into separation was always an option because the earth was designed to allow people to outplay the lower potential for free will. The forbidden fruit in Genesis represents the duality consciousness, but it was not truly forbidden. There was however a warning given to these early actors in the theater because duality leads to separation from the teacher and it makes life a struggle. For a very long time, none of the early inhabitants of the earth went into duality. They made use of the spiritual path offered by the ascended masters and raised their consciousness from the 48th to the 144th level, whereupon they could ascend from earth to the spiritual realm and continue their growth there.

After a long period of time, there was a shift and some of the inhabitants of the earth did go into duality. This caused them to lose contact with the ascended masters, which is what Genesis depicts as Adam and Eve being cast out of Paradise. As mentioned, they were not forcefully cast out, but by entering the duality consciousness, they lowered their consciousness to a point where they could no longer perceive the ascended masters. Now, their self-created worldview became what I have called a self-validating, self-reinforcing illusion that trapped them almost completely in identifying themselves with the dualistic roles they had created. These dualistic roles led to the creation of collective entities that could overpower individuals and make it more difficult for people to rise above the predefined roles.

People had entered the School of Hard Knocks because they could no longer receive direction from a higher level and therefore had to be taught by the physical circumstances they created through their minds. They had no frame of reference form outside their own minds. This became a self-reinforcing illusion because the people no longer remembered that it was their own minds that created their external circumstances.

Their suffering was steadily increasing, but they did not see that they had created their suffering through their own minds.

Take note that the dualistic consciousness must always have two opposite polarities that cannot exist alone, such as God versus the devil, good versus evil or capitalism versus communism. There is an epic conflict between the two, and this leads to conflict between people. Conflict inevitably leads to suffering, and after most people went into duality, the collective consciousness was quickly lowered to the point where we had to struggle to provide for the needs of the physical body. Since we see ourselves as separated from nature, we cannot work with nature and receive what we need. We think we have to struggle against the planet and force it to give us what we need.

Over a long period of time, this caused humanity to create numerous collective entities and to define numerous roles based on duality and separation. This lowered the collective consciousness far below the level at which it was created. This eventually led to a situation where the earth was no longer fulfilling the role of raising people's consciousness. Hardly anyone was growing because people were stuck in their dualistic roles. This was not a condition that was unforeseen by the ascended masters. There are numerous planets in our universe with self-aware beings, and most of them are at a much higher level of spiritual evolution than earth. Thus, there is a wide experience base for helping planets that have become stuck in duality.

The particular conditions on earth had led to much suffering created by conflict between groups of people. This had led the inhabitants of earth to form a society in which they attempted to eradicate conflict by eradicating differences. It was believed that if society could force all people to accept certain ideas and live within certain parameters, then conflict could be avoided. This had led to a very uniform society with little external conflict, but it had not removed the internal conflict in people's psychology. It had made it very difficult for people to raise their consciousness above the 48th level because people were literally brainwashed to follow the norms of society. They could not develop the individuality that is needed to raise oneself above the mass consciousness and grow towards the 144th level.

Because such a condition is not unforeseen, there is a certain safety mechanism built into any reality simulator. It is that if the people on a planet create a society that becomes a closed system, then there is a force in nature that will cause that society to break down. This is illustrated by the second law of thermodynamics. The principle is that if ever one dictator managed to suppress all human beings on earth, his regime would begin to break down so the people would be set free.

The ascended masters realized that the only way to put earth back on an upward path was to break up the very uniform society that had been created. Instead of waiting for it to self-destruct, the masters allowed some beings to embody here who were not part of the original inhabitants. These people came from vastly different backgrounds. Some were extremely narcissistic beings who would break up the existing order in society by setting themselves up as dictatorial leaders. Some had a higher level of awareness than the people on earth because they came from more evolved planets. These "avatars" had volunteered to come to earth to help bring this planet forward. If this idea resonates with you, read my novel *My Lives with Lucifer, Satan, Hitler and Jesus,* as it goes into much more detail.

The result of allowing many different people to embody on earth is that the uniform societies have been dissolved. This has clearly led to more chaos and conflict. But it has also led to a steady raising of awareness, which has so far culminated in the modern democracies but is far from having reached its highest potential. There is much more growth that can happen, and the ascended masters have a plan for taking us much higher, thereby removing the lower manifestations created by the most narcissistic beings. As we continue to raise the collective consciousness, there will come a point where such beings are no longer allowed to embody on earth. Yet for this to happen, a critical mass of people need to raise themselves above the level of consciousness represented by people like Hitler, Mao and Stalin. We also need to decide that we will no longer allow this level of consciousness on earth.

How do we raise consciousness?

In summary, the earth is a schoolroom that offers us a path whereby we can raise our consciousness. We do this step by step until we reach the 144th level and can graduate from earth by becoming ascended masters. This now raises the question of how we go from one level of consciousness to the one above or below? Or we could also say: "What is it that can go up of down in consciousness?" The answer to that question determines our success in raising our consciousness, so let me describe the process I have gone through and the understanding I have come to.

The ascended masters have been working with humanity for all of known history (even for much longer), and they have done this by releasing ideas and teachings through individuals who were able to receive them. People who are below the 48th level cannot receive ideas from the ascended masters, but people above that level can receive some ideas. However, here is the crucial understanding about the relationship between ascended masters and embodied humans. The ascended masters are at a fundamentally higher level of consciousness than anyone on earth or in the emotional, mental and identity realm. In a sense, we could say that the ascended masters have the absolute truth about the universe. Yet even though the masters know the truth, they are not seeking to give it to human beings on earth. The reason being that earth is a dense planet with a low level of collective consciousness, so there is no way we can fathom the truth as long as we are in embodiment.

The ascended masters do not have the goal to give us the absolute truth. The idea that a religion, a political ideology or Materialism could define the absolute truth does not come from the ascended masters but from beings in the serpentine consciousness. The ascended masters are practical realists so they are looking at a particular group of people and they are seeking to give them ideas that could help them rise to the next level up. There is no way a person can jump from the 48th level of consciousness to the 144th in one giant leap. It can only happen one level at a time. So for people at the 48th level, the ascended masters are seeking to give teachings aimed at helping them go a few steps above that level.

As we raise our consciousness towards the 144th level, we can grasp a progressively more comprehensive teaching, and that is why the ascended masters have given what they call progressive revelation. The purpose is to reach as many people as possible, and because of the wide range from the 48th to the 144th level, no single teaching can reach all. This means that it is meaningless to talk about a spiritual teaching being higher or better than others. The most useful spiritual teaching for you right now is the one that can help you rise above your present level of consciousness. If you are at the 48th level, a teaching given for the 140th level will not be useful to you as you cannot grasp it. The point being that I am not trying to make it sound like the teaching I will give you here is better than other teachings based on a dualistic value judgment. It is simply a teaching that I have found helpful at my level of consciousness.

I first heard about ascended masters in 1984, so quite a long time ago. At that time, I was not ready for the teaching I can grasp now, so I needed a more straightforward version. You might have noticed that so far I have not really used the word "soul." The reason is that soul is a term that has been used by so many different religious and spiritual teachings that it doesn't have a clear definition. What one teaching calls the soul may be very different from what another teaching means with that word.

When I found my first ascended master teaching, it defined human beings as spiritual beings by saying that we were more than our physical bodies. We were actually souls that had taken embodiment in our present bodies. It was the soul that had descended from the spiritual realm and that embodied from lifetime to lifetime. The soul had made karma and it was this karma that prevented it from ascending back to the spiritual realm. We could balance our karma, partly by our actions and partly by invoking spiritual light. Once we had balanced our karma and overcome our egos (and fulfilled certain other requirements) the soul would ascend and become an ascended master.

For about 20 years this teaching worked well for me, and I am not trying to say it is wrong. However, I gradually came to suspect that there was more to understand about the process leading to the ascension. This started with an intuitive realization that the ascension is an absolutely final step. The teaching I had, made it seem a bit like an automatic process. Once you had balanced your karma, you would automatically pop up there. I realized that once we ascend, we will *never* come back to earth, we leave it behind forever, and this must relate to free will. We made a choice to descend to earth in order to have certain experiences, so there is no way we could permanently leave until we feel we have finished what we came here for. I saw that when we are ready to ascend, we are standing in front of a gate. If we step through it, we will enter the ascended realm. Yet before we can take that step, we have to look back towards earth and see if there is anything on earth that pulls us back here. If there is anything at all that we have not finished, we cannot make the choice to leave the earth behind forever. We have to go back into embodiment and finish what we have not yet resolved.

The next step was that I read about the life of the Buddha. The story is that when he was ready to enter Nirvana (the word used back then for a non-dualistic state of consciousness) he had one last initiation. While he was sitting under a tree, he was confronted with the "Demons of Mara," meaning the forces of this world. In the terminology I have used here, this is the collective entities created by humankind and the beings in the serpentine consciousness. These forces were attempting to make the Buddha react to them, and the only way for him to pass the initiation was that he had nothing in his four bodies that these forces could use to pull him into a reaction of any kind. This is what the Buddha called non-attachment, and I realized that in order to ascend, I had to be non-attached to anything on earth. Or as Jesus expressed the same teaching: "The prince of this world cometh and has nothing in me."

Over several years I deeply considered these concepts, and I started to see that in order to become completely non-attached to anything on earth, there could not be anything in my emotional, mental and identity bodies (no subconscious program or self) that I had developed in reaction to what I had experienced here on earth. As we are exposed to various outer circumstances, we create these internal spirits or selves in response to them. I was very fascinated by a statement made by Jesus: "No man can ascend back to heaven, save he that descended from heaven." I realized that I originally descended from the spiritual realm in a state of purity in which I had no reactionary patterns to anything on earth. I could only ascend back to the spiritual realm by returning to that purity, meaning I had to dissolve everything in my mind that was developed as a reaction to conditions on earth.

I started considering how I could possibly do this. Combined with he work I had done on my psychology through various kinds of therapy and self-observation, I started seeing that my reactionary patterns actually made up what most people call the soul. So I started questioning whether the general concept of the soul taught by most spiritual and religious teachings was adequate to describe what descended. But if the soul did not descend from the spiritual realm, then what did?

We created our souls and must uncreate them

I then received a teaching from the ascended masters that contained a for me revolutionary idea. It said that what descended from the spiritual realm was something that did not have any internal structure. It was difficult to relate this being to the normal concept of a soul because the soul clearly has an internal structure. That is why our souls can react to circumstances on earth. It is the internal structure of the soul (the subconscious programs and selves) that causes us to react and that determines our reaction. The idea is that there was a being that originally descended, but it can best be described as "pure awareness." The ascended masters called this being the Conscious You because it is what gives us self-awareness as a distinct individual. It makes us conscious that we are a "you."

As we descended into our first embodiment, this Conscious You started to create the soul by defining structures in the identity, mental and emotional bodies. In other words, the soul did not descend from the spiritual realm but was created by the Conscious You as its vehicle for interacting with the four levels of this world. In the beginning, the Conscious You created the soul based on its individuality, which is anchored in our higher selves. These selves reside in the spiritual realm and are too complex to descend into embodiment. So the higher self, what the ascended masters call the I AM Presence, sends the Conscious You into the material world in order to have experiences that help the higher self expand its awareness.

To me, this teaching was revolutionary because it suddenly gave me a new perspective on the mystical experiences I have had since childhood. I had experienced that "I" could step outside of my normal consciousness, my normal perception filter. "I" could directly experience something outside of what I normally saw as "me." I could never explain this, but now I saw an explanation. What I normally call "me" is my soul vehicle. I am normally seeing the world from inside this vehicle. Yet a part of me can obviously step outside my soul and experience the world without seeing through the soul vehicle. In a mystical experience, we do not see the world through the beliefs and value judgments we normally have. We see the world through something that I can best describe as neutral awareness. Some mystics talk about a "silent witness" that simply observes without judging. This was put into words with the concept of the Conscious You, which is pure awareness, meaning neutral awareness.

Why is all this important? Because I am not my soul. I am the Conscious You, which is a neutral spiritual being. My Conscious You is residing in my soul, just as my body can enter a car. My soul cannot by itself change who it is. The soul cannot change its reactionary patterns because it cannot step outside itself and thus cannot see that its reaction is not the only possible one. However, I (the Conscious You) can step outside my soul and see that a particular reactionary pattern is just one among many possible patterns. Thus, I can consciously choose to change my reactionary pattern. I can even become aware that I do not need any reactionary patterns because when I reclaim my neutral awareness, I do not need to react to anything on earth. If I was the soul, I simply would not be able to do this, as the soul is created to give me certain experiences, experiences that are a product of my reactionary patterns.

Obviously, I have created my soul vehicle in order to have certain experiences here on earth, and it is the structure and contents of my soul that determines (or creates) the experiences I am having. There is nothing wrong with this, but my soul can indeed become a closed system, a self-validating illusion.

How we raise our consciousness

If the way I see the world is created by the soul vehicle, how can I ever come to see that the way I currently experience the world is just one among many possible experiences? When I have had enough of having my current experience, how can I shift to a different experience when my current experience seems completely real and seems like the only possible one?

The answer is that my soul vehicle is currently at one of the 144 levels of consciousness possible on earth. It is at this level because it has a self (a sense of identity) that is based on a certain illusion (each of the 144 levels has its particular illusion). To the self, this illusion seems completely real and even as the only way to look at life on earth. The self simply cannot shift because its self-reinforcing illusion will keep it at its current level. Yet I am not my soul or my self. I am the Conscious You, which has only entered my soul in its current form. This means I have the potential to step outside my current level of consciousness, my current sense of self, and have a mystical experience. What does such an experience demonstrate? It does not give me the absolute truth. It demonstrates that there is a reality beyond my current perception of reality, my current sense of self. And this means I can begin to question the "reality" of my current perception, opening up for a shift to a higher level of consciousness. In other words, the self is defined at a certain level of consciousness and cannot shift on its own. What can shift to a different level of consciousness is the Conscious You, but it can only do so when it realizes it is not my current sense of self.

It took me some time to integrate these ideas, and I had some resistance to accepting them. This is because at any one of the 144 levels of consciousness we have a certain self. This self is created like an individual entity, meaning it has a certain level of consciousness and wants to survive. The self at any level is based on a certain illusion and it will pull our minds into not questioning that illusion. The reason is that the self can sense that if we see through the illusion, the self will no longer receive our energy and it will die. As a result of its survival instinct, it will pull on our emotional, mental and identity bodies to stay within the parameters of that illusion. It will try to make us think that if we question the illusion of the self, *we* will die.

I then realized that Jesus had made some very profound statements that describe this process. He had said that if we seek to preserve our lives, we shall lose them, but if we are willing to give up our lives in order to follow Christ, we shall find eternal life. I had always thought these were somewhat enigmatic statements because I thought it related to the death of the physical body, meaning we had to be willing to die in order to follow Christ. With the concept of the Conscious You, they gained an entirely new meaning.

Our current sense of life is defined by the soul vehicle, or rather the current entity or self that we have. Since this self is defined here on earth, it is obviously a temporary form of life, it is a *mortal* self. If we seek to hold on to that sense of self, we cannot grow to a higher level of consciousness, and that means we are losing the point of life, we are in a sense losing the higher sense of self. Yet if we are willing to let our current self die, we can now "follow Christ." Christ is a symbol for the process of raising our consciousness towards the ascension, and it is only by gradually raising our consciousness until we are at the 144th level that we gain the eternal life in the spiritual realm. So rather than being the leader of a suicide cult, Jesus is actually describing the process towards the ascension.

There is of course more to say about this process than what I can give here, and it can be found in some of my other books. Yet if you can intuitively grasp (not just intellectually understand) the concept that there is a part of you that has no fixed sense of self, then it will be so much easier for you to make progress on the spiritual path. This can help you over-come the inner resistance that we all feel as we rise from one level to the next.

It can often feel as if part of us is going to die, and this has caused many spiritual seekers to stop their progress out of fear of losing part of their identity. What we lose is not part of our true identity, it is only part of the soul vehicle that we have cre-ated in order to have certain experiences on earth. If you have not had enough of the experience you are currently having, by all means hold on to the sense of self that gives you that experi-ence. But if you have had enough, then what you need to do is to let that self die. Of course, you cannot do this if you identify with the self and think this is who you are. But once you have experienced the pure awareness of the Conscious You, you know you are not the current self. So by letting one self die, *you* do not die, you simply rise to a higher sense of self. This self may still be limited, but you can continue to let selves die until you reach the 144th level and can let the final self die and ascend to a permanent sense of self as an ascended master. I can witness to the fact that once we have let certain selves die, we find an entirely new level of mental freedom and inner peace. The Conscious You can actually enjoy life on earth— when it is not perceiving life through a limited self.

I know this idea of a Conscious You can sound abstract, but I am fairly sure that since you have read to this point, you have already had some mystical experiences of stepping outside your normal awareness or sense of self. If not, here is a simple exercise.

So far, you have been reading this book and you have probably focused most of your attention on it. I am now asking you to mentally take a step back and become aware that you are sitting here, reading this book. You can even envision that you mentally step outside of your body and you are now standing behind your body, watching it sitting with the book. What part of you is able to step outside your body and become aware of what you are doing, looking at yourself from the outside? Well, that is the Conscious You. This part of you is normally focused inside your current sense of self, looking at the world through the perception filter of that self. Yet it has the potential to, at any moment, step outside your outer self and experience that there is a wider state of consciousness, a broader perspective, a non-judgmental, non-dualistic way of looking at the world. What pulls the Conscious You into your current sense of self is the beliefs and the energies in your emotional, mental and identity bodies. As you clear out these beliefs and energies (for example by using the techniques given by the ascended masters), you will find it much easier to step outside your current self and have a mystical experience. After 44 years of clearing my higher bodies, I can pretty much step outside my current sense of self by just becoming aware and making a decision to go into a neutral state of awareness. This is an invaluable perspective that prevents me from being fully identified with (attached to) my present situation.

To me, these ideas gave me a much more meaningful sense of what kind of being I really am. The teachings about coming to identify a certain self and letting it die have allowed me to make more progress on the spiritual path in two years than I had made in the preceding 42 years. I hope you will not have to wait 42 years until you can make use of these ideas.

27 | RE-PARENTING OURSELVES

I have talked a lot about my father and how his entire life was set on a course by his childhood, but obviously he is not the only one. I have met thousands of people who are affected by their childhoods for life, and one could argue that we all are. Some years ago as I was contemplating this, I suddenly had an intuitive breakthrough that gave me a different perspective on this for myself as a spiritual person.

I realized that I had grown up in a society that doesn't give its citizens even a basic understanding of human psychology and how we can take command over our psyches instead of beings passive victims of them. This means that each generation had received no help to deal with their psychology, so what could they do but live their lives with their psychological limitations and thereby pass them on to their children? Meaning we live in a society that for generations has passed the same psychological issues on from generation to generation. The sins of the fathers are visited upon the next generation.

I recognized that this was not an ideal situation. I also recognized that saying it was not ideal didn't really get me anywhere. It doesn't actually help me to blame my great-grandparents, my grandparents and my own parents for the fact that they had psychological limitations that ended up affecting me. My society was the way it was, and my childhood was the way it was. The empowering question wasn't really how things *should have been* but what *I can do* about things the way they are, so they affect me as little as possible.

I then recognized that I am a spiritual person. I accept reincarnation so this is by no means my first lifetime on earth. Even though my parents had certain psychological limitations, my present psychology is not primarily affected by them, but by my entire history.

I also recognized that as a spiritual person, my life is not determined by fate or chance. Before I came into embodiment, I met with my spiritual teachers and developed a plan for this lifetime. We can call it a life plan or a Divine plan. This plan involves many facets, but it sets certain goals for this lifetime that are independent of my childhood. In other words, I can't let the specifics of my childhood stand in the way of me fulfilling those goals.

Finally, I recognized that I do not live on an ideal planet. Earth is a planet characterized by a lot of chaos and conflict. In practical terms, this means that it is not easy to find a set of ideal circumstances into which one can be born. There is a limited number of children being born, meaning there is a limited number of opportunities for taking embodiment. I didn't have unlimited options for where I could be born so at some point I had to make a practical-realist decision and just get into a physical body and take it from there.

My conclusion was that as a spiritual person, I need to shift my attitude so that I do not let the specifics of my childhood stand in the way of the goals I defined in my life plan. In practical terms, this means that I recognize that even if I did not have an ideal childhood, I do not have to be affected by it forever. If my childhood can affect my psyche, it means my psyche is pliable, changeable. So I can then change it back, or rather heal my wounds, so I can get back to a neutral starting point. To say it another way, I accepted that as an adult, it is my responsibility to re-parent myself so my childhood will not prevent the fulfillment of my life plan.

Obviously, it took some time to integrate these realizations, but it caused me to go into a phase where I actively pursued psychological healing instead of hoping it would one day happen automatically as a result of me doing spiritual exercises. This is a syndrome I have seen in several spiritual movements. Each movement has a basic outlook on life and it usually also has a spiritual practice. My first movement promoted meditation, my second one promoted invoking spiritual light through a form of high-speed chanting, called decreeing. In both movements, I saw the same tendency for people to think that if only they faithfully did the spiritual practice, then one day their psychological issues would magically dissolve and they would have reached a higher state of consciousness without having looked at the beam in their own eye, meaning their own psyches. I see this as a non-constructive belief, even a dangerous illusion. As I said, we can create limiting beliefs without being consciously aware of it, but we cannot overcome them without looking at them and consciously changing them.

I even came to a point where I realized that I had used my spiritual practice as an excuse for not looking at my own psychology. I had thought that decreeing to improve world conditions was such an important goal that it took precedence over working on my psychology. I have seen numerous examples of how clever our egos are in coming up with excuses for why we do not have to look into our subconscious minds (and thereby expose the ego).

Healing my childhood wounds

I have said that I had an easy childhood compared to many people I have met on the spiritual path. So I don't want to imply that what I went through will be sufficient for everyone. If you have been exposed to abuse or severe trauma, it might require more healing work than what I did.

In 1990 I did some work with a concept called the "inner child." The basic idea is that if we have experienced difficult situations or even situations where our expectations were not met, we can have an entity or self in our subconscious minds that is still looking at and reacting to situations the way we did when we were children. In other words, we are normally reacting as adults, but in certain situations, this inner child is triggered, and we now react to that situation the same way we did when we were, say, five years old. Once the situation has passed, we revert back to our adult selves as if nothing had happened.

In order to avoid walking through adulthood with the reactionary patterns we built in early childhood, we need to become conscious of these inner children and use various techniques to basically re-parent the inner children and dissolve them. The mechanism is in my view quite similar to what I have talked about, namely that we create these psychological entities or selves and carry them with us.

I found the concept and the exercises helpful to resolve certain things, but after a while I realized that I needed some additional work. I then found a certified psychotherapist who also had a spiritual outlook on life, which I realize is not that easy to find. But I think it can also be helpful to work with therapists who are not themselves spiritual, as long as they are not antagonistic to your spiritual outlook. I did weekly sessions with her for about six months, and we did talk therapy and a new technique called EMDR (Eye Movement Desensitizing and Reprocessing).

We also did gestalt therapy, and it was especially helpful for me to do a couple of sessions where I was talking to my father and letting him respond. Obviously, he wasn't there (he was dead by that time), but the idea of gestalt therapy is that you have two chairs facing each other. First, I sat in one chair and imagined my father was sitting in the other. I then told him some of the things I had never told him, especially about how he affected me. I then switched to the other chair and I was now supposed to be my father responding to what I had said. It sounds a bit out there, but I found it very helpful, especially because it allowed me to experience that my father was simply a human being like myself. I directly experienced that every-thing he did was simply the result of his psychological wounds, meaning he had not done it deliberately in order to hurt me. This helped me forgive him and let go of any sense of hurt.

In the following years I also did some hypnotherapy, which is not actually that you are hypnotized. You go through a guided meditation for connecting to and processing difficult situations from your past. As I look back, I feel that it took me a couple of years to get to a point where I was not dragging my childhood baggage after me with every step I took. Obviously, with a more difficult childhood, it might have taken longer.

This did not mean that I had resolved all of my psycholog-ical issues. The fact that I had now resolved my major issues from this lifetime only meant that I was now freed up to start working on the issues I was dragging with me from previous lifetimes. And this is a process that is ongoing to this day. I have come to realize that I have had many lifetimes on this planet, and I think this is the case for most people who are open to a spiritual outlook on life. A couple of decades ago, I was very impatient with myself, always waiting for the big breakthrough so that I would be "home free" and completely over my psychological issues. I wanted to be enlightened in five minutes—well, perhaps I could settle for five years, but I was often thinking: "I have resolved so many issues in my psychology, how much can still be left?"

Today, I look at it entirely differently. I have indeed had some big breakthroughs and I feel I am much more at peace with myself and with life on this very difficult planet. But I now see that I will be working on psychological issues as long as I am in embodiment, because there are illusions to overcome until we reach the 144th level of consciousness and are finally ready to ascend. Accepting this was a big breakthrough because now I no longer need to feel hat I am always behind. Instead, I have accepted that earth is a difficult planet and that we will be working to overcome one illusion at a time, until we rise to that 144th level of consciousness. The reason is that if we did not have any illusions left, we simply could not hold on to a physical body but would leave the body and ascend right there.

Since most of us have things in our life plans that we want to experience and accomplish on earth, we are not ready to leave until we have either done what we came here for or given up on doing what we came here for. But this is a subtle topic that I will talk more about in the next book. For now, I want to assure you that if you can overcome your childhood issues, you will feel a new degree of inner peace and freedom. Whatever work it takes for you personally, it will be well worth it.

28 | WHY SPIRITUAL PEOPLE ARE ON EARTH

For me, the concept of the 144 levels of consciousness has given me a perspective on life on earth that has been invaluable on many different levels. First of all, it has given me a new perspective on my personal life. As I have described, I always had a longing to find a deeper sense of meaning and a deeper knowledge. I now see that this is something we develop when we reach a certain level among the 144 levels, meaning self-actualization becomes the main focus of our lives. People below that level simply do not have this longing, they are not seekers—and they don't have to be.

During my youth I very much felt like an outsider. I felt a tension between my seeking a deeper understanding and the fact that most people around me did not have that longing. I felt a projection that because I was different, this was somehow wrong or unacceptable. I even experienced from my family and society how they saw me as a threat because I was different.

There was obviously an entity in the collective consciousness that wanted me to surrender to it and be like everyone else.

I have now made peace with this experience. I realize that I had reached a certain level of consciousness in my last life-time and that is why I was born as a spiritual seeker. Most of the people I met during my childhood had not reached that level. Some of them did not have the longing I have, but they were not threatened by me. Others were at lower levels of consciousness where they were more identified with their roles so they felt threatened by me being different.

I now see this as a perfectly natural consequence of the fact that we have made different choices in past lives and therefore are at different levels of consciousness. I realize there is nothing wrong with people being at different levels of consciousness. Nor is there anything wrong with me being at my level of consciousness and striving to go higher. The earth is simply an educational institution that is set up to give people at many different levels of consciousness an opportunity to grow. And it does so by mixing us all together in this big melting pot. Yet I have also claimed my right to be different. This means I have accepted that I do not have to get other people to accept my spiritual outlook, just as I do not have to accept their non-spiritual outlook.

I have given up any desire to convince other people that they too should be seeking a higher understanding of life or that they should accept my spiritual teaching. I realize that some people are below the level of consciousness where they can discover the spiritual path. Trying to convince them of the reality of something they cannot see, is futile.

I used to feel that since people at these levels of consciousness are obviously struggling and suffering, I wanted to help them overcome their suffering and find the freedom I had found. I even felt I was here on earth to help raise the earth beyond suffering and that it was my responsibility to help other people. I felt I had to convince other people, and if I could not, it was me who wasn't good enough at reaching people. All of this I have been able to let go of. It took me a number of years, but I have been able to let go of all sense that I am responsible for others, and it has been like having the weight of the world fall from my shoulders. This is because before, I was literally struggling against the weight of the collective consciousness.

I know many spiritual people will feel that if we are not here to make the earth a better place, then what is our purpose for being on this planet? When I was younger, I experienced being on earth as a sacrifice because I felt so many things were not natural on this planet. When I found spiritual teachings, I started seeing that I am here to help improve conditions on this planet, and this made my sacrifice bearable. For a number of years, I was so focused on doing something positive for the planet that I felt life would be unbearable if I was not making a contribution to improving life on earth.

The frustration of spiritual people

I can see today that my drive to improve life on earth was in large part driven by my own reactionary patterns. It pained me to see other people suffer. I wanted to remove suffering so that I could feel better about being on this planet. I can go even further and say that I felt threatened by the warfare, violence and suffering on earth so I wanted to remove such conditions in order to give myself a sense of security, a sense of having my life under control. In other words, my desire to improve the earth had a clearly compulsive element. I felt *driven* to do something, and it made me obsessive-compulsive about how I practiced spiritual techniques.

The simple fact is that I was not at peace with being on this planet, and in order to gain a sense of peace, I wanted to change the world—preferably within the next five minutes. What happened over the years (or rather decades) was that I started resolving many of my reactionary patterns or inner selves. I gradually transformed the fear-based energies in my three higher bodies and I resolved many of the beliefs that prevented me from being at peace with how this planet functions. It was especially a deeper understanding of free will that helped me accept the concept that earth is a reality simulator. Nothing here is truly real so it doesn't have an epic importance whether this or that happens. This led me to accept the concept that people are learning and the planet is moving forward, even if everyone does not accept my spiritual teaching. Most people are in the School of Hard Knocks, and it causes them a lot of suffering, but they are still moving forward. And since they will not listen to a spiritual teaching, I cannot reach them, so why should I feel responsible for their suffering?

The stark reality, that it took me a long time to grasp, was that when I found my first spiritual teachings, I was still affected by the dualistic state of consciousness and the epic mindset. I have seen the same in thousands of other spiritual people I have met. This had several elements:

- I felt the suffering seen on earth was wrong and that the cause of suffering should be removed, by force if necessary. This doesn't mean I was ready to kill other people, as I had transcended that in past lives. But I did feel that some level of force (such as democratic societies enacting laws) was justified in order to remove suffering.

- I felt it was of epic importance to remove suffering and to restore the earth to a state with no war, crime and conflict.

- I saw that the only way to do this was to raise people's consciousness, and I thought this could only be done if all people accepted a spiritual outlook on life, preferably the one I had found.

- I was in a constant tension because I had experienced people's opposition to changing their outlook on life, and I felt powerless to actually change other people. Yet I felt a compulsion to try what I realized was impossible. It is very hard to feel that you *have* to do something, but you know it's impossible. There is not a high success rate in this sort of thing. It's like that old movie *The Princess Bride,* where one of the characters says: "There's not a lot of money in revenge." Well, neither is there a lot of profit in trying to do the impossible.

- For a time, I was becoming increasingly frustrated because I could not fathom how people could continue to suffer and still not be open to a spiritual outlook. I could not fathom how democratic societies could have the ideals they have and still not be willing to adopt a more spiritual outlook that could bring forth the kind of society I thought everybody wanted (peace, prosperity and happiness).

I am not saying all spiritual people feel the same frustration, but I have certainly met many who did. I have been in two spiritual movements that both had a clear intent of changing the world through the ideas and techniques they were promoting. What I was not seeing at the time was that this is actually a spiritual version of the epic mindset that springs from duality.

I see many spiritual movements that promote the idea that the key to a better world is to get everybody to accept a specific outlook on life and practice a certain spiritual technique. At the same time, these movement are completely convinced that they are entirely peaceful and that they are doing something completely different from what all of the violent people have done. But is this really true, or is it what psychologists call cognitive dissonance, meaning we don't see the contradictions in our worldview or the contradictions between our worldview and our actions?

How people in duality seek to save the world

I look at history and I see that a large number of groups have attempted to save the world. My standard example is the Catholic church. I have obviously been very critical of the church, but I can also see that most people, even many of the leaders, have been well-meaning people. They had much the same dream about improving the world that I had. And they had much the same approach as I had, namely that everyone should come into the fold of one worldview and one organization. Now, I saw the disastrous consequences of what the Catholic church did, such as the Inquisition, the crusades and the witch hunts. But I still thought that if my spiritual movement was given the same power over society that the Catholic church had, we would do better. But what evidence did I really have to support that theory? All power corrupts and absolute power corrupts absolutely, and the road to hell is still paved with good intentions.

Now, let's make things a bit more radical. When I was 18 I went to a university in Denmark for a year. This was in the late 1970s when a certain portion of people in Denmark were firmly invested in the dream of a communist (or at least social-ist) Utopia. I had never met some of these people while I was growing up, but I met them among the students and teachers at the university. These people were very negative towards my spiritual outlook on life while completely failing to see that their dream of improving the world was much the same as that of spiritual people. They were negative towards spiritu-ality because they thought the only solution to improving the world was the theories of Karl Marx (who said religion was the opium of the masses—today it's OxyContin). Now, when I am honest, I can see that they were the same well-mean-ing, enthusiastic people as myself and many spiritual people. I can also see today that they were as naive as myself and many spiritual people. They were, however, ready to force socialism upon society, with violent means if necessary. And that is one difference between them and most spiritual people because we have generally had enough of violence in past lives.

Okay, so now we take this to its logical extreme. As I said, the big evil in my upbringing was Nazism. Yet when I am hon-est, I can see that even among Nazi leadership (not at the top but lower down) and the followers there were many well-mean-ing people. They also had the dream of creating a better world, and the way they went about it was not so different from what the communists and the Catholics had done. The Nazis were blinded by the epic mindset. They thought it was of epic importance for the future of humanity that certain changes had to happen (like the Catholics and the communists). They had crossed that line where they thought the goal was so important and the consequences of failure so severe that the ends can justify the means (like the Catholics and the communists). Thus, they reasoned that killing other people was necessary in order to prevent a greater evil (like the Catholics and the communists).

I clearly saw that killing was not an acceptable way to save the world. I can only reason that in a past life, I had seen so many disasters result from the attitude that the ends can justify the means that I had internalized the lesson that no goal can justify the killing of other people. This was self-evident to me from early childhood. Yet I had not seen that the epic mindset can also have a non-violent aspect. I still thought that since it was so epically important to create a more peaceful world, it was acceptable to use a non-violent force to get people to accept my spiritual outlook on life. I didn't really have a clear idea of how this could happen, but I was always waiting for society to wake up and recognize the truth of my spiritual beliefs. I thought that if society enacted laws that forced people to see the spiritual side of life, that would be acceptable for the greater good. Since this wasn't happening, I felt frustrated, and what did that mean? My frustration caused me to generate fear-based energy, and where did the energy go?

I have explained previously how many of the activities in the world are driven by these collective entities that are overpowering people's individual minds and manipulating them into generating fear-based energy that the entities can then use to sustain themselves and even grow. From a certain perspective, we could say that one of the major factors that is preventing the shift to a better world is precisely these entities. They don't want a peaceful world because they live off the energy generated through conflict.

So if I am a spiritual person who wants to improve the world, what sense does it make that I have used my spiritual knowledge to put myself into a state of mind where I am feeding my energies to some of these entities? We have the concept that you are either part of the solution or part of the problem. Well, I was convinced that I was part of the solution, but in reality I was feeding my energies to upholding the problem, meaning I was actually part of the problem. And I was part of the problem because I had not resolved the reactionary patterns that caused me to react to circumstances on earth.

When I am brutally honest, I can now see that I was disturbed by the violence and conflict on earth. And while this is understandable and shared by many spiritual people, the question is whether I was part of the solution or part of the problem. I would not have been willing to see this back then, but I was actually part of the problem because I was willing to use force in order to remove war and conflict. But what is war and conflict except the use of force? Can more force remove force, can two evils make a right, can we solve a problem with the same state of consciousness that created the problem?

The conditions on earth had taken away my inner peace. I did not have the knowledge of how to overcome this problem by dealing with my own psyche. So I had taken the most common approach seen on this planet, namely thinking that the only way to change my inner condition was to change the external circumstances that I thought was the cause of the condition. And since conflict was caused by certain people using force against others, I thought it was acceptable to force these people to stop using force against the rest of us. I was trying to change my inner condition by changing something outside myself. I was trying to change other people instead of looking at my own psychology.

Yet let us now take an honest look at people like Hitler and Stalin. After having read about both of them at length, it is clear to me that they were both driven by their unresolved psychology. They never felt at peace within themselves because they never felt they had enough power. They basically both felt that they could not be at peace until they had conquered the entire world. And I felt I could not be at peace until I had changed the entire world.

Now, I am not trying to say that I, or other spiritual people, had the same level of unresolved psychology as Hitler and Stalin. Yet I realized that it was cognitive dissonance that I was essentially taking the same approach as Hitler and Stalin, namely to change the entire world in order to change how I felt inside myself. I can also say that I was seeking to change the world in order to avoid changing my psyche. I am not here trying to blame myself or other spiritual people. I am simply describing that I went through a shift where I realized I had to overcome this very subtle mechanism of seeking to force other people.

The conclusion I eventually reached was that if I am a truly spiritual person and if I am truly dedicated to improving the world, I cannot allow myself to be in a state of mind where I am feeding the very entities that are blocking progress. I need to resolve all reactionary patterns in my psyche so I can overcome what the Buddha called attachments. I need to live up to the ideal presented by Jesus when he said: "The prince of this world (the collective entities and narcissistic beings) cometh and has nothing in me." In other words, as a spiritual person I simply have to do better than all of the other well-meaning idealistic people who have tried to save the world from inside the bubble of the epic mindset.

How the reality simulator really works

It took me more than a decade to truly wrap my mind around these concepts and to resolve my attachments to improving the world. How this happened is a complex story that I will give in a future book. But the core of it was the understanding of free will and the idea that I can let these internal selves die.

Another important element was that I realized the collective consciousness has two sides. During most of my life I had felt that the collective consciousness was like a weight that was burdening me and holding me back. It was like dragging a heavy anchor behind me as I was climbing a mountain. Yet I eventually came to see that I felt this weight because I am part of the collective consciousness. This means that as the collective consciousness can drag me down, I can also pull up on the collective consciousness. And when I do so, it will affect other people so they gradually come to see things that they cannot see today.

I am not forcing them to see this, I am simply pulling them up, and when they get their heads above the water, they suddenly see what they could not see before. And when they truly see it, they naturally choose not to suffer. As the ascended masters say: "If people knew better, they would do better." However, knowing better is not a matter of intellectual or factual knowledge. It is a matter of raising consciousness so we can see what was hidden at lower levels. I used to think that I simply had to give other people the spiritual knowledge that I had found, but that isn't it at all. Only a raising of consciousness will truly make a difference.

I came to see that the most common approach to improving society is based on force. For example, the medieval

Catholics thought it was epically important to get people baptized into the Catholic faith and to make them follow the outer rules defined by the church. The focus was on changing people's outer behavior, and they used physical force and the fear of hell in order to force such a change. Their belief was that the change in outer behavior would qualify people for entry into heaven. After many deliberations, I eventually saw the flaw in this approach.

The earth is a reality simulator. The entire purpose of it is to give people an opportunity to see the physical outpicturing of their state of consciousness so that they eventually have an inner experience where they see the limitations of their current state of consciousness and thus consciously choose to raise themselves to a higher level. To say it bluntly, there is nothing wrong with warfare and violence on earth. Earth is simply the type of reality simulator where this is allowed. The purpose is that people outplay their inner violence until they have an inner experience where they see how this limits them and traps them on a merry-go-round of seeking revenge for revenge. In other words, they are not forced from without to give up violence, They come to an inner resolution where they *consciously* and *voluntarily* give up the state of consciousness that causes them to respond with violence. Most people in democratic nations have had this experience in a recent past life, and that is why they embodied in a democratic nation in this lifetime.

What the Catholic church did was to define certain types of behavior as sinful, saying these forms of behavior would disqualify you from entering heaven (in my language, this means exiting the reality simulator). Thus, if the church could force people to change their behavior so they were no longer sinning, they would qualify to enter heaven. I came to see that this was flawed reasoning. First of all, I realized that in the spiritual realm, there can be no selfishness, no unresolved psychology, no disrespect for free will or willingness to force others. In other words, until we completely transcend the lower states of consciousness, there is no way we can enter heaven. Entering heaven is not a matter of changing outer behavior, being members of a particular religion or following a set of rules. Entering heaven requires a fundamental shift in consciousness that takes us beyond all selfishness. I also realized that we have entered the reality simulator of earth in order to have certain experiences, and we will not get out of here until we have truly had enough of acting as separate individuals, giving up the entire state of identifying ourselves as separate beings.

I therefore realized that as a spiritual person, I need to develop a total respect for free will. I need to realize that what shifts our consciousness to a higher level is that we have an inner experience. This often comes about because we have experienced certain outer conditions for so long that we have finally had enough of them, and thus we reach the point that is the key to a growth in consciousness. That point is when we stop believing that our outer conditions have nothing to do with our psychology. For example, we might reach a point where we ask: "Why am I always in conflict with other people? Is it because there is something in my psychology that attracts those kind of people?" We can then realize that the only way to get away from such people is that we change ourselves so we no longer attract those kinds of circumstances.

I realized that a reality simulator works in a very simple way. In reality, we are spiritual beings who can create our circumstances through our own minds, we are co-creators with spiritual beings. Yet in order to fully recognize this, earth gives us an opportunity to experience that we live in an environment that is limiting us in many ways. Earth is the kind of reality simulator where most people are still choosing to have the experience that they are living in a world that they themselves have not created, and thus this world has power over them, perhaps even that the world defines them or that the world has produced them the way they are. This means they must reason that the only way to change their outer circumstances is to change something outside themselves. And this can only be done through force, which means they are locked in a perpetual struggle against nature or other people.

As a spiritual person, I have started to overcome this illusion. Yet I did so in past lifetimes as a result of me going through the process I just described. I had experienced certain outer circumstances for so long, and I had tried to change my outer circumstances through force for so long, that I eventually became open to the need to change my own state of consciousness. This experience was triggered by outer conditions, but it was an inner experience. The experience shifted my consciousness beyond intellectual understanding because it involved my emotional, mental and identity bodies. I literally came to see myself as a different person after the shifting experience.

In my recent past lifetimes, I had many of these shifting experiences, which means I came into this lifetime having internalized a lot of realizations. Many things were self-evident to me, but I didn't fully realize that this was because I had shifted. I thought it was because I had acquired certain spiritual knowledge, so if only I could give that knowledge to others, they would also see it as self-evident. But how could they see it when they had not had their personal, inner shifting experiences?

In other words, I had a desire to improve the world. And I thought this could be done by converting other people to a certain spiritual philosophy. And I thought people would accept this philosophy if only it was presented to them. It took some hard knocks to realize this was not the case, and it left me in a state of confusion. How could I then fulfill my reason for being on this planet, which at the time I could only see as making a contribution to improving the world?

What really changes the world

The key is to realize that even if I could get most people to accept a certain spiritual philosophy, this would not actually change the world for the better. Getting everyone to accept a spiritual philosophy as an outer belief system would be no better than when all people in Europe were members of the Catholic church. The only thing that can change the world is to change the collective consciousness. And the only way to change the collective consciousness is that individual people have an inner shifting experience. Getting them to believe in a certain spiritual teaching is not the same as helping them have such an experience.

It took me several decades, but I was eventually able to give up the dream that most people could or should be converted to a particular spiritual teaching. I saw that it is not a matter of which outer organization people are members of or which outer beliefs they have. The only thing that counts is their level of consciousness. I saw that it is only by raising the level of the collective consciousness that we can change the world.

This is how positive changes have happened throughout history. My favorite example is slavery, as I mentioned before. There was no violent revolution that ended slavery. There simply came a point where it became self-evident to a critical mass of people that a democratic society could not allow slavery. I know you can point to certain events, people and ideas who from a traditional perspective brought about this change. But I came to see that these people were simply the forerunners and what made them have an impact was that there had already been a raising of the collective consciousness. This was beyond finding some ultimate arguments for ending slavery. Certain arguments had been used a century before, but back then they had no impact.

For me, this was a fundamental shift in approach. The epic mindset always defines things in black-and-white terms, meaning something is right and the opposite is wrong. When we are in this mindset, we think that our way of looking at the world is right. The people who are creating problems do so because they cannot see the right way, meaning they are in the wrong state of mind and if only we force them to change, all problems will be solved.

This is the same mindset I had and that I saw in my first spiritual movements. The problems on earth are wrong, and they are created because people don't have our truth. Thus, people should be forced (non-violently but still forced) to accept the truth and then our problems would be over. I took a look at history and saw how many times different groups of people had tried that approach, and I saw that it has never, *ever* worked. I then remembered Einstein: "If you keep doing the same thing, and expect different results, you are insane." I recognized that it was a form of insanity to believe that my particular spiritual outlook could do what none of the other thought systems seen on earth could do.

People are not blinded because they have certain beliefs. They have certain beliefs because they are blinded. They are blinded because they are at a certain level of consciousness where they cannot see certain things. They cannot see the forest for the trees because they have not climbed high enough on the ladder of the observation tower. Once they raise their consciousness, they will naturally see the broader perspective. This is not a matter of them believing what they are told by an authority figure (not even a spiritual leader). It is a matter of them seeing that something is hurting themselves.

When they see this, they will spontaneously shift their consciousness and this will have the effect of changing their behavior because only very few people will continue to do what hurts themselves when they truly see it. I therefore realized that the quintessential key to changing the world is to raise the collective consciousness. Meaning that if I let go of all desires to change specific conditions and instead focused on raising consciousness, I could accomplish far more in terms of lifting the planet.

Changing myself

How can I raise the collective consciousness as an individual? By raising my own consciousness. It may seem naive that one individual can raise the collective consciousness, but I am not just one individual. There are millions of spiritual people who for decades have been working on raising our individual consciousness. I clearly see that this has had an impact, although it has not brought about the results I dreamed of when I was young. Yet those dreams were simply out of touch with reality, and this brought me to another liberating insight.

As I have said, many years ago I became open to the idea that there is a group of spiritual beings, the ascended masters, who are working actively to raise the earth to a higher level. I even found an organization that had many teachings released directly by the ascended masters. In the popular culture of this organization, it was assumed that the masters have a detailed plan for exactly what kind of political, economic and other changes should happen. I eventually came to see that this was not the full picture.

Sure, the ascended masters want to end poverty, war and hunger, and sure they have a plan for how this could be accomplished. But the ascended masters do not want to force this upon humanity, they want it to come about as a result of people's free choices. And how can people's choices become free? Only by raising the collective consciousness so people can see what they cannot see today, for example, they can see why slavery simply is not in their own best interest.

When I was a member of this movement, I spent countless hours invoking spiritual light in order to bring about a change in specific conditions. I am not saying this didn't have an effect, but I came to see that I (and the organization as a whole) was too focused on and attached to bringing about specific changes. Even to the point of being willing to use some element of force to change society. For example, most people in the organization thought it was acceptable to enact laws that forced people to live according to the organization's worldview.

I gradually started questioning this, and I eventually had a breakthrough where I realized that the ascended masters are primarily working on raising the collective consciousness. As this happens, and it *is* happening, people will gradually come to see things they cannot see, and this will bring about changes in people's individual lives and in society. Yet it will not have to be forced upon people; it will happen because they suddenly see what is in their enlightened self-interest and they naturally choose what they see is best for themselves and society.

Again, there are two forces seeking to change the world. There is a dark force that seeks to control and force people and then there is the ascended masters who seek to raise people's consciousness so they can make more aware choices. I then saw that if I truly want to support the ascended masters, I cannot allow my reactionary patterns and unresolved psychology to cause me to feed my energies to the dark forces. I made a shift where I stopped focusing on specific changes that needed to happen. Instead, I am now focused on raising the collective. I can see that this does cause people to make better choices, but it is very difficult to predict exactly what changes this will bring about and when it will happen. It is impossible for me to predict when a certain group of people will shift their consciousness so they let go of a particular behavior. But I don't have to know when specific changes will happen. The Buddha talked about a concept of interdependent originations. The way I understand this is that everything is connected, almost like humanity is a giant river. The entire river is moving as one giant whole so humanity is moving towards higher levels of the collective consciousness. This is in part because of the millions of spiritual people who are raising themselves, but also because many people who are not openly spiritual are changing their consciousness and pulling up on the collective. Of course, the ascended masters are also doing many things to help raise consciousness, but they only work as far as people respond.

So the river is moving and the water is swirling around in a very complex pattern of movement, like a giant dance. When you look at a fast-flowing river, it can seem quite chaotic, and it can be very difficult to predict how one particular swirl will move and evolve. That is why it can be difficult to predict when specific changes in society will come about. Thinking, as I used to do, that a certain change in society should happen at a certain time, can only lead to frustration. Yet giving up this desire for specific results at specific times helped me be at peace with being part of the stream and playing a part in speeding up the flow. I may not see *specific* changes in my lifetime, but I *will* see changes because I am pulling up on the collective and thereby changing the interdependent originations that produce outer circumstances.

I also realized that any change at the physical level has to be preceded by changes at the identity, mental and emotional levels—and this takes time. So I cannot expect instant results but must allow the change to cycle through the three higher levels before there can be a physical change.

All in all, this helped me overcome my previous frustration, and I am now at peace with being on earth and raising my own consciousness, seeking to help others do the same, and then allowing the river to flow in its own way and produce the results that can be produced at any given time. If a result is not forthcoming, then I reason that it is because not enough people have made the decision that they have had enough of this condition on earth. Too many people still have not had enough of a certain condition, and thus I must allow free will to outplay itself so these people stay in the School of Hard Knocks a while longer. I do not have to feel frustrated because some people want to learn the hard way. But neither do I have to let other people's way of learning take away my inner peace.

Overcoming judgment

After a very long process of working with these deep issues, I did shift my consciousness to where I saw that a very real problem on earth is that we human beings have a tendency to think that our subjective experience should have some universal validity. Say I lived several lifetimes where I was a warrior who fought for various causes, thinking that by winning the ultimate battle over the bad people, I could bring a better world. So I thought I could bring peace through some ultimate form of violence. I eventually had enough of this and saw the futility of creating peace through war. I had an inner experience where I did shift my consciousness so I had a higher sense of identity and no longer saw the world through this illusion that the ends can justify the means.

I now come into my next lifetime having integrated this. I have a direct experience that if only other people could see what I see, we could have a peaceful world. So I start preaching to them based on my shifting experience. Yet how did I have my experience? Only by first experiencing fighting to an extreme degree. Could I have had the shifting experience only through words? Obviously not, or I would not have been a warrior for so many lifetimes. So what sense does it make that I think other people can change based on *my* inner experience? What sense does it make that I think other people can change through me telling them something that I only internalized through experience?

How will other people ever change unless they have their own inner shifting experiences? And how will they have that unless they also experience having had enough of certain outer circumstances? I realized I will never actually improve the world by seeking to get other people to change based on my shifting experience or by making them believe my conclusion. The only way I might change the world is by seeking to help other people have their own inner shifting experiences—whatever that takes for each person individually.

For some people, there is nothing I could do or say that will shift them. They need to have more experiences in the School of Hard Knocks, but why should I have any judgment of that? I do not know the specifics about my past lifetimes, but I am fairly sure I have done a lot of different things. In other words, I have followed a very complex path to where I am today, and why shouldn't everyone else be allowed to do the same? Why should I judge, why should I even have an opinion about, how another person follows his or her individual path? This caused me to realize that one of the major problems in the world is that so many people are judgmental of others. Again, this could be said to simply be part of the experience we can have in Reality Simulator Earth. But I realized that if I am a spiritual person and want to improve the world, it makes no sense that I am feeding my energies to the collective entities of judgment. And by judging other people, by engaging my mind in evaluating what is right and wrong with their behavior and state of mind, I am indeed feeding my energies to these entities. Where my attention goes, there go my energies and eventually my sense of identity must follow.

I came to see that in the spiritual movements I had been a part of, there was a clear judgmental attitude towards those who were not in our movement. I lived in Utah for five years as one of the few non-Mormons in the state. The Mormons are generally very nice people, but they do have a clear judgmental attitude towards non-Mormons, whom they call "Gentiles." I saw the same in fundamentalist churches in the United States and I have seen it in the Catholic church as well. When I was young I experienced how believing Marxist were judgmental towards the rest of us and I have experienced in Israel how many Jews are very judgmental of the Palestinians (and the rest of us Gentiles) and how the Palestinians are very judgmental of the Jews.

So I simply came to a point where I realized that I no longer want to be part of this judgmental consciousness. I don't want to engage my attention in playing this game of judging others based on some artificial standard—and *all* standards on earth are artificial.

Being able to speak freely

Once I started overcoming my tendency to judge, I found that I was much more free to talk about my spirituality, even with people who are not spiritual or who are anti-spiritual. This is partly because I no longer have any intent of convincing people, and that means I am setting both myself and them free. Consider how you react when you are confronted with an aggressive salesperson, whether on the phone or when you are walking down the street. You might feel they are sending out an aggressive energy in order to convince you to buy their product, and you almost always react by pulling back. This is the reaction I often got when I was younger and attempted to tell people about my spiritual beliefs. I can see today that I was in a certain state of mind of feeling compelled to tell other people and I had a clear desire to convert them so I would not feel rejected. I did not feel free in myself and that meant I could not set other people free. I was pulling them into my own little stress spiral and they often resisted it, which is quite understandable to me today. Now that I have overcome the conditions in my own psychology that caused me to feel this stress, I am free in myself. I don't feel I need to convert anyone to my spiritual beliefs and I don't feel rejected if they don't respond. Yet I also don't feel I have to avoid talking about my spiritual beliefs in order to please them. I give them the right to talk about anything they want, and I claim my right to talk about what I want—giving them freedom to react as they want.

This means I am setting myself free to talk and I am setting them free to react. Interestingly, this means I often get a completely different reaction. In the beginning I was often surprised at how much I could say without getting a negative response, because I could still remember how I used to get a negative response for talking about the same topics. The difference is partly that I no longer have an intention of convincing others, but also that I am now merely talking about spiritual ideas and not about a specific philosophy, movement or guru. I am not trying to convert them to come into the fold, I am simply throwing out ideas—I am sowing seeds but I am non-attached to if or when they sprout.

I know from myself that it took me time to accept certain ideas. When I first came across an idea, I wasn't ready to seriously consider it, but a seed was planted in my subconscious mind. Over time, it sprouted, and one day the idea came back to my conscious mind and now I was ready to consider it. While I was in the convert-or-die mode, I was not content to sow seeds. I wanted a positive reaction from others in order to avoid a negative reaction in myself. It was an incredible relief to get over this inner tension and feel free to share my spiritual views without expecting a particular reaction. But the freedom rests on the fact that I have given up the desire to convert other people or society to a particular spiritual movement or guru. As mentioned before, I no longer believe that the world will be changed by getting as many people as possible to join a particular spiritual movement. The world will be changed by raising consciousness and by ideas that are universal, meaning that they are not exclusive to a particular thought system. For example, democracy did not come about because a particular religion promoted democratic ideals. The ideas were so universal that many people could accept them, including people from different religions. If democratic ideals had somehow been monopolized by the Christian religion, we would have had far fewer democratic countries. Again, I realized that if I really want to make a difference as a spiritual person, I can't take the same approach as so many religious and political people have done.

Admitting that I can be wrong

As I look back at my youth and adulthood, I can see that I had a very strong self that wanted me to never be wrong. Actually, I had several selves related to being wrong. One self projected at me that it would be an absolute, total disaster if I was proven wrong in any way. It would literally be the end of the world and thus it was a matter of life and death to never be wrong. Another self projected that this impending disaster could be avoided if I never *admitted* that I was wrong, meaning it had created an elaborate process for interpreting anything that happened in such a way that I did not have to admit that I had been wrong. There were other selves who were very adept at coming up with an intellectual interpretation for why I had not been wrong after all—and the intellect can argue for or against any case. There were even selves who had created an entire worldview according to which there was only one absolute truth: Kim Michaels can never be *really* wrong. In retrospect, I can see how much of my attention and psychic energy was tied up in trying to avoid being wrong. It was a constant inner tension to uphold this image, especially after I started writing books.

I have later realized that this mechanism can be traced back to past lives where I was manipulated by narcissistic beings into situations where I did something with the best of intentions. I was later proven wrong and humiliated in a very public manner. This was a shock to me, and I created a self that was tasked with making sure this could never happen again. Through a long and gradual process (too complex to explain here), I came to accept that it is perfectly acceptable for me to be wrong. My selves projected at me that in order to avoid being wrong, I had to live up to a superhuman standard of perfection, meaning I had to judge all of my thoughts, feelings and actions. It was an incredible relief for me to let go of this entire conglomerate of selves.

The key was the realization that although these selves are indeed in my four lower bodies, even my identity body, they are not who I am. I am the Conscious You, which is neutral awareness. As neutral awareness, I cannot interact with the world, I need certain selves in order to do that, and they naturally color the way I look at the world. If I go through a situation where it seems I was wrong, then it is because I was looking at that situation through a limited self. In reality, it is constructive to come to see that I have had a limited perception of the world because it can free me to attain a broader perspective. Any given self was created to give me a certain type of experience. If the perception of that self is proven wrong or limited, it is an opportunity for me to rise above that experience and have a higher experience. Yet in order to rise, I need to admit that I have a self with a limited perception and I have to let that self die. Obviously, the self has a survival instinct and doesn't want to die, so it will project at me that I must not admit that the self's perception was wrong. I must defend it as if it was a matter of life and death, which it is—for the self.

So what I need to do is to use the Conscious You's ability to step back and look at the situation neutrally. I can come to see that I am not the self and the self is not me. I can come to see how the self is limiting me and I can decide that I want a higher experience, meaning I can let the self die. Take note of the essential distinction here. I do not have to prove that the self was right after all, I do not have to defend the self or any viewpoint, I do not have to solve any problem. I simply have to let the self die and accept that I am free from that previous perception filter.

In a sense, one could say that I truly can never be wrong, meaning that the Conscious You, which is neutral awareness, cannot be wrong. It was an important step for me to realize that even if a belief was wrong, it didn't mean that *I* was wrong—if I didn't identify with the self holding the belief. In other words, it is my selves that can be wrong. Of course, I can only be wrong according to a dualistic evaluation that operates with right and wrong, and since the Conscious You is neutral awareness, it is not in duality. So once I let go of the dualistic thinking, I started thinking beyond right and wrong. It wasn't a matter of being right or wrong, it was a matter of seeing which viewpoints limited me and which set me free. I realized that once I saw that a certain viewpoint was limiting me, I also saw a broader perspective (or I could not have seen that my previous perception was limited). If I resisted seeing the limited view, I could not be free of it.

In a sense we can say that Kim Michaels can indeed be wrong because Kim Michaels is a conglomerate of selves that are created as a reaction to this world. These selves all have a limited perception because they are based on some illusion, so they can be proven wrong. It was an incredible relief when I came to the point where I could say: "Yes, I was indeed wrong. My view of that issue or my behavior in that situation was not the highest possible. I admit it, I learn from the situation and now I move on." This meant that every time Kim Michaels was proven wrong, it was an opportunity for the real me, the Conscious You, to free itself from another self that limited me. I could now see the self and let it die, so I could be reborn at a higher level of awareness. I stopped resisting being proven wrong, and this made it so much easier for me to interact with other people.

I also realized that there are some incredibly powerful collective entities that want all of us to feel that we are wrong and that we can never be free of having been wrong. It took me some time to free myself from their pull, but once I was willing to admit that I can be wrong, but that I can also rise above any mistake, they lost their pull on me. I saw that a viewpoint or behavior can be wrong, but that doesn't mean there is anything wrong with *me*. I have a right to experiment with free will and learn from my choices. I learn by making choices so I don't have to be perfect before I choose.

I can see today that this dynamic applies to many spiritual people. We can be incredibly hard on ourselves if we don't live up to the standard we have created in our own minds. And this standard often leaves no room for failure You are either perfect of no good. It is not only an incredible relief on the personal level to let go of this mess. I also think it is the only way that we spiritual people can have an impact on society.

If we go out (as I used to do and as I have seen many spiritual people do) with the attitude that we need to prove our spiritual teaching right by proving all other teachings wrong, we will only add to the conflict and the fear-based energies in the world. But if we can provide an alternative, if we can provide a different voice, then I think we can gradually make people listen. Because I think many people are ready to listen for something that does not spring from duality or unresolved psychology. Many people are ready to follow the examples of people who demonstrate that we can indeed attain mental freedom. I hope this book has been a different voice.

Why I wrote this book

One might now ask a logical question: "Why am I writing this book?" Is not this book an attempt to tell other people that they should change based on my personal experience? And I fully agree that people can see it that way and I am sure some will. Personally, I look at this book as my best possible attempt (based on where I am at in consciousness right now) to help people have their own shifting experiences so they do not have to have as many hard knocks as I have had. The simple fact is that we all need a certain amount of hard knocks in order to shift, but we don't necessarily all need to have the same amount of hard knocks. We can actually learn from observing other people have their hard knocks and deciding we do not want to go through the same.

I used to like the following example. Say you are walking into a parking garage in order to get your car, and you see a man who is running at great speed and then slamming his head into the concrete wall. After a few moments of disorientation, he picks himself up and repeats the procedure. You naturally ask him what he is doing, and he explains that he is convinced that if he slams his head against the wall long enough, he will eventually manage to break down the wall.

Back then, I looked at this as an example of how there are certain things in the world that we simply cannot do, and trying to do them is as futile as slamming our heads against a concrete wall. In other words, I thought it was stupid to slam your head into a concrete wall.

Today, I look at it differently. One of the things we human beings can do is to slam our heads against concrete walls. Another thing we human beings can do is to make ourselves believe that slamming our heads against concrete walls will accomplish some goal, perhaps even an epic goal of saving the world. One of the things we need to do as humanity is to try to do anything and everything that we can do in the reality simulator of earth. How do we know that slamming our heads against a concrete wall will not save the world until we try it? Yet do all of us have to slam our heads against a concrete wall in order to find out that it doesn't work, or can the rest of us learn that particular lesson by observing other people slam their heads against a concrete wall? In science, this is called the process of induction where we observe a certain amount of individual cases and then conclude that this can be applied as a general rule. If we throw a certain number different things into the air and observe that they all fall back down, we eventually reason that anything we throw into the air will fall back down. So we don't have to spend the rest of our lives throwing things into the air.

Obviously, if I see a man slamming his head against a concrete wall (and screaming in agony), it doesn't mean I now have to start slamming my head against a wall in order to have a direct experience of whether this works or not. I can shift my consciousness with regards to concrete walls by observing the other person's behavior and then letting this observation produce an inner shifting experience in me. It is this inner experience that shifts my consciousness, so the only question is what can bring about that shift in me? Can I shift based on observing other people slamming their heads into a wall or do I have to have the direct experience of doing it myself?

So if I observe a person slamming his head against a wall, and it is self-evident to me that this will accomplish nothing more than giving him a headache, it is because in the past I have had an inner shifting experience so I have experienced the reality that this doesn't work. Yet if the other person is slamming his head against a concrete wall, he obviously has not had that shifting experience yet. And obviously, he could not have that experience by observing others so he has to go through the direct experience.

I need to have no judgment of the fact that billions of people need to have the direct experiences they are having. I need to have no judgment of the fact that they cannot have an inner shifting experience by observing me or by me telling them about the experiences I have had. Yet by describing my experiences, *some* people might actually be able to have an inner shifting experience based on what I have gone through, and that would make it worth it for me to write the book.

There is a story about the Buddha having experienced Nirvana, which is essentially freedom from the dualistic mindset and the illusion of separation. He formed the desire to go back to earth and tell other people about his experience. He was then confronted by the forces of this world who told him that this was pointless because no one would be able to understand him. The Buddha thought about this and then said: *"Some* will understand!"* It is my vision that when a critical mass of spiritual people come out of the closet and start telling our stories of having shifted our consciousness, then *some* will understand and this will shift the collective consciousness.

NOTE: In this book I have focused on how I experienced being a spiritual person relating to an anti-spiritual society. Therefore, I have not gone into details about how I followed my personal path and I have given few specifics about the teachings and movements I was involved with. In the next book, I will give a much more detailed description of the process I have gone through. I will also describe how I have been involved with several spiritual movements, from one that thought meditation was the one solution to all problems to another that had profound teachings from the ascended masters, but nevertheless took a detour into being a survivalist cult that built nuclear bomb shelters and bought machine guns to defend them. It has been a rather wild ride, and I hope it will be both entertaining and enlightening to read about it.

29 | THE NEUTRALIST MANIFESTO

1. I am a non-material being, which means that nothing in the material world defines me. Neutralism does not define me, it is an approach I have adopted in order to facilitate my interaction with the material world.

2. As a Neutralist, I observe that human beings exhibit many different types of behavior and live in many different ways. I see that the difference in outer behavior is linked to the inner state of people's psychology. We human beings are psychological beings and everything we do as individuals or as societies is affected by the conditions in our psyches.

3. As a Neutralist, I observe that there is a wide range between the most selfish people and the most unselfish. The explanation is that the most selfish people are controlled by their psychology, by their reactionary patterns. Yet all human beings are limited by our reactionary patterns that compel us into reacting a

certain way rather than freely choosing not only our reactions but also our state of mind.

4. As a Neutralist, I observe that the differences in our reactions are determined by our level of consciousness. There is a scale of possible states of consciousness, ranging from the most selfish to the most unselfish. The most selfish people are entirely controlled by their psychological conditions, meaning they are the least free. The more unselfish have started moving towards having control or mastery over their own psyches, meaning they have the freedom to choose their reaction to external circumstances as well as their general state of mind. I have therefore decided that psychological freedom is a goal towards which I am actively striving.

5. As a Neutralist, I observe that most people live their lives as if their psychology was a product of inheritance, their environment and other factors over which they have no control. Yet I realize that there has always been an alternative to this approach, namely a systematic path whereby I can raise my consciousness from lower to higher levels. This path has been expressed through many spiritual or mystical traditions, yet beyond the outer expressions is a universal path to higher awareness. I have made the conscious decision to dedicate myself to following this path and making as much progress as possible.

6. As a Neutralist, I observe that people at lower levels of consciousness have the same desire for inner, psychological peace that I have. Yet because they cannot see how to work directly with their own psyches, they have become trapped in thinking the only way to change their *internal* circumstances is to change their *external* circumstances. I am dedicated to

freeing myself from this trap and to learn how to change my state of mind by working directly on my own psyche.

7. As a Neutralist, I observe that people at lower levels of consciousness have become trapped in thinking that the key to changing their external circumstances is to follow a thought- or belief system, be it religious, political or scientific materialist. They believe the only way to change the world is to get all other people to accept their system, or to force those who will not accept it voluntarily. I am dedicated to freeing myself from this approach and to avoid seeking to change other people as a way to change my state of mind.

8. As a Neutralist, I observe that many people at lower levels of consciousness have become trapped in a dualistic view of the world, where black-and-white thinking defines two opposite polarities, one right, one false, one good, one evil. They see the world through an epic mindset and they think the key to their inner peace is to destroy what their system defines as evil. I am determined to free my mind from even the most subtle influences of dualistic polarities, black-and-white thinking and the epic mindset.

9. As a Neutralist, I observe that it is virtually impossible to have a neutral, constructive conversation with people in the dualistic, epic mindset. I am dedicated to making peace with this fact so I do not seek to change these people but let the School of Hard Knocks be their teacher. Instead, I will focus on interacting with people who are not completely blinded by duality and the epic mindset. I will seek to change the public discourse in my society so it is not dominated by dualistic polarities.

10. As a Neutralist, I observe that people in the epic mind-set are judgmental of those who do not accept their "one and only truth." I am dedicated to overcoming all judgment of others so I do not seek to force them to conform to any thought- or belief system. Instead, I will seek to help them raise their level of consciousness based on my personal experiences.

11. As a Neutralist, I observe that humanity has been in an era where many people have believed that we human beings are capable of defining an ideology or thought system, and then we can get the universe to conform to our system. If the universe refuses to do so, then we seek to force other people to conform to our system. I am dedicated to freeing myself from this mindset and helping other people do the same without forcing them.

12. As a Neutralist, I observe that the universe does not conform to man-made ideas. I am dedicated to looking at human activities and evaluating them based on a neutral observation of their consequences. I will look at more than physical consequences, namely the psychological consequences. Does an action, policy, idea or thought system help us grow towards higher levels of consciousness or does it have the effect of trapping us at lower levels of consciousness?

13. As a Neutralist, I have total respect for the free will of other people and for democratic principles. I will not seek to force any system upon my society. I will promote the idea that it is a natural consequence of democratic ideals that we make a shift from material welfare to psychological well-being. It is natural for a democratic society to give not only political freedom to its citizens, but to also help them acquire psychological freedom.

14. As a Neutralist, I am dedicated to using non-forceful means to help democratic societies make the shift where they make it a priority to teach all people about the human psyche and give them the tools to free themselves from their psychological limitations. It is my goal to personally attain psychological freedom and to help other people do the same.

15. As a Neutralist, I realize that there is no thought system or methodology that can solve all problems. We can never solve a problem with the same state of consciousness that created the problem. I am dedicated to helping individuals and democratic societies see that raising the consciousness (individually and collectively) is the only realistic way to overcome problems. We create a problem through a certain state of consciousness, and we can only see a way out of the problem by rising to a higher level of consciousness. When we raise our consciousness, what we could not see when we created the problem, becomes self-evident.

16. As a Neutralist, I realize that no thought system on earth can be the absolute or final truth. Humankind is in the process of raising the collective consciousness, and we will progressively discover new knowledge. Therefore, I am dedicated to seeing any thought system as one step in our ongoing process of discovery and self-discovery. Closed-ended systems led to stagnation and only open-ended systems lead to ongoing growth.

NOTE: The Neutralist Manifesto is not copyrighted, and you are free to use and distribute it as you see fit.